ave become Tour champions. The year
f 1971 officially marked the birth of The
uropean Tour and following the second
ace to Dubai in November, 2010, there
ad been in total 387 champions.

MOST VICTORIES BY COUNTRY
THE TOP TEN

1.	England	257
2.	Spain	156
3.	Scotland	126
4.	USA	120
5.	Australia	106
6.	South Africa	94
7.	Sweden	89
8.	Germany	60
9.	Ireland	46
10.	Wales	44

18 JAPAN
Number of wins: 1
Number of winners: 1
Leading performer: Isao Aoki (1)

19 KOREA
Number of wins: 6
Number of winners: 4
Leading performers:
Y E Yang (3); KJ Choi, Noh Seung-yul
Charlie Wi (1)

20 THE NETHERLANDS
Number of wins: 4
Number of winners: 3
Leading performers: Robert-Jan
Derksen (2); Maarten Lafeber,
Rolf Muntz (1).

21 NEW ZEALAND
Number of wins: 25
Number of winners: 7
Leading performers: Michael Campbell
(8); Frank Nobilo (5); Bob Charles,
Greg Turner (4)

22 NORTHERN IRELAND
Number of wins: 37
Number of winners: 7
Leading performers: Darren Clarke (12);
Graeme McDowell; Ronan Rafferty (7);
David Feherty (5)

23 PORTUGAL
Number of wins: 1
Number of winners: 1
Leading performer: Daniel Silva (1)

24 SCOTLAND
Number of wins: 126
Number of winners: 21
Leading performers: Colin
Montgomerie (31); Sam Torrance (21);
Sandy Lyle (18); Bernard Gallacher (10)

25 SINGAPORE
Number of wins: 1
Number of winners: 1
Leading performer: Mardan Mamat (1)

26 SOUTH AFRICA
Number of wins: 94
Number of winners: 27
Leading performers: Ernie Els (25);
Retief Goosen (14); Hugh Baiocchi (6)

27 SPAIN
Number of wins: 156
Number of winners: 28
Leading performers: Seve Ballesteros
(50); José Maria Olazábal (23);
Miguel Angel Jiménez (18)

28 SWEDEN
Number of wins: 89
Number of winners: 28
Leading performers: Robert Karlsson
(11); Niclas Fasth, Anders Forsbrand,
Per-Ulrik Johansson, Henrik Stenson (6)

29 SWITZERLAND
Number of wins: 1
Number of winners: 1
Leading performer: André Bossert (1)

30 TAIWAN
Number of wins: 2
Number of winners: 2
Leading performer: Yeh Wei-tze,
Lin Wen-tang (1)

31 THAILAND
Number of wins: 6
Number of winners: 3
Leading performers:
Thongchai Jaidee (4); Chapchai Nirat,
Thaworn Wiratchant (1)

32 TRINIDAD and TOBAGO
Number of wins: 2
Number of winners: 1
Leading performer: Stephen Ames (2).

33 USA
Number of wins: 120
Number of winners: 52
Leading performers: Tiger Woods (38);
Phil Mickelson (7); Tom Watson (5);
Bob Byman, Mark O'Meara (4)

34 WALES
Number of wins: 44
Number of winners: 9
Leading performers: Ian Woosnam
(29); Stephen Dodd, Phillip Price (3)

35 ZIMBABWE
Number of wins: 29
Number of winners: 3
Leading performers: Mark McNulty
(16); Nick Price (7); Tony Johnstone (6)

The European Tour
Yearbook 2011

OFFICIAL PUBLICATION

I was born in England.

Thomas Lyte Bespoke offers the finest craft and workmanship in silver and leather. The Hornchurch Briefcase is designed and made in our London workshops. Selecting only the best vegetable tanned Breuninger and Bridle leathers, the Hornchurch is expertly cut and hand sewn by one of the country's most skillful bag makers. The hallmarked sterling silver furnishings are hand crafted and fitted by our master silversmiths who are responsible for some of the world's most iconic trophies. Fully lined in Jacquard silk, the Hornchurch is truly craftsmanship at its finest.

Discover Thomas Lyte at 12-13 Burlington Arcade, Mayfair, London, W1. thomaslyte.com

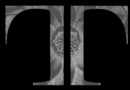

THOMAS LYTE

EUROPEAN TOUR

OFFICIAL SUPPLIER

CONTENTS

A Message from George O'Grady

Many expert commentators have judged the 2010 season as the most successful in the history of The European Tour. I invite you to share the moments of this extraordinary season as captured here in our European Tour Yearbook and to form your own opinion. We hope you enjoy this very special publication.

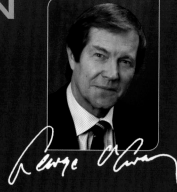

George O'Grady CBE
Chief Executive, The European Tour

ACKNOWLEDGEMENTS

Executive Editor
Mitchell Platts

Deputy Executive Editor
Scott Crockett

Production Editor
Frances Jennings

Editorial Consultant
Chris Plumridge

Picture Editors
Andrew Redington, Rob Harborne

Art Direction
Tim Leney, Andrew Wright
TC Communications Ltd

Print Managed by
Peter Dane
Mark Baldwin
The Print House Ltd

The European Tour Yearbook 2011 is published by The PGA European Tour, Wentworth Drive, Virginia Water, Surrey GU25 4LX.

Distributed through Aurum Press Ltd.
7 Greenland Street, London NW1 0ND
© PGA European Tour.

A Year to Cherish

Colin Montgomerie's astute leadership of Europe's victorious 2010 Ryder Cup Team, Lee Westwood's admirable arrival as World Number One and Martin Kaymer's winning of The Race to Dubai were sublime moments in a landmark year during which European Tour Members claimed ownership of three of the four Major Championships in one calendar year for the first time.

Graeme McDowell, Louis Oosthuizen and Kaymer himself completed the historic hat-trick and, similarly, Ernie Els, Ian Poulter and Francesco Molinari won a record-breaking three of the four World Golf Championships in the same season. It is difficult not to agree with the assessment of many knowledgeable observers of the game that this has been the best year in the history of The European Tour.

European Ryder Cup Captain Colin Montgomerie celebrates victory with the fans at The Celtic Manor Resort

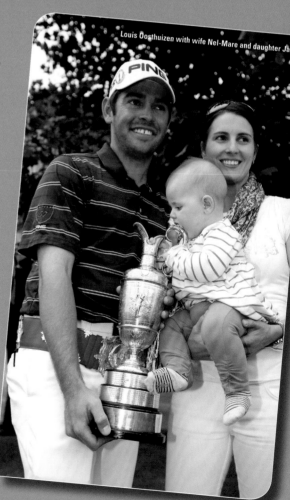

Louis Oosthuizen with wife Nel-Mare and daughter Ja...

At The Celtic Manor Resort four days of unrivalled excitement reached a crescendo when Europe secured a thrilling 14 ½ - 13 ½ triumph. Unquestionably The Ryder Cup footprint now stretches way beyond followers of golf, and this victory further enhanced global recognition of The European Tour. Captain Montgomerie received Sam Ryder's golden chalice from the Rt Hon Carwyn Jones, First Minister for Wales, where The Ryder Cup had been played for the first time, and said: "This means the world to us; the world to The European Tour."

At Pebble Beach Golf Links, Graeme McDowell followed Jack Nicklaus, Tom Watson, Tom Kite and Tiger Woods as the winner of the US Open on this iconic course and became the first European to succeed since Tony Jacklin in 1970. Graeme said: "To win at Pebble Beach and join those names is a pretty amazing feeling."

At St Andrews, Louis Oosthuizen captured The 139th Open Championship by a spread-eagling seven shots – the largest winning margin since 2000 - on the revered Old Course and said: "I think seven years on The European Tour made me a bit tougher; the win in Andalucia earlier in the year gave me a different mindset."

At Whistling Straits on the shores of Lake Michigan, Martin Kaymer became the second German golfer after Bernhard Langer to win a Major and the 40th European Tour Member to receive one of these prized trophies since Seve Ballesteros won The Open Championship in 1979. Martin said: "The European Tour has done an enormous job over the last few years; it's cool to see my name next to so many greats of the game on this trophy."

Ian Poulter's win in the WGC-Accenture Match Play was the 250th English victory in Tour history.

Seve Ballesteros: 1983 Masters Tournament champion

Ernie Els completed his 25th European Tour win with his success in the WGC-CA Championship and became the leading money winner in The European Tour Official Career Earnings with more than €25,000,000. Francesco Molinari also created history as his win in the WGC-HSBC Champions marked the first time three different Italians – following his brother Edoardo and Matteo Manassero – had won in the same season and the first time since Seve and Manuel Ballesteros in 1983 that two brothers had celebrated victory on the same schedule.

At the Emirates Golf Club in Dubai, Le Golf National in Paris, and Club de Golf Valderrama in Andalucia, Miguel Angel Jiménez captured the Omega Dubai Desert Classic, Alstom Open de France and Omega European Masters respectively to become, aged 46 years and 243 days, the oldest player to win three tournaments in a single season on The European Tour International Schedule.

At Club de Campo del Mediterráneo in Valencia, Matteo Manassero became, by winning the CASTELLÓ MASTERS Costa Azahar at 17 years and 188 days,

> Seve is everything that is European golf. He is our icon, our hero. We won The Ryder Cup for him. Colin? He's been amazing. For the last two years he's been right up for this. There's no-one quite like Colin Montgomerie. He is everything that The Ryder Cup is about and to be able to do that for him and for Seve is really special
>
> **Graeme McDowell**

Matteo Manassero aged four

Miguel Angel Jiménez and Matteo Manassero

YOUNGEST AND OLDEST WINNERS ON THE EUROPEAN TOUR

YOUNGEST

PLAYER	AGE	EVENT
Matteo Manassero	17 and 188 days	2010 CASTELLÓ MASTERS Costa Azahar
Danny Lee (AM)	18 and 213 days	2009 Johnnie Walker Classic
Noh Seung-yul	18 and 282 days	2010 Maybank Malaysian Open
Seve Ballesteros	19 and 121 days	1976 Dutch Open
Paul Way	19 and 149 days	1982 KLM Dutch Open
Sergio Garcia	19 and 176 days	1999 Murphy's Irish Open
Seve Ballesteros *	19 and 191 days	1976 Trophée Lancôme
Sergio Garcia	19 and 267 days	1999 Linde German Masters
Rory McIlroy	19 and 273 days	2009 Dubai Desert Classic
*Approved Special Event		

OLDEST

PLAYER	AGE	EVENT
Des Smyth	48 and 34 days	2001 Madeira Island Open
Neil Coles	48 and 14 days	1982 Sanyo Open
Eduardo Romero	47 and 362 days	2002 The Barclays Scottish Open
Christy O'Connor	47 and 187 days	1972 Carrolls International
Mark McNulty	47 and 95 days	2001 Mercedes-Benz South African Open
Mark O'Meara	47 and 54 days	2004 Dubai Desert Classic
Harold Henning	46 and 295 days	1981 KLM Dutch Open
Miguel Angel Jiménez	46 and 243 days	2010 Omega European Masters
Miguel Angel Jiménez	46 and 180 days	2010 Alstom Open de France

Graeme McDowell and father Kenny

the youngest winner on The European Tour International Schedule. It was also a victory which persuaded the judging panel to vote the Italian teenager as the winner of The Sir Henry Cotton Rookie of the Year. Matteo said: "I never dreamed of winning on the Tour so soon and then to be named the Rookie of the Year is something to cherish. It's incredible. A dream. Winning on the Tour, and now this award - wow!"

Elsewhere, Simon Khan regained his Tour card by finishing first at the European Tour Qualifying School at the end of 2009 and the value of that success was evident to all when in the BMW PGA Championship – The European Tour's flagship event – he completed a famous win at Wentworth Club.

It was not Simon's first win although there were maiden victories for Fredrik Andersson Hed, Rhys Davies, who ran Manassero close for The Sir Henry Cotton Award, Andrew Dodt, David Horsey, Hunter Mahan, Edoardo Molinari, James Morrison, Noh Seung-yul, Louis Oosthuizen, John Parry, Ritchie Ramsay Martin Wiegele and Manassero himself on The 2010 European Tour International Schedule on which players from more than 40 countries competed in 48 tournaments at 27 destinations.

All these fine achievements are chronicled in depth elsewhere in the following pages, chapters which also celebrate and rejoice in the global nature of The European Tour. It is this worldwide feel that has always been one of the Tour's main strengths and never has that been better illustrated than this year on the Official World Golf Ranking, crowned by the rise of Lee Westwood to the top.

At the time of the Englishman's ascension to Number One on the afternoon of Sunday October 31, Europe had six players in the top ten compared to only two in 2000; ten in the top 20 compared to six in 2000; 17 in the top 50 compared to ten in 2000 and in all, half the top 50 were European Tour Members. At the end of 2000, Europe still had only half the number of players in the top 200 as the United States – 47 to 94 – with 59 from the Rest of the World. There is now almost parity between the three regions.

However, the plaudits rightly go to Westwood who has been doing special and spectacular things throughout his 17 year professional career. There have been fewer more determined golfers made in England and it is to his lasting credit that he has changed little in the process of turning from an unknown into a major sporting celebrity recognised throughout the sporting world.

George O'Grady, Chief Executive of The European Tour, led the tributes to Westwood's phenomenal performance. "Lee's ascent to Number One in the world is a landmark achievement in a career

Ernie Els with wife Liezl and daughter Samantha

that most professional golfers can only dream of emulating," he said. "His level of performance over the last two years has set a new benchmark for consistency in world golf. The fact that Lee reached the Number One spot playing most of his golf on The European Tour International Schedule gives everyone involved with our Tour an immense amount of satisfaction, and we congratulate Lee and his team on this tremendous accomplishment."

With 20 victories on The European Tour International Schedule, and 32 in all worldwide, Westwood is unquestionably one of the finest golfers to grace the fairways in the history of the Royal and Ancient game. He is also one of sport's most respected and well liked players with exemplary credentials.

Over the two year time span during which the Official World Golf Ranking is calculated he amassed 23 top ten finishes. This included being runner-up in both the Masters Tournament and The Open Championship in 2010, and third in both The Open Championship and the US PGA Championship in 2009. All this and victory in the inaugural Race to Dubai last year, secured by his success in the Dubai World Championship presented by: DP World, and the small matter of his talismanic role in The 2010 Ryder Cup triumph despite his persistent calf injury problems. No question, then, that the quality of his golf and the consistency of his results deservedly earned Westwood his rise to the top of the world.

Only 12 players had previously held such a position since the Official World Golf Ranking was devised in 1986. These include five regular European Tour Members – Bernhard Langer, Seve Ballesteros, Sir Nick Faldo, Ian Woosnam and Ernie Els. Westwood himself spent 180 weeks in the top ten between 1998 and 2001 but by May 2003, however, he was down to 266. His revival came with the support of many people. His wife, Laurae, and their children, Sam and Poppy; his parents, John and Trish; his manager,

Francesco Molinari

Andrew 'Chubby' Chandler, head of the International Sports Management group; his caddie, Billy Foster; his coach, Pete Cowen; and his fitness coach, Steve McGregor, among them.

Westwood is aware that he is one of the most blessed players of his generation. Yet it has always been his refusal to allow his feet to leave the ground and his

abiding loyalty and commitment to his family and lifelong friends in Worksop that most warmly charms public and critics alike. "When you are growing up and people say what do you want to achieve everyone says I want to be the best in the world," he said.

"Right at this moment I can show people the World Rankings and say I am the best

Ian Poulter with children Aimee-Leigh (left) and Luke

Simon Khan

L-R: Francesco Molinari, Matteo Manassero and Edoardo Molinari - the first time three Italians have triumphed in a single season on The European Tour

on the planet. It is a fairly large achievement when you look at the people who have gone before me in that spot. It is an elite list. It is the most satisfying moment of my career."

The global strength of European golf was further magnified on the 2010 Senior Tour won by Thailand's Boonchu Ruangkit ahead of South Africa's Chris Williams, Paraguay's Angel Franco, Scotland's Gordon Brand Jnr and England's Carl Mason, while on the Challenge Tour – where Spain's Alvaro Velasco finished Number One in the Rankings – the international top ten was completed by England's Matt Haines, Denmark's Thorbjørn Olesen, Netherlands' Floris de Vries, Austria's Bernd Wiesberger, Sweden's Oscar Floren, Australia's Daniel Gaunt, England's Robert Dinwiddie, Chile's Mark Tullo and George Murray of Scotland.

Four graduates from the 2009 Challenge Tour – Rhys Davies, Edoardo Molinari, James Morrison and John Parry – equalled a record by winning on their arrival to The 2010 European Tour International Schedule and the new graduates have now joined the next Race for Number One honours – a prize which Martin Kaymer captured ahead of Graeme McDowell following a thrilling end of season tussle between the German and the Northern Irishman which went down to the wire in Dubai.

It truly was a year to cherish.

Mitchell Platts

Martin Kaymer

OFFICIAL WORLD GOLF RANKING RECORDS FOR WORLD NUMBER ONE POSITION
(as at the end of The Race to Dubai 2010)

BERNHARD LANGER	6.04.86 to 20.04.86	(3 weeks)
SEVE BALLESTEROS	27.04.86 to 7.09.86	(20 weeks)
	22.11.87	(1 week)
	30.10.88	(1 week)
	13.11.88 to 19.03.89	(19 weeks)
	2.04.89 to 13.08.89	(20 weeks)
		(Total 61 weeks)
GREG NORMAN	14.09.86 to 15.11.87	(62 weeks)
	29.11.87 to 23.10.88	(48 weeks)
	6.11.88	(1 week)
	26.03.89	(1 week)
	20.08.89 to 26.08.90	(54 weeks)
	14.10.90 to 27.01.91	(16 weeks)
	6.02.94 to 7.08.94	(27 weeks)
	18.06.95 to 13.04.97	(96 weeks)
	27.04.97 to 8.06.97	(7 weeks)
	29.06.97	(1 week)
	7.09.97 to 4.01.98	(18 weeks)
		(Total 331 weeks)
SIR NICK FALDO	2.09.90 to 7.10.90	(6 weeks)
	3.02.91 to 31.03.91	(9 weeks)
	29.03.92	(1 week)
	19.07.92 to 30.01.94	(81 weeks)
		(Total 97 weeks)
IAN WOOSNAM	7.04.91 to 15.03.92	(50 weeks)
FRED COUPLES	22.03.92	(1 week)
	5.04.92 to 12.07.92	(15 weeks)
		(Total 16 weeks)
NICK PRICE	14.08.94 to 11.06.95	(44 weeks)
TOM LEHMAN	20.04.97	(1 week)
TIGER WOODS	15.06.97	(1 week)
	6.07.97 to 31.08.97	(9 weeks)
	11.01.98 to 5.04.98	(13 weeks)
	10.05.98	(1 week)
	14.06.98 to 21.03.99	(41 weeks)
	4.07.99 to 1.08.99	(5 weeks)
	15.08.99 to 29.08.04	(264 weeks)
	6.03.05 to 13.03.05	(2 weeks)
	10.04.05 to 15.05.05	(6 weeks)
	12.06.05 to 24.10.10	##(281 weeks)
		** (Total 623 weeks)
ERNIE ELS	22.06.97	(1 week)
	12.04.98 to 3.05.98	(4 weeks)
	17.05.98 to 7.06.98	(4 weeks)
		(Total 9 weeks)
DAVID DUVAL	28.03.99 to 27.06.99	(14 weeks)
	8.08.99	(1 week)
		(Total 15 weeks)
VIJAY SINGH	6.09.04 to 27.02.05	(26 weeks)
	20.03.05 to 3.04.05	(3 weeks)
	22.05.05 to 5.06.05	(3 weeks)
		(Total 32 weeks)
LEE WESTWOOD	from 31.10.10	(4 weeks)

Total of 1286 weeks

Lee Westwood - World Number One

** Record number of weeks at No.1   ## Record successive weeks at No.1

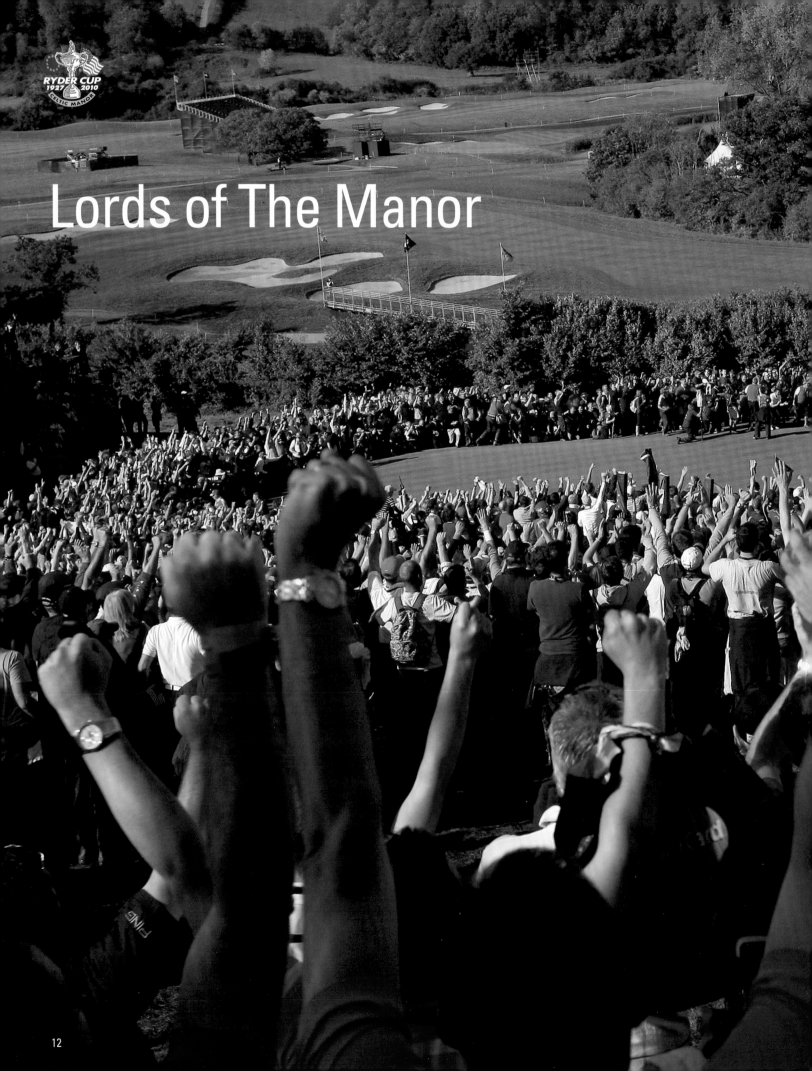

Lords of The Manor

When Sir Terry Matthews first conceived his bid for The Ryder Cup more than 15 years ago, he did so in the hope that one day it would end with precisely the pictures that were beamed around the world yesterday

Paul Kelso (Daily Telegraph)

The latest story of The Ryder Cup is captured for most people in the photographs and television pictures of that thrilling ending, of the teeming, happy and chaotic throng that surrounded players on the 17th green of The Twenty Ten Course at The Celtic Manor Resort as Europe claimed a dramatic 14 ½ - 13 ½ victory.

This public memory seized on the throbbing emotion of the moment and filed it away in a special place. For the overwhelming majority The 2010 Ryder Cup ended up being about champagne and laughter, big cigars and little moments of serious comradeship. This is understandable.

Yet for those of us privileged to have observed at close quarters the body language of the defeated as well as the victorious and to have listened to their words when the American and European teams came into the sprawling media centre an hour or so after this extraordinary final day ended, there were other, more intimate memories on offer to pull along life's highway.

Many of the players became more eloquent than they had been all week. Freed by either disappointment or elation from the constraints of considering what they should say, they said what they really felt. In Hunter Mahan's case this eloquence consisted of a few words as he described his deciding singles match against Graeme McDowell before he choked up, the tears rolling into his eyes and closing his throat.

Corey Pavin and Colin Montgomerie

Lisa Pavin (left) and Gaynor Montgomerie lead the
wives and partners at the Opening Ceremony

Carries golfers, bags **and your operation to a new level.**

CAN A GOLF CAR
REALLY DO THAT?

Increase revenues, reduce expenses, manage your key assets and deliver a superior customer experience. Only a Club Car fleet can deliver all of these. Sound too good to be true? Contact your Club Car representative today.

YES, IF IT'S A **Club Car** ®

www.clubcar.com
info_esa@clubcar.com
(+44) 777 180 5463

Sir Terry Matthews, Chairman of The Celtic Manor Resort, John Jermine, Chairman of Ryder Cup Wales and HRH Prince Charles

The Rt Hon Carwyn Jones, First Minister for Wales

Katherine Jenkins

Sir Terry Matthews and President of the European Commission José Manuel Barroso

HRH Prince Charles (seated centre, front row) with the Captains, players, officials, wives and partners of both teams at Cardiff Castle

This simple, physical expression of despair from a young man who blamed himself for Europe's victory said much for his own competitive instinct but more about where this compelling contest now sits in the psyche of the players as well as in our own imagination.

It is now a Ryder Cup tradition that the vanquished come in to talk to the media first. Eventually these players will dissect their week and will come to the reasonable conclusion that, but for a missed putt here or a wayward drive there, they could have won. Even Mahan will realise that mis-hitting a straightforward chip a few yards short of the 17th green is not the worst mistake he will make in his life.

But for this moment in Wales it clearly was the focus of his tearful distraction and we all felt for him. His team-mates felt for him too and indeed Phil Mickelson quickly grabbed a microphone to reinforce the thought that whatever they had done, they had done it as a team. Even the great individualist Tiger Woods nodded emphatically while a stony-faced Jim Furyk suggested that anyone who had thought they did not share the Europeans' passion for the old duel had now been disabused of this fanciful notion.

George O'Grady and Joe Steranka, CEO of the PGA of America, explain the change in playing format to the world's media

Jim McKenzie (front centre), Director of Golf Courses and Estates Management at The Celtic Manor Resort with his greenkeeping staff

Ross Fisher

Vivid Sensations

HEREDEROS DEL
MARQUÉS DE RISCAL

Fundada en 1858

www.marquesderiscal.com
www.sensacionesvivas.com

Lee Westwood

Then it was the European Team's turn. Separated from Corey Pavin's side by just one point but by several miles of satisfaction, they wandered in. Colin Montgomerie, a genuinely distinguished Captain as events turned out, confirmed he would not be seeking a second spell in the hot seat. "No, no," he said. "I am handing the baton on."

There was some sentimentality as well as much inevitable banter. Lee Westwood, the rock upon whom Montgomerie built his campaign, interrupted Rory McIlroy's soliloquy to ask the Northern Irishman what he now thought about an occasion he had somewhat recklessly referred to as "an exhibition" some 18 months earlier. McIlroy paused, laughed and said: "I think it's the greatest 'exhibition' in the world and I've just enjoyed the best week of my life."

Soon enough they had retreated, a gang in search of a good time, a few more beers and perhaps even some Rioja. Not all hit the exit however. Westwood, clearly enjoying his time at the centre of the Team, stayed to one side chatting to reporters. McDowell, too, remained, sitting in his seat cradling a beer.

Steve Stricker and Tiger Woods

It has been some year for him. Victory in the US Open Championship at Pebble Beach and now this. You could see him trying hard to grasp the detail of the most significant four months of his career and trying even harder to work out exactly what had happened as he nursed a slender lead home.

What had happened, of course, was that he had hit the approach shot of his life at the 16th and then curled the best birdie putt of his life into the hole to move from one hole up to two. "I didn't want to knock it several feet past but when it went in my heart jumped," he said. "It was a slippery putt alright."

What followed then was a concession by Mahan on the 17th green to confirm Europe's triumph. Would McDowell not have preferred to hole a putt on that green to win the Cup? "No, Hunter did the right thing," said the Ulsterman. "I was only five feet away with two for the hole, the match and The Ryder Cup. When he missed his chip shot I swapped to a putter and just nudged my ball up there. I could hardly hold the club I was so nervous. I've played a lot of golf with

Hunter, starting with college golf in the States. I know him well so I felt for him. It could so easily have been the other way round. I'm just lucky I guess."

Fortunate, perhaps, but also undeniably very, very good and, over time, McDowell will be very proud of the fact that when the biggest question of his golfing life was asked he came up with the right answer. Over time, European golf will also thank their collective lucky stars that it was he who Montgomerie selected to sashay on to the course to play out the role of last man standing.

Yet before this historic, blue-sky Monday took place it had seemed that The Ryder Cup in Wales had been cursed by some particularly malevolent spirit as half a month's worth of water fell in less than 24 hours, meaning even The Twenty Ten Course's mammoth irrigation system gurgled in alarm and temporarily gave up the ghost. With play suspended after just a couple of hours of fourball action on the Friday and more rain forecast overnight, many feared this Ryder Cup was irretrievably lost.

José Maria Olazábal

Colin Montgomerie and Rhys Davies

Jim Furyk and Darren Clarke

Stewart Cink

Ross Fisher and Padraig Harrington

Lee Westwood and Martin Kaymer

Sergio Garcia

Francesco and Edoardo Molinari

Miguel Angel Jiménez and Peter Hanson

RYDER CUP
1927 2010

OFFICIAL PARTNERS OF
THE 2010 RYDER CUP

OFFICIAL PARTNERS OF
THE 2010 RYDER CUP

EUR	5	OVERALL STANDINGS	6	USA
6 & 5	DONALD WESTWOOD	F	STRICKER WOODS	
3 UP	McDOWELL McILROY	11	Z. JOHNSON MAHAN	
1 UP	HARRINGTON FISHER	10	FURYK D. JOHNSON	
1 UP	HANSON JIMENEZ	9	WATSON OVERTON	
1 UP	E. MOLINARI F. MOLINARI	8	CINK KUCHAR	
3 UP	POULTER KAYMER	7	MICKELSON FOWLER	

They had not, however, reckoned with the sheer determination and never say die attitude of the organisers to get the show going again. A hundred miles away, Wentworth Club's own greenkeeper Chris Kennedy purloined whatever water-moving machinery he could find at his and adjoining clubs and hurled it into a lorry before setting off down the M4 for Wales to join Jim McKenzie, Director of Golf Courses and Estates Management at Celtic Manor and his 110-strong greenkeeping staff who waited patiently for reinforcements.

Their efforts were prodigious and in the end they worked. Heroes were not just to be found playing golf at The Ryder Cup. Heroes at The Celtic Manor Resort also wore Wellington boots caked with layers of mud and worked through the night.

The same may be said of the paying public who turned up in their thousands and refused to be bowed by delayed play and squelching ground.

In many ways, the fans made The 2010 Ryder Cup with their good humour, their songs, their support for Europe and their good-nature towards the American Team. "They were never, ever, disrespectful and we thank them for that," said Pavin.

It meant Friday's fourballs were completed on the Saturday morning with the Americans ending the session 2 ½ - 1 ½ to the good. We then enjoyed a unique sight in Ryder Cup history of six foursomes being played at the same time, each one of the 24 players out on the course in an attempt to make up the time lost to the elements. "What's happening?" one fan shouted to a pal. "I've no idea," came the reply. "But it's magnificent, whatever it is."

It was too. It was a fall-back defensive plan that had been hatched some time before and one which hoped to see all 28 points played for and contested, as planned, by the close of play on Sunday night.

Thomas Björn

Graeme McDowell and Rory McIlroy

It nearly worked too but rain came again overnight on Saturday meaning Sunday morning was washed out too. By then, the six foursomes had been completed midway through the day on Saturday with the United States taking the session by 3 ½ - 2 ½ to open up an overall lead of 6-4. The new format then saw two further foursomes and four fourballs take to the course on Saturday afternoon and this proved to be the session where, effectively, Europe won The 2010 Ryder Cup.

When darkness drew a halt to proceedings, Montgomerie's side were ahead in all six matches on the golf course and they continued the surge when play eventually resumed on Sunday afternoon, taking five and a half points out of the six available to turn a two point deficit into a 9 ½ - 6 ½ point lead. "Momentum," said Montgomerie. "At last we've got the momentum."

After a hectic period of thrust and counter-thrust it meant the final singles session would now, for the first time in history, have to take place on a Monday - the three-day Ryder Cup had become a four-day Ryder Cup.

Ian Poulter

Luke Donald

As the additional day dawned there was no rain. Instead the sun dangled hesitantly over the course, a slim veil of fog causing brief irritation but no more than that. Walking down into the valley to see play offered a beautiful autumnal scene while behind the first tee the spectators gathered, sang and laughed.

On early morning television Sir Terry Matthews was asked how upsetting it was to have had all this rain and now for The Ryder Cup to have to go into Monday. "Upsetting?" he laughed. "We bought into a three day match and now we've got an extra day for free. How good is that?" Positive-thinking man is Sir Terry, the driving force behind The Celtic Manor Resort and the architect of its audacious original bid for the match.

The serious worry had been that Monday play would see a diminished crowd, that the spark would go out of the spectacle. But, if there were fewer fans on Monday than any other day, then the absentees must have been hiding in a small shed somewhere for no-one could tell the difference as over 35,000 people flooded in.

Miguel Angel Jiménez

Luke Donald and Ian Poulter

Peter Hanson

Edoardo and Francesco Molinari

When the competition changed in 1979 from the United States versus Great Britain and Ireland to the US versus Europe, people were unsure whether the amorphous European mass would have any collective identity. But if you wanted an answer to that, you would have had it on the first tee yesterday morning when Miguel Angel Jiménez arrived. He received the loudest cheer of the day, he took his cap off and he conducted the singing. And next, in succession, came the Molinari brothers; and boy have these (mainly) British crowds enjoyed hugging two Italians to their hearts. There is something about The Ryder Cup that is marvellously, healthily international.......suddenly we are all a big family. Not just the players, the spectators belong here too, and that is why they come back in the rain or when they should be at work, and serenade players from foreign countries......and the rivalry works so well. Right on the edge, gentlemen at war, with the enemy, the Americans, being applauded heartily for their every good shot, too. I am writing this as a reporter who has been privileged enough to cover pretty much every big sport and every big sporting event. Olympics, World Cups, it is a vain brag to have pretty much bagged them all. They all have their own wonder and their own joy. But for pure, unadulterated, non-stop magic, The Ryder Cup beats them all.

Owen Slot (The Times)

Paul McGinley

> So to a putt that will be recalled as long as golf is played, to a scene that left 35,000 people thanking the Lord for genial bosses, and a nerve-shredding conclusion to a manic Monday that left a brilliant captain to surely reflect this was the major he never won. So to McDowell. So to another unforgettable day when the European colours of gold and blue were tinged once again with a magical splash of green

Derek Lawrenson (Daily Mail)

Graeme McDowell

The denouement is detailed elsewhere and, anyway, you know it. You know that a gracious Steve Stricker started an impressive American assault on Europe's three point lead by defeating Lee Westwood thanks to some startling, quality play. You know that Stewart Cink missed two short ones coming in and that Rory McIlroy held his nerve to pull in a half; that Luke Donald continued to impress everyone with his laser-like precision that dispatched Jim Furyk and that 46 year old Miguel Angel Jiménez likely signed off from Ryder Cup playing duty with a special victory of his own over Bubba Watson. Of course, you also know that Graeme McDowell held his nerve against Hunter Mahan when it mattered most.

So a relieved Montgomerie, his career already defined by The Ryder Cup as a player, finally had his victory as a Captain and drew the whole shebang into a final, golden circle. It was, he said, his proudest moment.

Over in Spain, such a sentiment would have been equally expressed by an exultant Severiano Ballesteros, freed for a short time from his pressing health concerns by this

Francesco Molinari and Sergio Garcia

wonderful spectacle. The great man played a central part in this stunning triumph however, his encouragement to the players on the eve of the contest – relayed on a speakerphone from his home – was a speech which impacted deeply on each and every one of them.

If, then, there was a more poignant sight all year than the vision of his great friend José Maria Olazábal – drafted in to bolster an already impressive backroom staff of Thomas Björn, Darren Clarke, Sergio Garcia and Paul McGinley – carrying away from the closing ceremony the giant photograph of the pair of them in Ryder Cup action, a picture that had illuminated the team-room for the week, then I, for one, did not see it.

"We won The Ryder Cup for ourselves, for Monty, for The European Tour and for all those wonderful fans but we especially won it for Seve," said McDowell. We all join with him in that sentiment.

Bill Elliott
Golf Monthly

Edoardo Molinari

Lee Westwood

Padraig Harrington

Martin Kaymer

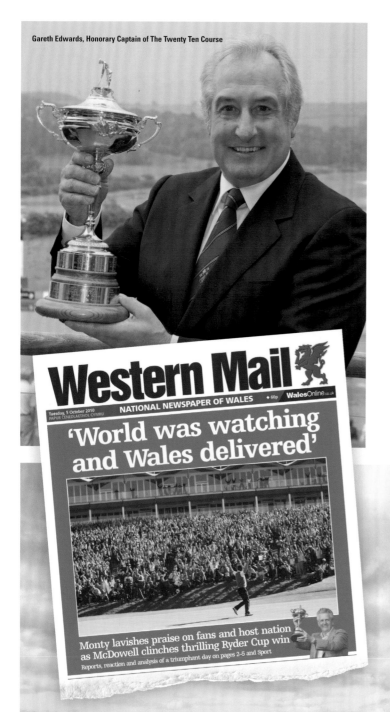

Gareth Edwards, Honorary Captain of The Twenty Ten Course

Western Mail

NATIONAL NEWSPAPER OF WALES

Tuesday, 5 October 2010
PAPUR CENEDLAETHOL CYMRU

WalesOnline.co.uk

◆ 60p

'World was watching and Wales delivered'

Monty lavishes praise on fans and host nation as McDowell clinches thrilling Ryder Cup win

Reports, reaction and analysis of a triumphant day on pages 2-5 and Sport

> Whether passing bottles of Heineken down the table at their news conference Monday night at Celtic Manor, or putting a well-placed hand around the shoulder of a teammate during a match at a crucial time, we have come to know the European Ryder Cup team as one of the tightest collective units in sports
>
> **Tim Rosaforte, Golf World (US)**

Colin Montgomerie

Magical Monday put me on a fairway to heaven

What a day Monday was. A day to burn in the memory. A day to lock away. A day to keep safe.

A day to resurrect when you need to remember how magical, how engrossing, how utterly riveting and visceral sport can be.

Watching a portly marshal fall over in the mud on the bank by the fifth tee and laughing because it made Tiger Woods smile.

Marvelling at the hush that fell over the crowd by the side of the 15th green on the extremities of the course as Graeme McDowell lined up a putt and all you could hear was the long grass rustling in the wind.

Studying American captain Corey Pavin as he put his hands on Ricky Fowler's shoulders when the rookie walked off the 14th green three down to Edoardo Molinari.

"See you on the 18th," Pavin said, "and make sure you're even." Pavin didn't make it but Fowler did. In one of the most courageous efforts of the competition, he halved his match. Gazing at Monty striding the wrong way down the 14th fairway, shoulders stooped, head down, realising it was all in the balance, realising his career might soon have no hiding place.

Squinting in the sunlight, seeing him disappear towards the 13th fairway where McDowell was holding Monty's fate in his hands.

Lying on a grassy knoll above the 16th green, pretty much behind McDowell as he rolled his putt, slowly, slowly, towards the hole and seeing it drop in

Seeing the army of fans swarming around the 17th green as McDowell and Hunter Mahan played out the final scenes of the epic.

Watching the ropes that usually separate the supporters from the players disappear and become irrelevant.

Wondering what would happen if the match went to the 18th, thinking that the chaos might be unmanageable.

Looking at the scenes around the 17th and thinking this was about as good as sport gets.

Thinking that golf, sometimes so sedate and so stuffy, has a capacity for drama that other more breathless sports cannot match.

Watching poor Mahan choke and fluff his chip from the edge of the putting surface. Knowing then that it was over.

Realising that when Mahan conceded, everyone was going to run on to the green. And running on with them.

Getting close enough to Monty in the crazy melee to be sprayed in the face by champagne aimed at him. Watching his emotional confusion in the very moment of his greatest victory.

Hearing a Welsh voice amid the cacophony of celebration. "Well done Monty boy," it was saying.

Leaving the 17th in a demented conga line of players, cameramen and journalists and turning round to see Rory McIlroy right behind me.

Thinking to hell with the journalists' convention of not getting involved, and shaking McIlroy's hand as a small gesture of thanks for the entertainment he had provided.

Strolling down the side of the 18th flecked with mud and happiness and looking back at the army of fans heading down the hill like soldiers following their generals.

Seeing a golf cart arrive at the 18th green and doing a wheelie, nearly tipping Lee Westwood and Ian Poulter off the back.

Getting caught in another scrum on the 18th when McDowell is interviewed by a television crew and the crowd drowns him out with its chanting.

Sitting in the media tent and seeing the other side of things, watching Mahan, tormented by guilt, break down in tears, sobbing and saying simply: "He beat me."

Watching Phil Mickelson intervene and take the microphone from Mahan, hearing Mickelson talk about the points he had lost for his team. Realising Mickelson was taking the blame for the defeat, that without actually saying it, he was telling Mahan it was not his fault. Realising everything they say about Mickelson being a classy guy is true.

Thinking then that I'd been dumb to mock the Americans, and particularly Pavin, so much before the competition.

Remembering how desperately close they had come to pulling off a remarkable victory.

Watching them in a long line on the dais, hearing them refuse to make excuses about mud or fog or partisan fans. Thinking they were about as dignified and as honourable in defeat as any team could ever be.

Thinking it didn't really feel as though anyone had lost the match, that it just felt as though everyone who had played a part in that day was a winner.

Riding the bus back up the hill in the darkness, seeing the lights in the clubhouse and the lights in the valleys.

Hoping that maybe, before too many years pass, a day like that would come again.

Oliver Holt
Daily Mirror

THE 2010 RYDER CUP
The Celtic Manor Resort (Twenty Ten Course)
City of Newport, Wales
October 1–4, 2010

FINAL RESULTS

EUROPE		UNITED STATES	

SESSION 1
FOURBALLS

EUROPE		UNITED STATES	
L Westwood & M Kaymer (3 & 2)	1	P Mickelson & D Johnson	0
R McIlroy & G McDowell (halved)	½	S Cink & M Kuchar (halved)	½
I Poulter & R Fisher	0	S Stricker & T Woods (2 holes)	1
L Donald & P Harrington	0	B Watson & J Overton (3 & 2)	1
	1½		**2½**

SESSION 2
FOURSOMES

EUROPE		UNITED STATES	
M A Jiménez & P Hanson	0	T Woods & Stricker (4 & 3)	1
E Molinari & F Molinari	0	Z Johnson & H Mahan (2 holes)	1
L Westwood & M Kaymer (halved)	½	J Furyk & R Fowler (halved)	½
P Harrington & R Fisher (3 & 2)	1	P Mickelson & D Johnson	0
I Poulter & L Donald (2 & 1)	1	B Watson & J Overton	0
G McDowell & R McIlroy	0	S Cink & M Kuchar (1 hole)	1
	2½		**3½**

SESSION 3
FOURSOMES

EUROPE		UNITED STATES	
L Donald & L Westwood (6 & 5)	1	S Stricker & T Woods	0
G McDowell & R McIlroy (3 &1)	1	Z Johnson & H Mahan	0

FOURBALLS

EUROPE		UNITED STATES	
P Harrington & R Fisher (2 & 1)	1	J Furyk & D Johnson	0
P Hanson & M A Jiménez (2 holes)	1	B Watson & J Overton	0
E Molinari & F Molinari (halved)	½	S Cink & M Kuchar (halved)	½
I Poulter & M Kaymer (2 & 1)	1	P Mickelson & R Fowler	0
	5½		**½**

SESSION 4
SINGLES

EUROPE		UNITED STATES	
L Westwood	0	S Stricker (2 &1)	1
R McIlroy (halved)	½	S Cink (halved)	½
L Donald (1 hole)	1	J Furyk	0
M Kaymer	0	D Johnson (6 & 4)	1
I Poulter (5 & 4)	1	M Kuchar	0
R Fisher	0	J Overton (3 & 2)	1
M A Jiménez (4 & 3)	1	B Watson	0
F Molinari	0	T Woods (4 & 3)	1
E Molinari (halved)	½	R Fowler (halved)	½
P Hanson	0	P Mickelson (4 & 2)	1
P Harrington	0	Z Johnson (3& 2)	1
G McDowell (3 & 1)	1	H Mahan	0
	5		**7**

EUROPE	**14½**	**UNITED STATES**	**13½**

INDIVIDUAL PLAYER PERFORMANCES

EUROPE

	PLD	W	L	H	PTS
Luke Donald	4	3	1	0	3
Ian Poulter	4	3	1	0	3
Martin Kaymer	4	2	1	1	2½
Lee Westwood	4	2	1	1	2½
Graeme McDowell	4	2	1	1	2½
Miguel Angel Jiménez	3	2	1	0	2
Ross Fisher	4	2	2	0	2
Padraig Harrington	4	2	2	0	2
Rory McIlroy	4	1	1	2	2
Peter Hanson	3	1	2	0	1
Edoardo Molinari	3	0	1	2	1
Francesco Molinari	3	0	2	1	½

UNITED STATES

	PLD	W	L	H	PTS
Steve Stricker	4	3	1	0	3
Tiger Woods	4	3	1	0	3
Stewart Cink	4	1	0	3	2½
Zach Johnson	3	2	1	0	2
Jeff Overton	4	2	2	0	2
Matt Kuchar	4	1	1	2	2
Hunter Mahan	3	1	2	0	1
Rickie Fowler	3	0	1	2	1
Dustin Johnson	4	1	3	0	1
Phil Mickelson	4	1	3	0	1
Bubba Watson	4	1	3	0	1
Jim Furyk	3	0	2	1	½

Efficiency and Focus

For those of us who have spent a lifetime admiring German efficiency and focus on the football field, the car factory and almost everywhere else, it is tempting to label each fresh German prodigy with the same serious epithet. Tempting, and in the case of Martin Kaymer, apposite.

The new Race to Dubai champion might be fun and possess a quietly wicked sense of humour off the course but inside the ropes he is indeed overwhelmingly focused while his game is the sort of finely-honed efficient fusion of movement and talent that marks a man out early as potentially something special.

At 25 he is now an integral part of the future of European golf, a player surely destined to further embroider his game into the global consciousness. As European Number One he is a worthy successor to a long line of outstanding champions. He is also one of the youngest.

"I am very proud of what I have achieved this year," he said. "It has been a fantastic season and to have accomplished all the goals I set out for myself at the start of the year, culminating in winning The Race to Dubai

is just wonderful. It will be a tough act to follow next year but I will be trying my hardest, you can bank on that."

It seems extraordinary when one reflects that it is only three years since he was voted The Sir Henry Cotton Rookie of the Year. The fact remains, however, that since that accolade was bestowed upon him towards the end of 2007, he has made the sort of progress others may only consider during their more dreamy moments.

Kaymer, mind, is no dreamer. Instead he endorses that other German strength – he is a practical man and a golfer who realised early that the harder he worked, the more he strived and the higher he reached, then the better he became. This may be a simplistic truth but too many talented young players fail to fully

Celebrating his US PGA Championship triumph

With brother Philip (left) and father Horst

grasp this thought,
confusing time spent on a practice ground
with actual, hard-graft practice. Not
Kaymer. Never Kaymer.

Petra Himmel, a golf writer who casts
an elegant eye over the German scene
from her base in Bavaria, has been one
of the keenest of observers of Kaymer
over the years and reports that he has
always been an intelligent, polite young
man whose ego has remained as small
by contrast as his achievements are
increasingly spectacular.

"Martin has always been a very nice
guy," she said. "He comes from a very
good family with good values and they
have always made sure he has remained
grounded. Because he lived a part of
his college life in Arizona he was not
as well known in Germany initially
as he should have been, but that has
changed now. He works very hard and
he is his own man. Even as an amateur
he impressed the others because he
practised so much and always seemed
to know exactly what he wanted."

Of course what he wanted was to be
the best that was available to him. The
interesting thing is that he is still finding
out how good this 'best' actually is.

Born in Dusseldorf on December 28, 1984,
he is the younger by two years of two
brothers. Like most German lads, their

imagination was originally captured by
football and no doubt they practised
penalties until darkness prevented them
once again beating England in a World
Cup Final played out in their back garden.

Their father Horst, however, was
increasingly drawn to golf. Bernhard
Langer was in his Masters Tournament-
winning pomp at the time and at last
the game was being driven forward by
positive publicity in the German media.
Happily also, just down the road from
the family home was Mettmann Golf

Club and swiftly this place became a
playground for the brothers and their dad.

Martin and Philip turned out to be
naturals. Enthused by the old game, they
brought their hand-eye co-ordination
away from the football field and onto
the golf course. Horst, meanwhile,
encouraged. He also challenged.

When they were big enough in their teens
to properly attack the ball he laid down a
template that the boys followed faithfully.
First, he encouraged them to play off the
back tees and then he challenged them
by outlawing tee pegs. Even for drivers.
"It meant that when we got to use tees in
competitions we thought driving the ball
was really easy," said Martin. Watch him,
he still does.

This was no considered and scary
Tiger Woods-esque preparation for the
professional stage by an overbearing
father. He never envisaged either of his
sons playing any game for a living, he
simply wanted them to play golf to the
best of their abilities. Indeed, he expected
them to enter other, safer and more
obvious professions; law, medicine, or the
business world.

In his late teens, however, Martin began
to entertain other ideas. He admits it took

With caddie Craig Connelly

Partnering for Success

As a proud sponsor of The European Tour, we are clearly focused on working with the right partner to succeed in our field. Since 2007 we have celebrated this partnership through performance in statistics.

Together. Celebrating Golf.

To learn more visit genworth.com

The official sponsor of the European Tour Statistics

courage to tell his father and mother, Rina, of his ambition but when he at last plucked up the courage, he found that his parents were surprised but supportive. Once committed, none of them looked back.

So he turned professional in 2005 and entered the first stage of The European Tour Qualifying School. Philip offered solidarity by entering alongside him. Martin finished first, Philip was last. A few days later Philip signed up for law school. Horst was happy.

Martin failed to go on to win his playing rights and therefore instead of a big adventure in 2006 he found himself grinding away for peanuts on the European Professional Development Tour. He soon prospered, however, entering 14 events and winning five of them.

This victory roll included the Habseberg Classic where he started with a par and then a bogey before strolling through the next 16 holes in 14 under par for a 59. It is a score that still irritates him. Four years later he told Sports Illustrated: "I'm still annoyed that I parred the 17th hole, a really easy par five." Never satisfied is always a sign of impending greatness.

His success moved him on to the Challenge Tour in August 2006. It was a very late start if he was to earn enough to secure a place on The European Tour the following year and few expected him to do it. No-one except Martin and his family. In the end he played in eight events and won two of them to do just that.

The first of these victories came at the Vodafone Challenge near his home in Dusseldorf but it was a crucial win that almost never happened. By then, sadly, his mother was ill and a fall saw her taken into hospital. Martin's instinct was to drop everything and head for her bedside.

Horst was down to caddie that week but instead asked Philip to set aside his law books and to do the job. When Philip got to the course he saw an upset Martin prepared to withdraw. It was then that

With father Horst at the culmination of his Race to Dubai victory

Philip made the motivational speech of his life, telling his little brother that it would not help their mother if they sat by her bed with tears in their eyes and if they wanted to do something positive then they should gear up and go out and win.

"After that he played with more focus than I have ever seen from him," Philip later reflected. Together, the Kaymer brothers won. That evening they presented the trophy to Rina in the hospital and of course there were tears. A second win a few weeks later in France saw Kaymer secure his card to play The European Tour in 2007. He was off, although, as it turned out, not yet running.

He missed the cut in his first five tournaments in 2007. He felt homesick and more than a little lost as he faltered during the Tour's early swing through the Far East. Once again Philip lobbed aside his law books and headed east to offer support off the course and to carry the bag on it. It worked and after Philip returned to his studies, a series of high finishes, highlighted by ten top 15s, saw a reinvigorated Martin end the year as top rookie.

A couple of months later in early 2008 he won his first big professional title at the Abu Dhabi Golf Championship. Six months later, Rina insisted he play

rather than spend time with her as she approached the end of a weary two year battle with cancer – he did just that and won the BMW International Open in Munich. The tearful victory was dedicated to his mum before, sadly, Frau Kaymer passed away a few weeks later and her son's stellar season understandably stuttered to a premature halt.

Since then, however, he has won another six titles including this year his first Major, the US PGA Championship, when he watched with co-leader Bubba Watson in the Whistling Straits locker-room as the unfortunate Dustin Johnson mistook a bunker for a building site to miss out on his place in a play-off. "Bubba and I looked at each other and said the same thing, 'that's sad'," he said later.

Sad or not, while Watson approached the play-off with a gung-ho strategy which ultimately backfired, Kaymer once again tapped into his reservoir of efficiency and focus to take the title after having holed one of the putts of the year from 12 feet on the 72nd green to make the play-off in the first place. He was, he admitted, more concerned initially with making sure of a place in the European Ryder Cup Team - the US PGA Championship, it seems, was no more than a really decent bonus. Everyone got the impression he wasn't kidding either.

He won on his next two outings as well, the KLM Open and the Alfred Dunhill Links Championship, to offer us a rare hat-trick of victories to savour. In so doing he set up a Race to Dubai lead that, though whittled away by a determined Graeme McDowell, proved significant enough to secure him The Harry Vardon Trophy at the culmination of the Dubai World Championship where he finished in a share of 13th place to see him end the season with record earnings of €4,461,011.

Martin (second left) and fellow members of the German team at the 2004 Eisenhower Trophy

Some season then and some golfer. Asked to sum up his rival for the Race to Dubai crown, Graeme McDowell thought for a few seconds before offering: "Nothing seems to faze him."

Meanwhile, his old, unflappable inspiration, Bernhard Langer, came up with his usual considered thought. "He has a good head on his shoulders. If he doesn't get distracted, he should be up there for a long time." Coming from Bernhard, that is by way of a coronation endorsement.

Herr Kaymer, sie sind der mann!

Bill Elliott
Golf Monthly

MARTIN KAYMER - FACTS AND ACHIEVEMENTS

Becomes the second German to finish The European Tour season as Number One, following Bernhard Langer (1981 and 1984).

Aged 25 years and 335 days is the youngest player to be crowned Number One since Ronan Rafferty in 1989, who was 25 years and 289 days.

His first season on The European Tour was in 2007, when he was crowned The Sir Henry Cotton Rookie of the Year, finishing 41st in the Order of Merit.

Follows Bernard Gallacher, Peter Oosterhuis, Sir Nick Faldo, Sandy Lyle and Colin Montgomerie as players to have been named The Sir Henry Cotton Rookie of the Year and go on to win The Harry Vardon Trophy.

Has improved his ranking in every one of his four years; 41st in 2007, eighth in 2008; third in 2009 and first in 2010.

Since The European Tour's first season in 1972, Kaymer becomes the 17th different player to be Number One.

Follows Seve Ballesteros (1976, 77, 78, 86, 88, 91), Bernhard Langer (1981, 84) and Robert Karlsson (2008) as Continental Europeans to win The Harry Vardon Trophy.

THE 2010 RACE TO DUBAI FINAL STANDINGS

			€
1	**MARTIN KAYMER**		**4,461,011**
2	Graeme McDowell		3,896,996
3	Lee Westwood		3,222,423
4	Ian Poulter		3,027,008
5	Francesco Molinari		2,799,692
6	Robert Karlsson		2,296,486
7	Ernie Els		2,261,607
8	Charl Schwartzel		2,207,965
9	Miguel Angel Jiménez		2,179,418
10	Louis Oosthuizen		2,070,763
11	Edoardo Molinari		2,009,337
12	Paul Casey		1,888,850
13	Rory McIlory		1,821,050
14	Alvaro Quiros		1,750,255
15	Luke Donald		1,678,072

"This is unbelievable and the perfect way for me to get The 2010 Race to Dubai underway. There was a lot of emotion out there – I am so happy"

Pablo Martin

ALFRED DUNHILL CHAMPIONSHIP

ALFRED DUNHILL CHAMPIONSHIP
Leopard Creek Country Club
Malelane, South Africa
December 10-13, 2009

1	**PABLO MARTIN**	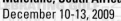	68	63	71	69	271	-17
2	Charl Schwartzel		67	69	68	68	272	-16
3	Anders Hansen		68	70	68	68	274	-14
4	Gareth Maybin		68	70	67	71	276	-12
	Robert Rock		69	68	70	69	276	-12
	Richard Sterne		72	66	72	66	276	-12
	Dale Whitnell		70	68	72	66	276	-12
8	Shiv Kapur		68	71	68	70	277	-11
	Michael Lorenzo-Vera		71	69	66	71	277	-11
	Damien McGrane		67	70	68	72	277	-11

Gaynor Rupert, wife of Johann Rupert, Group Executive Chairman of Richemont and Pablo Martin

Total Prize Fund €1,000,000   **First Prize €158,500**

Sister Act

The first tournament of the second Race to Dubai on The European Tour International Schedule was significant in its own right but Pablo Martin ensured it was history-making too when he became the first player since The European Tour began in 1972 to win titles both as an amateur and a professional.

The 23 year old Spaniard captured the Estoril Open de Portugal as an amateur in April 2007 but his first two full years in the paid ranks were less productive and, indeed, he only secured his playing rights for the 2010 season on the final day of the penultimate event of 2009 in Hong Kong.

But all that changed in the Alfred Dunhill Championship where a superb second round 63 proved the catalyst for a fine victory over the host nation's Charl Schwartzel who made a bold bid for the title. The South African attacked all the flags on the back nine on Sunday, an approach which yielded five birdies but also three bogeys which allowed the steady Martin to par the last five holes for a one shot triumph.

As well as his fellow Spanish professionals, Martin was cheered on by his sister Maria, who had watched him win in Portugal and who took in events at Leopard Creek on holiday. "She can't go home now, she'll have to come to every tournament with me," he joked.

Gareth Maybin

Richard Sterne

Barry Lane – who had the honour of hitting the first shot in The 2010 Race to Dubai – and Richard Hills of The European Tour

"Wherever you are in the world, whatever tournament you are playing in, there is no greater feeling than winning."

Richie Ramsay

1	**RICHIE RAMSAY**		67	75	68	65	**275**	**-13**
2	Shiv Kapur		71	68	69	67	275	-13
3	Anders Hansen		66	69	72	69	276	-12
4	Fredrik Andersson Hed		71	68	68	70	277	-11
	Edoardo Molinari		68	69	69	71	277	-11
6	Darren Fichardt		73	71	68	66	278	-10
	Pablo Martin		65	68	72	73	278	-10
8	Michiel Bothma		68	73	68	70	279	-9
	Søren Hansen		70	72	70	67	279	-9
	Michael Jonzon		68	75	69	67	279	-9
	James Kingston		72	66	69	72	279	-9
	Chris Swanepoel		72	69	68	70	279	-9

Richie Ramsay and Enver Hassen, President of the South African Golf Association

Total Prize Fund €1,010,637   **First Prize €158,500**

Richie Rich

Three years after becoming the first Scot to win the US Amateur Championship in 108 years, Richie Ramsay took the next step up the golfing ladder with his first European Tour title in the South African Open Championship.

The 25 year old struck a truly rich vein of form in the final round to come from five behind leader Pablo Martin – looking for consecutive victories following his win in the Alfred Dunhill Championship seven days previously – to storm to 13 under par 275 with a best of day 65.

As Martin slipped back, the final obstacle to his success stood in the shape of India's Shiv Kapur who matched the Scot's total following his own final round

67. But when he found the rough from the tee on the first play-off hole – the long 18th – he could do no better than par five, leaving Ramsay's textbook birdie four good enough for victory.

Ramsay was not the only European Tour Member celebrating in the Western Cape as Anders Hansen's third place finish confirmed the Dane as the winner of the 2009 Sunshine Tour Order of Merit. From the moment he won the Joburg Open in January, Hansen was in control and his supreme consistency over the season saw him become the first European golfer to top the ranking since 1972, finishing almost two million rand ahead of second placed Charl Schwartzel.

Anders Hansen

Shiv Kapur

Fredrik Andersson Hed

Edoardo Molinari

AFRICA OPEN
East London Golf Club
East London, Eastern Cape, South Africa
January 7-10, 2010

1	**CHARL SCHWARTZEL**		**67**	**70**	**68**	**67**	**272**	**-20**
2	Thomas Aiken		67	67	69	70	273	-19
3	Jbe' Kruger		69	68	67	70	274	-18
4	Trevor Fisher Jnr		66	66	71	72	275	-17
	Rick Kulacz		72	69	67	67	275	-17
	James Morrison		68	70	69	68	275	-17
	Chris Swanepoel		71	68	68	68	275	-17
8	Michiel Bothma		69	69	70	68	276	-16
	Pelle Edberg		69	68	70	69	276	-16
	Branden Grace		70	70	70	66	276	-16
	James Kingston		68	69	71	68	276	-16
	Miles Tunnicliff		68	71	67	70	276	-16

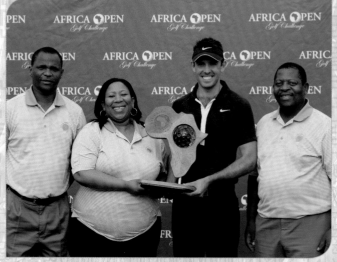

L-R: Mayor of Amathole Alderman Sakhumzi Somyo, Mayoress of Buffalo City Alderman Zukisa Faku, Charl Schwartzel and Khaya Ngqula, CEO of the Africa Open

Total Prize Fund €1,000,000   **First Prize** €158,500

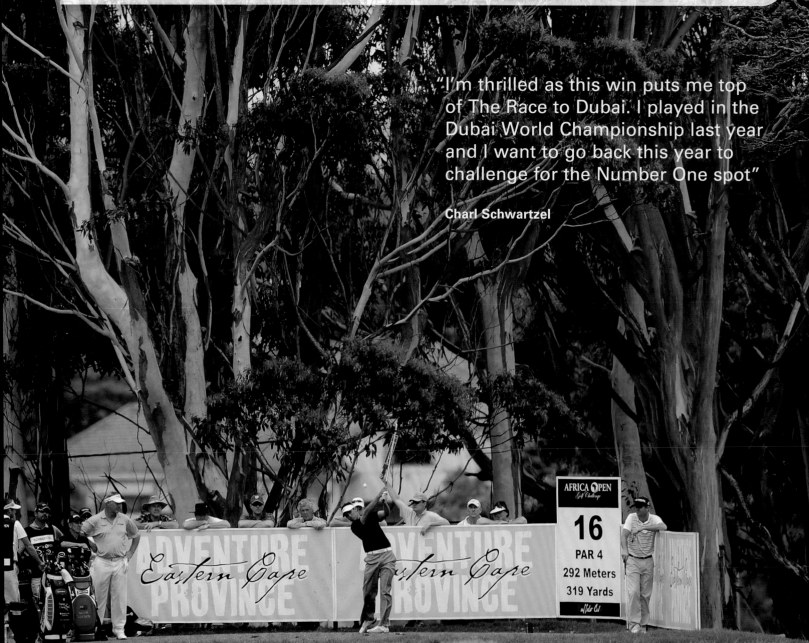

"I'm thrilled as this win puts me top of The Race to Dubai. I played in the Dubai World Championship last year and I want to go back this year to challenge for the Number One spot"

Charl Schwartzel

...h Moore's colourful fan club

James Morrison

Pelle Edberg

Out of Africa

Golf, by its very nature, is a difficult sport in which to predict winners. The perfect example of that came last season when you would have been given very long odds by your local bookmaker on the winners of the four Major Championships being Angel Cabrera, Lucas Glover, Stewart Cink and Y E Yang.

However, on the odd occasion, the favourite for the tournament does come out on top as was the case in the Africa Open when Charl Schwartzel picked up his fourth European Tour title. The 26 year old began the week as the highest ranked player in the Official World Golf Ranking in the field and lived up to his billing with an assured performance to

take the title, a victory which saw him move to the top of The Race to Dubai.

Opening rounds of 67-70-68 saw Schwartzel enter the final round two shots adrift of his fellow countrymen Thomas Aiken and Trevor Fisher Jnr but his flawless Sunday showing saw him pick up seven birdies in the first 17 holes to move two shots clear of Aiken.

His error-free day ended on the 18th where a pushed drive led to a bogey five, throwing down the gauntlet to Aiken, in the final group, who knew a birdie three on the same hole would force a play-off. Although he tried gamely from 15 feet, the ball stayed above ground to give Schwartzel victory.

Thomas Aiken

"I'm delighted as, not only does this strengthen my position at the top of The Race to Dubai, it gets me into the Masters through my World Ranking – I could not have had a better week"

Charl Schwartzel

Jo!burg
Open 2010

JOBURG OPEN
**Royal Johannesburg and Kensington Golf Club
(East and West Courses)
Johannesburg, South Africa**
January 14-17, 2010

1	**CHARL SCHWARTZEL**		**63**	**68**	**64**	**66**	**261**	**-23**
2	Darren Clarke		63	69	67	68	267	-17
	Keith Horne		68	65	70	64	267	-17
4	James Kamte		67	66	69	68	270	-14
	Danny Willett		65	67	70	68	270	-14
6	Søren Hansen		66	70	68	68	272	-12
	Joost Luiten		66	69	69	68	272	-12
	Hennie Otto		67	66	69	70	272	-12
	Peter Whiteford		66	69	70	67	272	-12
10	Josh Cunliffe		68	70	67	68	273	-11
	John Parry		66	67	71	69	273	-11

Charl Schwartzel and Councillor Amos Masondo, the Executive Mayor of Johannesburg

Total Prize Fund €1,313,847   **First Prize** €206,050

James Kamte and Danny Willett

Søren Hansen

Keith Horne

Darren Clarke

Homecoming Hero

The winner might have been the same as the previous week's Africa Open but the manner of victory for Charl Schwartzel in the Joburg Open could not have been more different.

Seven days ago at the East London Golf Club in the Eastern Cape, the 25 year old began the final round in arrears but came from behind to triumph. This time though, the Johannesburg native relished his homecoming by taking a four shot lead into the final round over the East Course at the Royal Johannesburg and Kensington Golf Club.

Earlier rounds of 63-68-64 had given him pole position before a superbly controlled final round 66 – where he brushed off the inconvenience of an early dropped shot at the third with

six birdies in the closing 13 holes – proved far too good for the chasing pack, led by Northern Ireland's Darren Clarke and Keith Horne of South Africa, who both ended the tournament six shots in arrears.

The winning margin equalled the biggest recorded throughout the entire 2009 season on The European Tour International Schedule; Schwartzel's recent dominance illustrated by the fact he was 52 under par for his last 11 competitive rounds.

His fifth Tour title also saw him move to a career high of 35th on the Official World Golf Ranking, bettering the 40th place he attained in April 2007, following his victory in the Open de España.

"Abu Dhabi will always hold a special place in my heart because it was where I recorded my first Tour win in 2008. So to come back here and win again, my fifth Tour victory in all, is awesome"

Martin Kaymer

ABU DHABI GOLF CHAMPIONSHIP
Abu Dhabi Golf Club
Abu Dhabi, UAE
January 21–24, 2010

1	**MARTIN KAYMER**		67	67	67	66	267	-21
2	Ian Poulter		65	70	67	66	268	-20
3	Rory McIlroy		66	69	67	67	269	-19
4	Shane Lowry		68	65	71	67	271	-17
5	Louis Oosthuizen		67	71	68	66	272	-16
6	Ariel Canete		70	65	74	64	273	-15
	Rhys Davies		66	68	72	67	273	-15
8	Anders Hansen		69	70	68	67	274	-14
	Søren Hansen		72	67	68	67	274	-14
	David Horsey		73	66	70	65	274	-14

His Highness Sultan Bin Tahnoon Al Nahyan, Chairman of the Abu Dhabi Tourism Authority and Martin Kaymer

Total Prize Fund €1,504,497   **First Prize** €250,000

Fast Track

Even in its relatively short existence on The European Tour International Schedule, the Abu Dhabi Golf Championship has developed a reputation for not only being a tournament everyone wants to play in, but also one which produces thrilling golfing theatre; and the 2010 vintage certainly lived up to that billing.

Everyone who watched the pulsating final day unfold was enthralled, including European Ryder Cup Captain Colin Montgomerie who saw three men in the final group who will all stake strong claims to be part of his Team at The Celtic Manor Resort – namely Martin Kaymer, Rory McIlroy and Ian Poulter.

In the end it was the supremely talented Kaymer who triumphed, maintaining the one shot lead he possessed going into the final round with a superb birdie four on the 72nd hole to hold off the determined challenge of Poulter and the fast-finishing McIlroy, who birdied two of the last four holes to finish one shot adrift of the Englishman in third.

Kaymer missed a large chunk of last season with a foot injury sustained while go-karting in the United States. It ultimately cost the 25 year old the chance of winning The 2009 Race to Dubai but, as he proved conclusively on the National Course, that episode is firmly behind him and he is once again, back in golf's fast lane.

Louis Oosthuizen

Shane Lowry

Ian Poulter and Rory McIlroy

"I've been to this tournament a couple of times and had a couple of close calls in the past. But I love this golf course, it's a great challenge, and to be able to win here at long last is fantastic"

Robert Karlsson

COMMERCIALBANK QATAR MASTERS PRESENTED BY DOLPHIN ENERGY
Doha Golf Club
Doha, Qatar
January 28–31, 2010

1	**ROBERT KARLSSON**		68	70	70	65	273	-15
2	Alvaro Quiros		71	70	68	67	276	-12
3	Brett Rumford		69	66	73	69	277	-11
	Lee Westwood		68	69	70	70	277	-11
5	Paul Casey		71	69	66	74	280	-8
	Bradley Dredge		67	69	70	74	280	-8
	Oliver Wilson		67	70	72	71	280	-8
8	Thomas Björn		73	70	70	68	281	-7
9	Niclas Fasth		70	68	73	71	282	-6
	Ricardo Gonzalez		72	72	71	67	282	-6
	Retief Goosen		73	71	66	72	282	-6
	Peter Lawrie		72	68	73	69	282	-6
	Camilo Villegas		70	72	70	70	282	-6

L-R: Andy Stevens, Group CEO of Commercialbank, Robert Karlsson and Hassan Al Nuaimi, President Qatar Golf Association

Total Prize Fund €1,760,945   **First Prize** €294,584

Lee Westwood

Oliver Wilson

Niclas Fasth

Brett Rumford

Commercial bank
Qatar Masters

PRESENTED BY

DOLPHIN دولفين
ENERGY للطاقة

Robert Karlsson
2010 Champion

3-6 February 2011
Doha Golf Club

For more information, please log onto www.qatar-masters.com

الاتحاد القطري للجولف
Qatar Golf Association

QATAR

نادي الدوحة للجولف
Doha Golf Club

Paul Casey

Back to the Future

It is fair to say, in his darker moments during 2009, there were times when Robert Karlsson wondered if he would ever find himself in such a position again.

Having not played a single event between May and October as a result of fluid behind the retina in his left eye which caused blurred vision and balance problems, his concerns were understandable. But a stirring four day showing in Qatar, including a final round 65 which represented the best score of the week at Doha Golf Club, proved conclusively to the 40 year old that he was not only back to the form he showed when he became the first Swedish player to win The Harry Vardon Trophy as European Number One in 2008, but that he

was also ready to look once again to the future with confidence.

Going into the final round it was Paul Casey and Bradley Dredge who led but as both slipped back to share fifth in the end, it was left to Karlsson and playing partner Lee Westwood to emerge as the main protagonists.

The Englishman surged with four birdies in five holes from the tenth but when he dropped a shot at the 16th, his momentum halted allowing defending champion Alvaro Quiros to charge into second place with three closing birdies. However, neither could seriously challenge Karlsson, who ended with two birdies of his own to win by three shots.

Bradley Dredge

Alvaro Quiros

OMEGA DUBAI DESERT CLASSIC
Emirates Golf Club (Majlis Course)
Dubai, UAE
February 4–7, 2010

1	MIGUEL ANGEL JIMÉNEZ		70	67	68	72	277	-11
2	Lee Westwood		72	65	68	72	277	-11
3	Thongchai Jaidee		70	66	69	73	278	-10
4	Martin Kaymer		71	70	68	70	279	-9
	Edoardo Molinari		68	70	70	71	279	-9
6	Rory McIlroy		68	70	69	73	280	-8
	Alvaro Quiros		69	69	67	75	280	-8
8	Grégory Bourdy		74	70	70	68	282	-6
	Henrik Stenson		76	69	69	68	282	-6
	Tom Watson		73	70	71	68	282	-6

L-R: Miguel Angel Jiménez, Adrian Flaherty, General Manager, Golf in Dubai, Mohammed Juma Buamaim, Vice Chairman and CEO of Golf in Dubai and Sheikh Ahmed Bin Mohammed Bin Rashid Al Maktoum

Total Prize Fund €1,765,104   **First Prize** €296,500

"I might not be 25 years old or hit the ball as far as the guys who are, but I am still healthy and strong and I can still play this game. I think, like a fine wine, I am getting better with age"

Miguel Angel Jiménez

Lee Westwood

Henrik Stenson

Thongchai Jaidee

Fringe Benefits

When Miguel Angel Jiménez was part of Europe's successful Ryder Cup winning side at Oakland Hills in 2004, he asked Captain Bernhard Langer to provide three things for the team room: an espresso coffee machine, a case of the finest Rioja and a box of cigars. Current European Captain Colin Montgomerie might be advised to have such items on standby for Celtic Manor.

There are several players who are energised in Ryder Cup years and the flamboyant Spaniard is most definitely one of them as he showed when he held off the challenge of Lee Westwood to win the Omega Dubai Desert Classic at the third play-off hole.

The Englishman had chances to win on both the first two extra holes but did not take them as Jiménez battled bravely to stay alive, getting up and down for par firstly from the fringe of the water hazard on the 18th and then from the back bunker on the same hole.

The move to the adjacent ninth hole coincided with a change of fortune for the Spaniard who was faced with a four foot putt for the title after Westwood failed to get up and down for par from the front of the green. Despite the left to right break, the destiny of the ball was never in doubt, giving Jiménez his 16th European Tour title with, incredibly, nine of those coming in his 40s.

AVANTHA MASTERS
DLF Golf and Country Club
New Delhi, India
February 11–14, 2010

1	**ANDREW DODT**		67	68	71	68	274	**-14**
2	Richard Finch		69	69	71	66	275	-13
3	Richard Bland		68	71	66	71	276	-12
	David Drysdale		68	67	71	70	276	-12
	Tetsuji Hiratsuka		73	62	70	71	276	-12
	Barry Lane		67	67	71	71	276	-12
7	Fredrik Andersson Hed		68	71	66	72	277	-11
8	Yin-Shin Chan		65	68	72	73	278	-10
	Darren Clarke		71	66	70	71	278	-10
	Oliver Fisher		70	67	71	70	278	-10
	Jeppe Huldahl		71	70	66	71	278	-10
	Jason Knutzon		70	67	72	69	278	-10
	Steven O'Hara		69	73	67	69	278	-10

Gautam Thapar, Chairman and CEO, Avantha Group and Andrew Dodt

Total Prize Fund €1,488,260   **First Prize** €250,000

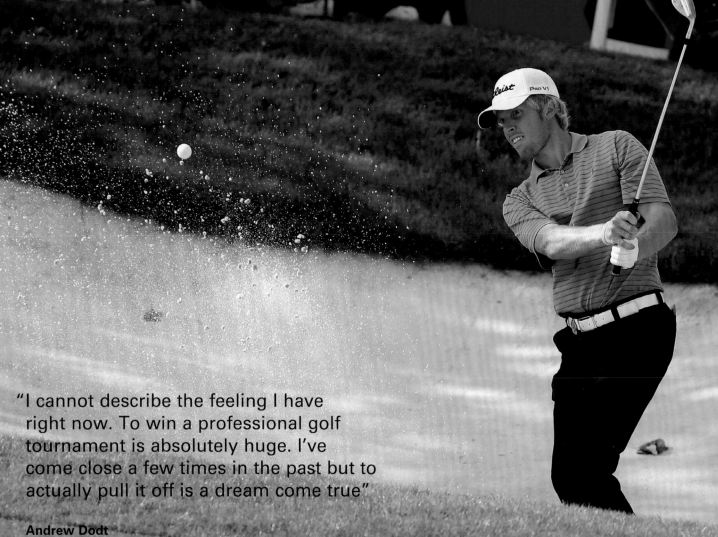

"I cannot describe the feeling I have right now. To win a professional golf tournament is absolutely huge. I've come close a few times in the past but to actually pull it off is a dream come true"

Andrew Dodt

Richard Finch

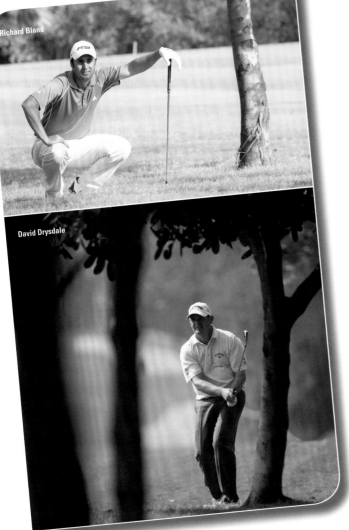
Richard Bland

David Drysdale

Barry Lane

Australia Day

He might be one of The European Tour's newest faces, having only taken up Affiliate Membership a week ago, but Andrew Dodt nevertheless continued Australia's long standing tradition of success with a fine victory in the inaugural Avantha Masters.

The 24 year old's one shot triumph at the DLF Golf and Country Club in New Delhi extended his nation's run of consecutive winning years on The European Tour to 27, dating back to the 1984 season; Australia second only to England in terms of that particular statistic.

Such figures are impressive but the only one which mattered to the young man from Brisbane was the fact his 14 under par total of 274 gave him the €250,000 first prize along with a European Tour exemption until the end of the 2012 season.

With seven players entering the last round level at the top of the leaderboard, it always promised to be a thrilling and exciting final day and so it proved. The lead changed hands several times with Richard Finch's spectacular 66, at one point, looking to have secured victory for the Englishman.

But Dodt – who was one shot off the leading group at the start of the day – birdied the 16th and 18th holes to be home in 35 for a 68 to pip Finch by a shot and become the 36th different Australian player to win on Tour since 1972.

> "It feels amazing to win a World Golf Championship and I certainly felt very comfortable and in control on the golf course all week. It's also great to move up to number five in the world"
>
> Ian Poulter

WGC - ACCENTURE MATCH PLAY
Ritz-Carlton Golf Club
Dove Mountain, Marana, Arizona, USA
February 17–21, 2010

CHAMPION	IAN POULTER
Runner-Up	Paul Casey
Third	Camilo Villegas
Fourth	Sergio Garcia

Final: Ian Poulter beat Paul Casey 4 and 2
Consolation Match: Camilo Villegas beat Sergio Garcia 5 and 4

Total Prize Fund €6,190,643 **First Prize** €1,019,635

Ian Poulter and William Green, CEO of Accenture

Paul Casey

Sergio Garcia

Camilo Villegas

Poulter-Heist

Given their respective match play pedigrees, it was perhaps no surprise that Ian Poulter and Paul Casey ended up facing one another in the 36 hole final of the World Golf Championships – Accenture Match Play.

Poulter had shown his prowess in the genre with a stirring showing in The 2008 Ryder Cup at Valhalla when he emerged the top points scorer, while Casey finished runner-up to Geoff Ogilvy 12 months ago and also triumphed in the original World Match Play format at Wentworth Club in 2006.

After requiring extra holes to defeat Justin Leonard in round one, Poulter was never seriously troubled and brushed aside Sergio Garcia by 7 and 6 in the semi-finals. Casey, incredibly, won his first four matches by the same 5 and 4 margin

before requiring six extra holes to see off Camilo Villegas in their epic last four encounter.

In the final, Poulter edged in front for the first time at the seventh and never looked back. Two ahead at lunch, birdies at the first and second holes of the afternoon round doubled his advantage and although Casey battled hard, his fellow Englishman refused to yield and closed out the match on the 16th green. It was the 34 year old's first WGC triumph and one that moved him top of The Race to Dubai and up to fifth on the Official World Golf Ranking.

It also capped a superb week for The European Tour in the desert with seven members – Retief Goosen, Thongchai Jaidee, Oliver Wilson, Casey, Garcia, Poulter and Villegas – featuring in the last eight.

Thongchai Jaidee

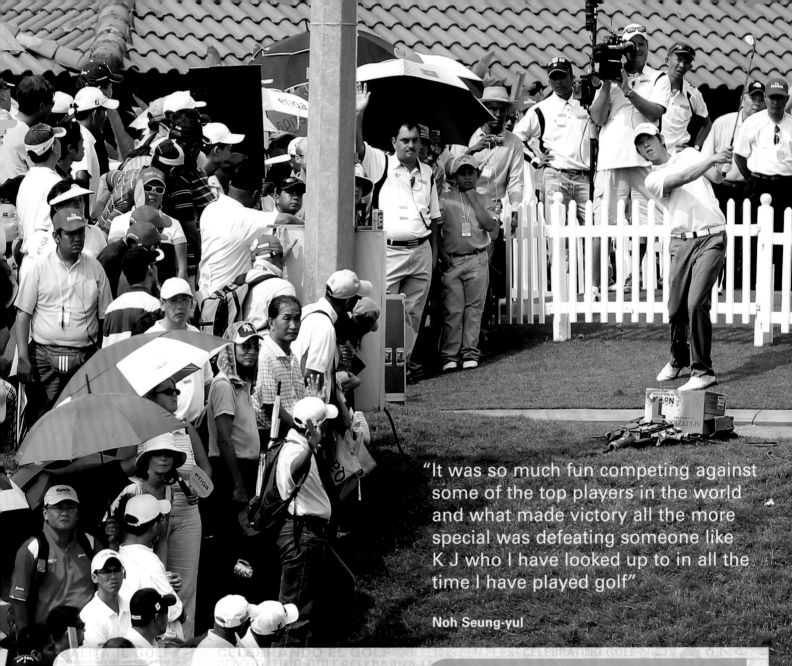

"It was so much fun competing against some of the top players in the world and what made victory all the more special was defeating someone like K J who I have looked up to in all the time I have played golf"

Noh Seung-yul

MAYBANK MALAYSIAN OPEN
Kuala Lumpur Golf and Country Club
Kuala Lumpur, Malaysia
March 4–7, 2010

1	**NOH SEUNG-YUL**		**69**	**70**	**67**	**68**	**274**	**-14**
2	K J Choi		67	70	69	69	275	-13
3	Kiradech Aphibarnrat		68	69	68	71	276	-12
	Rhys Davies		65	69	71	71	276	-12
	Søren Hansen		70	67	69	70	276	-12
6	Danny Willett		72	69	68	68	277	-11
7	Johan Edfors		69	69	69	71	278	-10
	Thongchai Jaidee		66	71	69	72	278	-10
9	Jason Knutzon		73	67	72	67	279	-9
10	Mark Brown		71	71	72	66	280	-8
	Rahil Gangjee		68	75	66	71	280	-8
	Peter Lawrie		69	72	71	68	280	-8
	Angelo Que		70	67	72	71	280	-8

Najib Razak, Prime Minister of Malaysia, and Noh Seung-yul

Total Prize Fund €1,497,605   **First Prize** €246,291

K J Choi

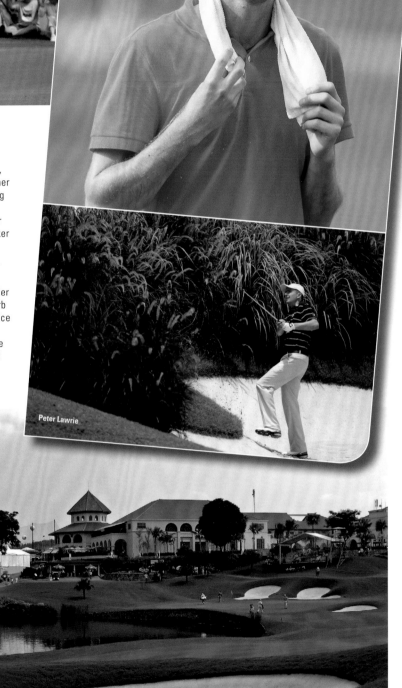
Rhys Davies

Peter Lawrie

Noh Surrender

The Maybank Malaysian Open is no stranger to making history. Back in 1999 it became the first tournament to be co-sanctioned between The European Tour and the Asian Tour when American Gerry Norquist triumphed at Saujana Golf and Country Club in Kuala Lumpur.

Fast forward 11 years and it was the turn of South Korean teenager Noh Seung-yul – across the Malaysian capital at the Kuala Lumpur Golf and Country Club – to pen himself a chapter in golf's record books when, at 18 years and 281 days, he became the youngest professional in history to win a European Tour event, edging out veteran compatriot K J Choi in a dramatic finalé to the tournament.

Noh beat the record - previously set by Dale Hayes in 1971 - by nine days, although he is not the youngest winner in Tour history; that honour remaining with New Zealand's Danny Lee who was 18 and 213 days and an amateur when he won the 2009 Johnnie Walker Classic in Australia.

Noh secured victory by holing a four foot birdie putt on the 18th green to card a four under par 68 for a 14 under par total of 274, after playing a superb chip shot from the edge of the practice putting green beside a hospitality marquee. Choi had earlier birdied the last to card a three under par 69 and post the clubhouse lead at 275.

WGC - CA CHAMPIONSHIP
Doral Golf Resort and Spa
Doral, Florida, USA
March 11–14, 2010

Ernie Els and Richard Hills, European Tour Ryder Cup Director

1	**ERNIE ELS**		68	66	70	66	270	-18
2	Charl Schwartzel		67	70	67	70	274	-14
3	Padraig Harrington		70	68	67	72	277	-11
	Martin Kaymer		70	72	66	69	277	-11
	Matt Kuchar		71	71	67	68	277	-11
6	Paul Casey		69	72	68	69	278	-10
	Bill Haas		71	66	70	71	278	-10
	Graeme McDowell		74	68	70	66	278	-10
	Alistair Presnell		72	70	72	64	278	-10
	Alvaro Quiros		72	69	69	68	278	-10

Total Prize Fund €6,207,143   **First Prize €1,022,353**

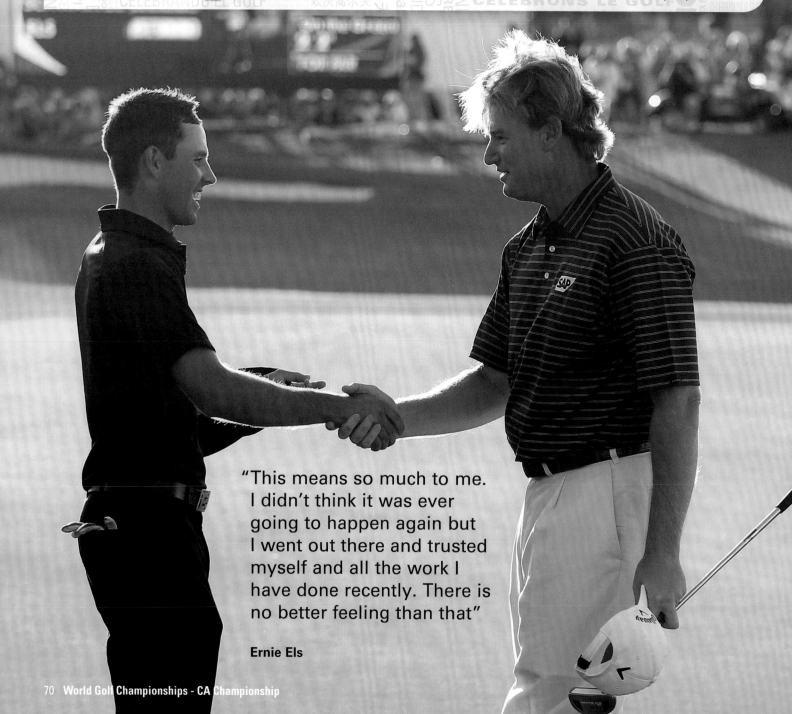

"This means so much to me.
I didn't think it was ever
going to happen again but
I went out there and trusted
myself and all the work I
have done recently. There is
no better feeling than that"

Ernie Els

Padraig Harrington

Francesco Molinari

Graeme McDowell

Martin Kaymer

Friends Reunited

Not having won for nearly 16 months, it was understandable that Ernie Els was a touch emotional following his fine victory in the World Golf Championships – CA Championship. However the success was made all the more poignant for the South African due to the young man across the fairway who provided his closest challenger.

Fellow Springbok Charl Schwartzel might never have scaled the heights of the game were it not for the help given to him in his formative years by The Ernie Els and Fancourt Foundation which was formed with the purpose of identifying and helping promote young golfers from families of limited resource. It is a friendship which has endured and, indeed, Schwartzel eschewed hotel accommodation to stay the week in Els' south

Florida home. Ironic then, that the housemates stood toe-to-toe as the final round teed off.

Schwartzel battled hard but Els always had the edge before the crucial moment arrived late in the back nine. One ahead approaching the 15th, Els saw his lead doubled when Schwartzel made bogey from the sand. Then, when Els birdied the 16th and Schwartzel bogeyed the 17th, the contest was over.

Els' cheque for €1,022,353 saw him move to the top of The European Tour career earnings and also back into the top ten on the Official World Golf Ranking. For Schwartzel, there was the consolation of moving back to the top of The 2010 Race to Dubai.

"I was comfortable on the Asian Tour but I wanted to be part of The European Tour and play with the best players. To win, however, is incredible and a bit surreal to be honest – it's all a bit of a blur"

Rhys Davies

TROPHÉE HASSAN II
Royal Golf Dar Es Salam (Red and Blue Courses)
Rabat, Morocco
March 18–21, 2010

1	**RHYS DAVIES**		68	64	68	66	266	-25
2	Louis Oosthuizen		70	64	64	70	268	-23
3	Thomas Aiken		67	68	67	71	273	-18
	Ignacio Garrido		67	67	69	70	273	-18
	Mikko Ilonen		71	69	67	66	273	-18
	Thomas Levet		69	65	68	71	273	-18
7	Christian Nilsson		71	68	70	66	275	-16
	Robert Rock		71	67	67	70	275	-16
	Danny Willett		73	67	64	71	275	-16
10	Peter Lawrie		66	70	73	67	276	-15
	Gareth Maybin		72	69	66	69	276	-15
	Francesco Molinari		66	70	70	70	276	-15

L-R: Her Royal Highness Princess Lalla Meryem, Rhys Davies and His Royal Highness Prince Moulay Rachid

Total Prize Fund €1,361,205   **First Prize €229,160**

Louis Oosthuizen

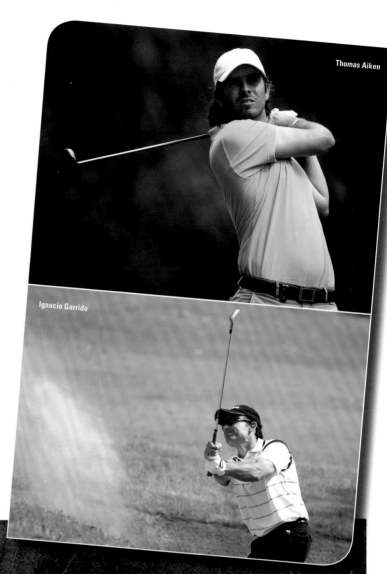

Thomas Aiken

Ignacio Garrido

Thomas Levet

Principal Boy

Given the excitement surrounding his maiden victory on The European Tour International Schedule, it was understandable that Rhys Davies admitted to feeling a little "surreal" in the immediate aftermath of his triumph in the Trophée Hassan II in Morocco.

Having played on the Asian Tour and come through the 2009 Challenge Tour Rankings, the Welshman had made progress with top ten finishes in Abu Dhabi and Malaysia but winning on The European Tour is a whole different ball game. However, the man who gave up cricket to pursue golf professionally refused to be stumped in the heat of the final round.

Two shots adrift of South African Louis Oosthuizen going into Sunday's action, a bogey on the third from Davies saw him fall three behind but five birdies in a wondrous spell either side of the turn saw the Welshman turn matters around to walk off the 11th green one ahead. Two further birdies at the 13th and 14th put him in the driving seat and late dropped shots from Oosthuizen ensured his two shot victory with a stunning total of 25 under par 266.

With The Ryder Cup being staged on its shores later in the year, golf in the Principality is very much in the spotlight and Davies ensured that focus is not merely outside the ropes.

OPEN DE ANDALUCIA DE GOLF
Parador de Málaga Golf
Málaga, Spain
March 25–28, 2010

1	**LOUIS OOSTHUIZEN**		67	63	66	67	263	**-17**
2	Richard Finch		68	65	66	67	266	-14
	Peter Whiteford		69	64	67	66	266	-14
4	Robert Coles		69	65	63	71	268	-12
	Francesco Molinari		68	68	65	67	268	-12
6	Gabriel Canizares		69	64	65	71	269	-11
	Jamie Donaldson		67	69	67	66	269	-11
	Gonzalo Fernandez-Castaño		68	66	67	68	269	-11
	Søren Kjeldsen		65	67	69	68	269	-11
	Joost Luiten		66	69	68	66	269	-11
	James Morrison		71	63	70	65	269	-11

L-R: Miguel Angel Jiménez, Louis Oosthuizen and Luciano Alonso, Minister of Tourism, Trade and Sports for Junta de Andalucia

Total Prize Fund €1,017,802   **First Prize** €166,660

"It has been seven years since I came through the Qualifying School which is a long time to wait for your first win but it makes it all the sweeter now it's here. This is a great feeling; unbelievable"

Louis Oosthuizen

Richard Finch

Take Two

As well as sharing a platform of professional golf and a love of the movies, Louis Oosthuizen and Peter Hedblom now also have a career experience to share on The European Tour.

Last season, Hedblom was in despair when his chance of a third Tour victory in the KLM Open was snatched away by England's Simon Dyson in a play-off. Instead of moping around and bemoaning his misfortune, however, the Swede dusted himself off and went about winning the very next tournament, the Johnnie Walker Championship at Gleneagles.

Fast forward six months and Oosthuizen found himself in precisely the same position. Having taken a two shot lead into the final round of the Trophée

Hassan II in Morocco, the South African seemed on the verge of his maiden Tour success only to see a hesitant final round allow Rhys Davies the opportunity to nip in and triumph.

Like Hedblom, Oosthuizen stored the experience in his memory banks and immediately went about putting what he had learned to good effect. Seven days later he once again took the lead into the final round – of the Open de Andalucia de Golf – but this time his tactics were spot on.

Three early birdies in the first five holes settled his nerves and from there on he was in control, thwarting the respective challenges of eventual runners-up Richard Finch and Peter Whiteford to win by three shots.

Søren Kjeldsen

HOYO / HOLE
13
PAR 3
172mts / 188yds

Open de Andalucia de Golf

www.andalucia.org

Robert Coles

Peter Whiteford

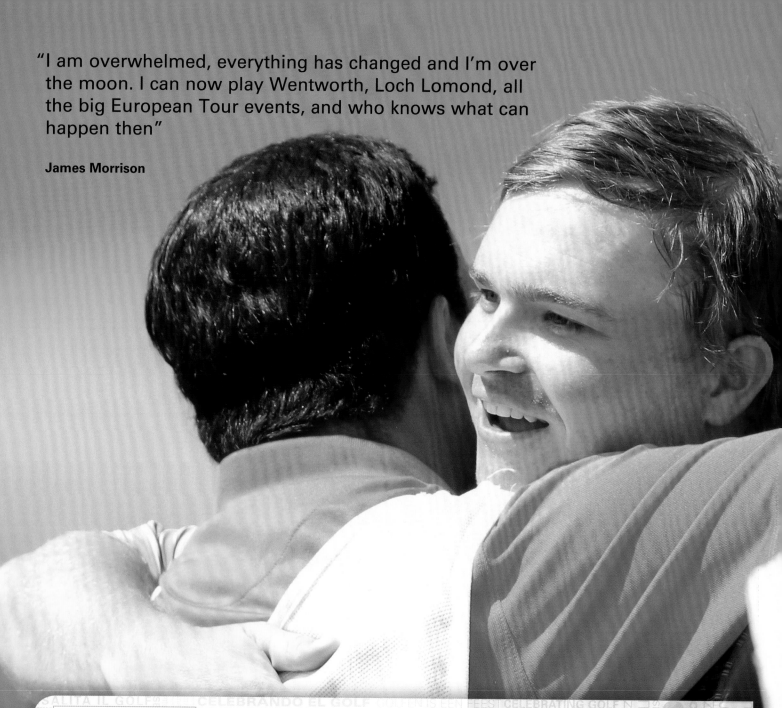

"I am overwhelmed, everything has changed and I'm over the moon. I can now play Wentworth, Loch Lomond, all the big European Tour events, and who knows what can happen then"

James Morrison

MADEIRA ISLANDS OPEN BPI - PORTUGAL
Porto Santo Golfe
Madeira, Portugal
April 8–11, 2010

1	**JAMES MORRISON**		67	65	66	70	**268**	**-20**
2	Oliver Fisher		67	72	65	65	269	-19
3	George Murray		66	67	68	73	274	-14
4	Charles-Edouard Russo		74	66	68	67	275	-13
5	Alessandro Tadini		68	71	71	66	276	-12
6	Gary Clark		69	70	68	70	277	-11
	George Coetzee		69	70	70	68	277	-11
	Michael Hoey		72	68	69	68	277	-11
9	Jean-Baptiste Gonnet		69	71	73	65	278	-10
	John Parry		71	66	70	71	278	-10

L-R: Francisco Taboada, President of Porto Santo Golfe, James Morrison and José Carlos Agrellos, Manager of Activities and Incentives - BPI Golf

Total Prize Fund €700,000   **First Prize €116,660**

George Murray

Michael Hoey

Gary Clark

Three and Easy

It is often said that things tend to come along in threes and the truthfulness of that particular idiom was illustrated once again by James Morrison who, through his victory in the Madeira Islands Open BPI – Portugal, became the third consecutive first time winner on The 2010 European Tour International Schedule.

Previously it had been Welshman Rhys Davies and South African Louis Oosthuizen who had basked in the glory of success but this time it was the 25 year old Englishman's turn after holding off a determined last day challenge from his compatriot Oliver Fisher.

Morrison had led since the conclusion of his second round 65, a remarkable effort which contained only 21 putts, and his third round 66 saw him take a three shot lead into Sunday, his nearest challenger being Scotland's George Murray. But when Murray's title quest failed to materialise, it was left to Fisher, who began the day six shots adrift of Morrison, to take up the gauntlet.

He did so in style, flying out of the blocks with four successive birdies from the third to close the gap before another birdie at the 14th took him to within two of Morrison, who then bogeyed the penultimate hole to set up a grandstand finish.

Fisher cranked up the pressure with a closing birdie but Morrison held his nerve admirably, getting up and down from the greenside bunker for his own birdie four to secure a one shot triumph.

Oliver Fisher

MASTERS TOURNAMENT
Augusta National Golf Club
Augusta, Georgia, USA
April 8-11, 2010

1	**PHIL MICKELSON**		67	71	67	67	272	-16
2	Lee Westwood		67	69	68	71	275	-13
3	Anthony Kim		68	70	73	65	276	-12
4	K J Choi		67	71	70	69	277	-11
	Tiger Woods		68	70	70	69	277	-11
6	Fred Couples		66	75	68	70	279	-9
7	Nick Watney		68	76	71	65	280	-8
8	Hunter Mahan		71	71	68	71	281	-7
	Y E Yang		67	72	72	70	281	-7
10	Ricky Barnes		68	70	72	73	283	-5
	Ian Poulter		68	68	74	73	283	-5

Phil Mickelson receives the Green Jacket from Angel Cabrera, 2009 Masters Champion

Total Prize Fund €5,595,094   **First Prize** €1,002,905

Who Dares Wins

"To win this tournament is the most amazing feeling. It has been a difficult year so to come out on top here at Augusta is very emotional and very special. It is something I will always cherish"

Phil Mickelson

The 13th hole at Augusta National might be the best risk-reward par five in tournament golf. It is here that the game's daredevils show off their audacious skills or fall flat on their faces. No question as to which side of that particular fence Phil Mickelson belongs. Not after a 74th Masters that will be remembered as long as golf is played.

This was a tournament that was all about three men: the gunslinger Mickelson, the chastened hero Tiger Woods and Europe's Number One, Lee Westwood. When it all came down to it, the destiny of the Green Jacket was decided on the way Mickelson played a single hole.

It was at the 13th on the opening day that a round going nowhere turned in the direction of a wonderful 67 thanks to an eagle three; that a Saturday afternoon in danger of falling flat was transformed into something completely different on the back of another eagle; and there, after all that and towards the end of a truly memorable final round, that he saved the best for last.

Fred Couples

Sometimes a stroke is played that is so special you simply cannot help your bottom jaw from involuntarily dropping. This is what happened to Westwood's caddy Billy Foster as he assumed the role of interested spectator as Mickelson surveyed his second shot. With the ball nestling on pine needles, a tree only feet in front of him blocking out half of the green, and with 203 yards to go to clear Rae's Creek, if truth be told, it did not seem that hard a decision to make.

According to Foster, not once but twice, Mickelson's caddy Jim 'Bones' Mackay implored his man to chip the ball down the fairway and hope for a pitch and putt birdie four. After all, he was in the lead following a two at the par three 12th. Why take any risk?

However, gunslingers do not think like that, do they? Particularly not this one. It is one of the reasons why Mickelson's gallery numbers in the thousands every time he tees up. 'I just fancy that I can pull this shot off,' he said to himself. So it was that he dispensed with the wedge that was Bones's weapon of choice and went with a six iron.

Imagine if he had failed to pull this stroke off? The ridicule would have been immense. Yet sometimes, it is true that he who dares wins. When the ball landed over the creek with hardly anything to spare, Foster knew that he had just been a privileged witness to greatness. Only once before, when caddying for Seve Ballesteros when he played a seemingly impossible shot with his ball nestling next to a wall in Crans-sur-Sierre, could Foster recall anything like it.

K J Choi

Where does it stand among the great strokes Augusta has seen? Surely alongside Gene Sarazen's three wood blow for an albatross at the 15th at the 1935 edition; Sandy Lyle's seven iron from the fairway bunker to set up victory in 1988; and Tiger Woods's miraculous chip from behind the 16th green in 2005. It was a stroke of sheer genius, and it illuminated a tournament that gripped from the moment Jack Nicklaus and Arnold Palmer hit their ceremonial drives and which never let go.

What made Mickelson's entire performance so extraordinary and why it captured everyone's imagination was the background of both his wife Amy and

Phil Mickelson

Lee Westwood

Anthony Kim

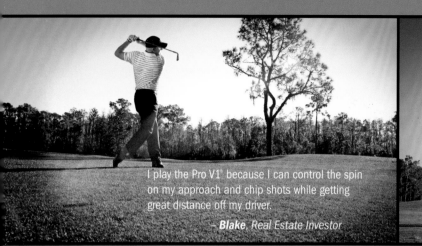

I play the Pro V1® because I can control the spin on my approach and chip shots while getting great distance off my driver.

— **Blake**, *Real Estate Investor*

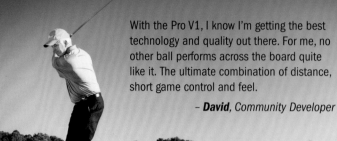

With the Pro V1, I know I'm getting the best technology and quality out there. For me, no other ball performs across the board quite like it. The ultimate combination of distance, short game control and feel.

— **David**, *Community Developer*

STORIES OF TRUST.

Played a Pro V1x for the first time last year. Never had a ball that was as explosive off the driver yet could spin that much off a long iron. Switched and never looked back.

— **Clint**, *Student*

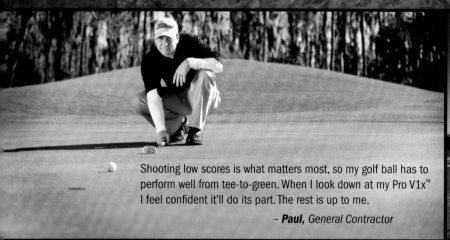

Shooting low scores is what matters most, so my golf ball has to perform well from tee-to-green. When I look down at my Pro V1x™ I feel confident it'll do its part. The rest is up to me.

— **Paul**, *General Contractor*

I play the Pro V1 for its consistency. I need to be able to control my distances. I also love the way it performs into and around the greens.

— **Hannah**, *Student*

Augusta National Golf Club Chairman Billy Payne (right) welcomes Honorary Starters Jack Nicklaus (left) and Arnold Palmer to the first tee

Ian Poulter

his mother Mary's ongoing treatment for breast cancer. This was his third Green Jacket success and fourth Major Championship title but, more importantly, it was the one that earned him his passport to the pantheon.

While celebrating his achievement, it was hard for anyone of European pursuasion not to feel sorry for Westwood. It says everything about how good he was that he knocked ten shots off his previous best 72 hole score at Augusta; everything about how good Mickelson was that, even if the Englishman had shot 69 in the final round instead of 71 to become the first man in Masters history to shoot four rounds in the sixties, he still would not have won.

Westwood's total of 275 would have won 25 of the previous 30 Masters Tournaments and been in play-offs for two more. How unlucky that his own personal best should coincide with Mickelson's.

Finally Woods. Only he could have played as badly as he did for long periods and still finished joint fourth. Whatever his limitations as a man, it was certainly good to have him back as a golfer.

Woods brought intrigue before the event started and before Nicklaus and Palmer delivered unabashed nostalgia as only they can. On day one we had Fred Couples and Tom Watson doing their twirl for the aged before, finally, we had Mickelson and Westwood, two of the great golfers of the age, going head to head to produce an absolutely classic Sunday.

No talk anymore about where all the roars have gone at Augusta National. Not after a sun-drenched week in Georgia, where one man blessed with magic in his hands dared to dream, and in so doing delivered a fantasy that remains with us still.

Derek Lawrenson
Daily Mail

Tiger Woods

VOLVO

VOLVO CHINA OPEN
Suzhou Jinji Lake International Golf Club
Suzhou, China
April 15–18, 2010

1	Y E YANG		68	66	68	71	273	-15
2	Rhys Davies		73	70	65	67	275	-13
	Stephen Dodd		69	71	66	69	275	-13
4	Jamie Donaldson		66	68	69	73	276	-12
	Johan Edfors		68	71	68	69	276	-12
	Mikko Ilonen		68	67	68	73	276	-12
7	Oliver Fisher		73	65	70	69	277	-11
8	Nicolas Colsaerts		69	72	68	69	278	-10
	Thongchai Jaidee		64	70	75	69	278	-10
	Do-Hoon Kim		64	69	73	72	278	-10
	Pablo Larrazábal		66	69	70	73	278	-10
	Graeme McDowell		70	70	70	68	278	-10
	Ross McGowan		71	68	69	70	278	-10
	Alex Noren		71	67	70	70	278	-10
	Henrik Stenson		68	73	68	69	278	-10

L-R: Zhang Xiaoning, General Secretary of the China Golf Association and Director of the Multi-ball Games Administrative Centre of State Sport ,Y E Yang and Per Ericsson, President & CEO of Volvo Event Management

Total Prize Fund €1,881,480   **First Prize** €311,708

"After the US PGA Championship I had a lot of expectation on my shoulders. I had a few high finishes which were good but now this wonderful win. I am definitely back on the right track"

Y E Yang

Rhys Davies

Stephen Dodd

Jamie Donaldson

Mikko Ilonen

Weight of Expectation

The history of golf is peppered with people who have not capitalised on the glory of winning one of the four Major Championships. Y E Yang was desperate not to be bracketed in that same category; hence the Korean's understandable joy at winning the Volvo China Open.

Ever since that memorable afternoon at Hazeltine National last August, when he held off the challenge of Tiger Woods to win the US PGA Championship, the world of golf has waited to herald his next triumph and, from the moment he grabbed a one shot lead at the end of the third round in Suzhou, this was always his best chance.

The 38 year old never surrendered his overnight lead completely although he was joined at the top of the leaderboard briefly during an enthralling final day by the two Welshmen who eventually ended up joint second; Rhys Davies and Stephen Dodd.

However, Yang produced a short game masterclass to secure a one under par 71 on his way to a two stroke victory overall. Three times the Korean found deep sided pot bunkers on the back nine but three times he scrambled to save par. In the end he recorded 50 consecutive holes without a dropped shot – from the third in Friday's second round to the 17th on Sunday. By the time he dropped a shot at the 72nd hole, his victory was already assured.

BALLANTINE'S CHAMPIONSHIP
Pinx Golf Club
Jeju Island, South Korea
April 22–25, 2010

1	**MARCUS FRASER**		**65**	**70**	**69**	**204**	**-12**
2	Gareth Maybin		68	68	72	208	-8
	Brett Rumford		67	70	71	208	-8
4	Oliver Fisher		68	70	71	209	-7
	Noh Seung-yul		71	70	68	209	-7
6	Robert-Jan Derksen		71	68	71	210	-6
	Jamie Donaldson		68	72	70	210	-6
	Mardan Mamat		68	70	72	210	-6
9	Ernie Els		68	69	74	211	-5
	Niclas Fasth		70	70	71	211	-5
	Tano Goya		66	70	75	211	-5
	Mikko Ilonen		69	73	69	211	-5
	Thongchai Jaidee		69	67	75	211	-5

Paul Scanlon, International Commercial Director for Chivas Brothers and Marcus Fraser

Total Prize Fund €2,196,793   **First Prize** €367,500

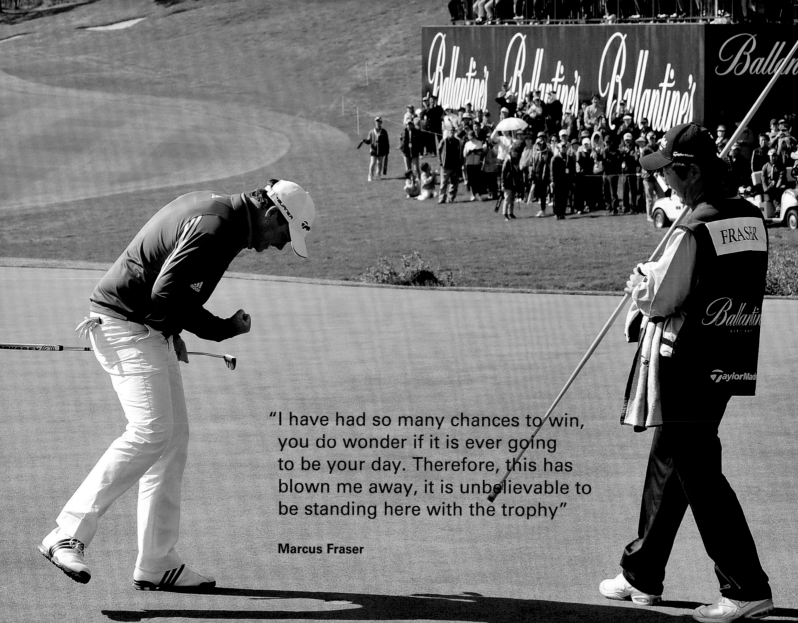

"I have had so many chances to win, you do wonder if it is ever going to be your day. Therefore, this has blown me away, it is unbelievable to be standing here with the trophy"

Marcus Fraser

Lam Chih-bing, Pablo Larrazábal and Anthony Kim

Gareth Maybin and Oliver Fisher

Brett Rumford

Destiny Calling

Professional sport can be an unforgiving place at times but, on occasion, things happen that appear destined to occur. So it was with Marcus Fraser's victory in the Ballantine's Championship in Korea.

A year ago, the Australian came to Jeju Island to play in the tournament but, in doing so, missed his uncle's funeral. The absence had played on Fraser's mind ever since that week and, therefore, it was no surprise to whose memory he dedicated his victory 12 months later.

Dense fog on the opening day forced officials to cut the tournament to 54 holes and by the time the mists had dissipated, Fraser had seen his way clear to open up a one shot lead going into the final 18 holes, the 31 year old looking to claim his first European Tour success since the 2003 Russian Open.

Among the chasing pack was the pre-tournament favourite Ernie Els and when the South African moved within a shot of Fraser at the turn, his charge looked ominous. But Els could not maintain the momentum on the inward half and slipped back as did Fraser's other serious challenger, Northern Ireland's Gareth Maybin, who eventually finished tied second with Fraser's fellow Australian Brett Rumford. When the dust had settled, Fraser's closing 69 gave him a 12 under par total of 204 and a four shot winning margin.

Ballantine's Birdie Hole

Ballantine's CHAMPIONSHIP

17

214 yds (196m) par 3

"To be the winner of your country's national Open is something really special. It is definitely one of the most important things I have done in my career so far"

Alvaro Quiros

OPEN DE ESPAÑA
Real Club de Golf de Sevilla
Seville, Spain
April 29–May 2, 2010

1	**ALVARO QUIROS**		68	72	67	70	277	-11
2	James Morrison		73	67	70	67	277	-11
3	Alejandro Cañizares		71	69	70	68	278	-10
	Mark Foster		69	66	69	74	278	-10
	Raphaël Jacquelin		69	67	71	71	278	-10
6	Nicolas Colsaerts		71	66	72	70	279	-9
	Stephen Dodd		69	68	71	71	279	-9
	Paul Lawrie		74	67	71	67	279	-9
	Paul Waring		66	75	72	66	279	-9
10	Grégory Bourdy		69	72	69	70	280	-8
	Jamie Donaldson		71	72	66	71	280	-8

L-R: Gonzaga Escauriaza, President of the Royal Spanish Golf Federation, Alvaro Quiros and Maximo Luvie, Director of Reale Seguros

Total Prize Fund €2,038,766   **First Prize** €333,330

Mark Foster

Exclusive Club

Prior to the week in Seville it was a very exclusive club, featuring only Seve Ballesteros, Sergio Garcia and Antonio Garrido. We are, of course, talking about the club which features home winners of the Open de España on The European Tour since 1972 and now it has a new member – Alvaro Quiros.

The powerful 27 year old was the highest world ranked player in the field at the start of the week and lived up to his pre-tournament billing as favourite in fine style, beating Englishman James Morrison at the first hole of a sudden-death play-off to claim his fourth European Tour title.

Morrison used to be a youth cricketer of some repute and indeed shared a room with England test player, Alastair Cook. However, the 25 year old chose golf and his decision was a wise one as he showed once again in Spain, only three weeks after his maiden European Tour triumph in the Madeira Islands Open BPI – Portugal.

His final round 67 tied Quiros on 11 under par 277 after the Spaniard had closed with a 70 but Quiros' greater experience told in the play-off which was over almost before it had begun. A cool head saw the Spaniard make par four on the 432 yard 18th, which was more than enough after Morrison pulled his approach shot into the water en route to a double bogey six.

Alejandro Cañizares

Raphaël Jacquelin

James Morrison

BMW ITALIAN OPEN
Royal Park I Roveri
Turin, Italy
May 6–9, 2010

1	**FREDRIK ANDERSSON HED**	**70**	**66**	**63**	**73**	**272**	**-16**
2	David Horsey	68	71	67	68	274	-14
3	Nicolas Colsaerts	70	67	69	70	276	-12
	Peter Gustafsson	71	69	70	66	276	-12
	Chris Wood	71	70	65	70	276	-12
6	Ignacio Garrido	70	67	70	70	277	-11
7	Stephen Dodd	68	74	69	67	278	-10
	Hennie Otto	68	69	71	70	278	-10
	Graeme Storm	67	73	69	69	278	-10
10	Alejandro Cañizares	71	66	74	68	279	-9
	Søren Kjeldsen	73	68	70	68	279	-9
	Anthony Wall	71	71	69	68	279	-9

L-R: Franco Chimenti, President of the Italian Golf Federation, Fredrik Andersson Hed and Gianni Oliosi, Communication Director BMW Italy

Total Prize Fund €1,300,000   **First Prize €216,660**

"It is the same tension in the Qualifying School as out here in contention so maybe that helped me but, obviously, after all I have gone through, it feels great to be standing here as a winner at last"

Fredrik Andersson Hed

Waiting Game

Good things, they say, come to those who wait and never can that have been truer in a golfing sense than for Fredrik Andersson Hed.

No less than 14 times has the affable Swede been forced to attend the Qualifying School to try and regain his playing privileges, with success forthcoming on only six occasions. Thankfully, for the 38 year old, the last of those was registered last December, a performance which guaranteed him a card for the 2010 season before finally in this, his 245th European Tour event, victory was secured for the first time.

A superb third round 63 saw him open up a six shot lead with statistics telling us that, of the 20 players who have held six shot leads going into the final day of a European Tour event in the past, 17 of those have won.

The last to lose was Simon Dyson who surrendered to Miguel Angel Jiménez in the 2004 BMW Asian Open and, ironically, the Spaniard began the final day as Andersson Hed's nearest challenger. But, as Jiménez struggled to make an impact, it was Englishman David Horsey who charged.

Seven shots adrift of Andersson Hed at the start of the day, by the time he walked off the 13th green he was level. But two late bogeys, allied to Andersson Hed's steadiness and strict adherence to par, saw the Swede win by two shots.

David Horsey

Chris Wood

BMW Sheer Driving Pleasure

Peter Gustafsson

Nicolas Colsaerts

"Sometimes it's good to have these special cameras and sometimes it's bad but the penalty was fair. But, obviously, after all that happened out there, it feels absolutely fantastic to win"

Peter Hanson

IBERDROLA OPEN CALA MILLOR MALLORCA
Pula Golf Club
Son Servera, Mallorca, Spain
May 13–16, 2010

1	**PETER HANSON**		72	69	67	66	**274**	**-6**
2	Alejandro Cañizares		68	70	70	66	274	-6
3	James Kingston		65	70	74	69	278	-2
4	Christian Cévaër		73	70	71	65	279	-1
5	Pelle Edberg		71	64	71	74	280	0
	Gonzalo Fernandez-Castaño		70	68	68	74	280	0
	Scott Hend		72	69	66	73	280	0
	Chris Wood		69	72	68	71	280	0
9	Mark F Haastrup		72	69	68	73	282	2
	Stuart Manley		70	68	74	70	282	2
	Andrew Marshall		70	69	71	72	282	2
	Marco Ruiz		70	71	73	68	282	2

L-R: Celia Jaume of Iberdrola Mallorca, Peter Hanson and Pedro Cañellas, President Hotels Association of Bahía de Cala Millor

Total Prize Fund €800,000   **First Prize** €133,330

Double Trouble

James Kingston

There are many ways to win an event on The European Tour International Schedule but perhaps no-one has done so in quite the dramatic circumstances Peter Hanson overcame to win the Iberdrola Open Cala Millor Mallorca title.

Witnessed by a super slow motion television camera double hitting his pitch to the 12th hole in the final round, Hanson, who had moved into control of the tournament at that stage, instantly accepted the one shot penalty imposed by Chief Referee John Paramor but it clearly rattled the Swede who subsequently bogeyed the 14th to fall behind the charging Spaniard Alejandro Cañizares.

However, showing immense mental strength and resilience, Hanson regrouped and holed birdie putts of 12 and 30 feet respectively at the 15th and 17th before saving par from a greenside bunker at the last. It matched the six under par total of 274 set by Cañizares, whose victory in the 2006 Russian Open saw him, together with his father José Maria, become only the third father/son combination to win in European Tour history following Antonio and Ignacio Garrido and Craig and Kevin Stadler.

Any hopes Alejandro harboured of adding a second European Tour title to his golfing portfolio quickly ended on the first play-off hole, the 203 yard 18th, where his tee shot found the same greenside bunker Hanson had been in during regulation play. Unlike the Swede though, he could not get up and down, giving Hanson his third European Tour title.

James Kingston

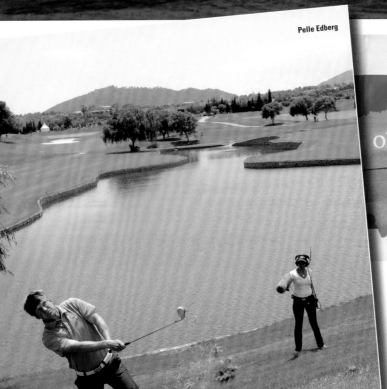

Pelle Edberg

Alejandro Cañizares

Christian Cévaër

Red Letter Day

BMW PGA CHAMPIONSHIP
Wentworth Club (West Course)
Surrey, England
May 20-23, 2010

1	**SIMON KHAN**		**72**	**69**	**71**	**66**	**278**	**-6**
2	Fredrik Andersson Hed		68	70	74	67	279	-5
	Luke Donald		68	68	72	71	279	-5
4	Stephen Gallacher		69	72	69	70	280	-4
5	Danny Willett		65	72	70	74	281	-3
6	Padraig Harrington		71	67	72	72	282	-2
	James Kingston		68	69	73	72	282	-2
	Paul Lawrie		71	69	71	71	282	-2
	Chris Wood		70	68	67	77	282	-2
10	Ross Fisher		67	70	76	70	283	-1
	Justin Rose		74	69	70	70	283	-1
	Lee Westwood		70	74	73	66	283	-1

Tim Abbott, Managing Director, BMW UK and Simon Khan

Total Prize Fund €4,553,916   **First Prize** €750,000

PGA Championship

"This is what I have always
dreamed of and it is unbelievable
to be standing here with the
trophy. I love The European Tour
so much and this tournament is
the reason I started playing golf"

Simon Khan

The globetrotting nature of today's professional golfers means they are always armed with the latest smart phone and laptop to ensure staying in touch. There are times, though, when the traditional pen and paper is all that is required.

Just ask Simon Khan, winner of the flagship event on The 2010 European Tour International Schedule – the BMW PGA Championship at Wentworth Club. The Englishman makes sure he is never far from notebook and ballpoint, ready to jot down his innermost thoughts. It is a proven process in benefiting his game.

At the lowest point of his career Khan sought solace with his note-taking. He was on the flight home from the 2009 UBS Hong Kong Open, disconsolate at the thought that his next undertaking would be the rigour of trying to regain his playing privileges over six rounds at the Qualifying School.

The 2004 Celtic Manor Wales Open champion began to write, noting that, in fact, his golf in the closing weeks of the 2009 season had not been that bad. "I thought that period had actually been a bit of a success compared with the earlier part of the year," he recalled.

Khan credits this moment of contemplation for the confidence that enabled him to go on and win the Qualifying School, passing golf's most stressful examination with flying colours. But although he was sure of staying on the circuit he had no guarantee of playing the Tour's biggest event at Wentworth Club.

By late April, therefore, it was time to again make use of pen and paper.

This time it was to fashion a letter to European Tour Chief Executive George O'Grady asking for an invitation to play in the BMW PGA Championship. "I thought I should write to George personally and explain that I wanted to play," he said. "I didn't want to put it in an email or anything like that, I wanted to send him something handwritten."

Khan is the sort of character who likes to do things properly and on the Monday of the tournament week itself he received the reply he wanted. He was in the field, as

Danny Willett

was Stephen Gallacher, the Scot who had penned a similar letter to O'Grady and who took similar advantage to eventually finish fourth.

Khan had plenty of fond memories of the tournament played in the shadow of The European Tour headquarters. He was runner-up in 2006 and two years later tied for tenth place. Wentworth had always inspired him and even more so the substantially remodelled version that staged this year's event.

The tournament attracted record crowds who bore witness to the £6 million investment made by the club's owner Richard Caring. Bunkers had been deepened, the greens re-laid and reshaped and at the 18th there was a new water hazard immediately in front of a raised putting surface that only the boldest were prepared try to hit in two blows.

Khan made a steady start with rounds of 72 and 69 while Robert Karlsson was convinced he was one of those who had failed the toughened test. An early finisher on the Friday, the 2008 European

Paul Lawrie

Fredrik Andersson Hed

Luke Donald

James Kingston

Lee Westwood

Padraig Harrington

Par 4
362m
396yds

7

BMW
PGA Championship

JOY DOES NOT COMPROMISE

Joy is having it all. The 320d ED is the most efficient BMW ever built, delivering just 109 g/km CO_2. But it only takes a few seconds in the BMW 320d EfficientDynamics Saloon to discover how responsiveness and responsibility go hand in hand. This discovery hits you in the eight seconds between 0 and 62 mph. On one hand, fuel-saving optimised aerodynamics. On the other, a lowered suspension. Under the foot, a heightened sense of power as you would expect from The Ultimate Driving Machine. The story of Joy continues at bmw.co.uk/joy

THE BMW 320d EFFICIENT DYNAMICS SALOON.
JOY IS FUTUREPROOF.

BMW EfficientDynamics
Less emissions. More driving pleasure.

9 mpg (4.1 ltr/100km). CO_2 emissions 109 g/km. BMW EfficientDynamics reduces BMW emissions without compromising performance developments

One of the many new innovations at this year's BMW PGA Championship saw BBC TV's Andrew Cotter stage a daily Q&A session in the Tented Village with leading players including David Howell (left) and Graeme McDowell

Special Olympic athletes Alan Booth, Hilary Thomas, Georgina Harris, Karen Oosthuizen and Scott Hastings enjoyed a full day of activities at Wentworth Club, the highlight of which was meeting Special Olympics ambassador Padraig Harrington

The Tour Players' Foundation awarded a grant of £25,000 to Sebastian's Action Trust, the designated local charity for the 2010 BMW PGA Championship. The charity was formed in the memory of Sebastian Gates who attended the same school as the children of Tour Members Anthony Wall and Retief Goosen who were there, along with TPF Chairman Mark Roe, to hand over the cheque to Sebastian's mother Jane

Tour Number One believed that, at three over par 145, he would miss the cut and therefore headed home to Monaco.

The Swede was within 500 metres of his house when he took the call that said he had been wrong to make the return journey. He immediately instructed his taxi driver to make a U turn before flying from Nice to Paris. Karlsson had a couple of hours sleep before a taxi ride to a private airport from where he jetted back to London, arriving at the course just before seven in the morning for his 8.55 am tee time.

Extraordinarily, this proved the ideal preparation for a stunning 62, a nine under par round that set a new course record on the West Course and propelled him from joint last place to alongside young Englishman Danny Willett, both players within two shots of third round leader Chris Wood.

Khan's Saturday 71 put him on the fringes of contention while Luke Donald, who began the final round three shots off the pace, was firmly in the mix.

While Karlsson, Willett and Wood were unable to sustain their challenges on the final day, Khan embarked on the round of his life from a starting position seven shots adrift of the 54 hole leader.

When a 20 foot birdie putt at the last was gobbled up by the very back of the hole, Khan snatched the clubhouse lead at six under

Stephen Gallacher

Robert Karlsson

par 278. He was quickly into the recorder's hut, pen in hand to sign for the joint lowest round of the day, a 66.

Still out on the course Donald was also at six under par, needing to birdie one of the two closing par fives to claim the biggest title of his career. But, at the 17th, the two time Ryder Cup player blocked his drive and ran up a double bogey seven.

It meant he needed to eagle the last to force a play-off. Dramatically, his wedged third skipped towards the hole and threatened to drop before spinning back past the hole to remain above ground and confirm victory for his fellow Englishman.

Moments later another pen was being put to use. It was inscribing the name of Simon Khan on a winner's cheque for €750,000 and with it the guarantee of a European Tour exemption until the end of the 2015 season.

The new champion continues making pertinent notes to bolster his rejuvenated career, but when you win an event as big as the BMW PGA Championship, the days of having to write letters asking for a place in any tournament are long gone.

Iain Carter
BBC Radio Five Live

Lee Westwood collected both The Harry Vardon Trophy as 2009 European Number One and The Players' Player of the Year Award at The European Tour Annual Dinner

Chris Wood (right) received The 2009 Sir Henry Cotton Rookie of the Year award from fellow Englishman and the winner in 2000, Ian Poulter

Mizuno unveiled its new state of the art workshop at Wentworth Club. Neil Coles, Chairman of the PGA European Tour Board of Directors, cut the ribbon watched by, L-R: Andy Kikidas, Tour Operations Manager for Mizuno, George O'Grady and Mitsuo Hasegawa, Head of Mizuno Europe

The European Tour and BMW announced a new four year extension to their partnership for the BMW PGA Championship through to 2014. Ralf Hussman, General Manager BMW Sports Marketing and George O'Grady shook hands on the deal in front of the world's media

MADRID MASTERS

MADRID MASTERS
Real Sociedad Hípica Española Club de Campo
Madrid, Spain
May 27–30, 2010

1	**LUKE DONALD**		65	67	68	67	267	-21
2	Rhys Davies		65	68	67	68	268	-20
3	Francesco Molinari		67	70	65	68	270	-18
4	Graeme McDowell		68	68	70	65	271	-17
5	Robert Rock		70	68	67	68	273	-15
6	Jamie Donaldson		65	70	70	70	275	-13
	Stephen Gallacher		69	73	66	67	275	-13
	Peter Lawrie		71	69	68	67	275	-13
9	Oliver Wilson		70	71	70	65	276	-12
10	Robert-Jan Derksen		71	71	67	68	277	-11
	Simon Dyson		70	69	70	68	277	-11
	Grégory Havret		68	74	69	66	277	-11
	Alvaro Quiros		69	70	64	74	277	-11
	Brett Rumford		67	71	71	68	277	-11
	Fabrizio Zanotti		71	72	65	69	277	-11

L-R: Ángeles Alarcó, CEO of Madrid Turismo, Luke Donald and Francisca Astillero, Communications Manager of Caja Madrid

Total Prize Fund €1,515, 687   **First Prize** €250,000

"The longer you go without a win the harder it becomes but this is a weight off my shoulders. To put last week behind me and to play the way I did this week makes me very proud indeed"

Rhys Davies

Cool Hand Luke

One of the difficult aspects about being a professional golfer is when the chance to win a tournament slips from your grasp. By the very nature of the sport, the opportunity to put that right can often be months away and, in some cases, years. For some, however, the wait can be as little as seven days.

A week ago Luke Donald stood in pole position to win the BMW PGA Championship at Wentworth Club before an errant tee shot on the penultimate hole of the final round cost him a double bogey seven and, with it, the title.

A mere 168 hours later and Donald again found himself in front as the clubhouse loomed on Sunday afternoon, this time his dogged challenger being Welshman Rhys Davies where last week it had been his fellow countryman Simon Khan. This time, however, there was no mistake with the pivotal hole being the par five 16th.

With some 252 yards left after a fine drive, Donald fired a sublime three wood to 12 feet from where he holed out for a crucial eagle three. Davies, looking for his second win of a fine rookie season, to his credit made birdie four but could not find another birdie over the closing two holes to force a play-off.

Donald's first win anywhere since 2006 moved him into the top ten on the Official World Golf Ranking and firmly into contention for his third Ryder Cup appearance.

Oliver Wilson

Francesco Molinari

THE CELTIC MANOR WALES OPEN
The Celtic Manor Resort (Twenty Ten Course)
City of Newport, Wales
June 3–6, 2010

1	**GRAEME McDOWELL**		72	70	64	63	269	-15
2	Rhys Davies		67	73	70	62	272	-12
3	Luke Donald		75	65	69	65	274	-10
4	Stephen Gallacher		70	73	63	69	275	-9
	Edoardo Molinari		67	71	70	67	275	-9
	Robert Rock		68	71	70	66	275	-9
7	Marcel Siem		69	67	66	74	276	-8
8	Miguel Angel Jiménez		70	68	70	69	277	-7
9	Thomas Björn		69	68	68	74	279	-5
	Niclas Fasth		69	72	67	71	279	-5
	Richard McEvoy		67	71	69	72	279	-5

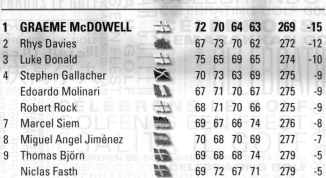

L-R: The Rt Hon Carwyn Jones AM, First Minister of Wales, Graeme McDowell and Sir Terry Matthews, Chairman of The Celtic Manor Resort

Total Prize Fund €2,118,254   **First Prize** €350,940

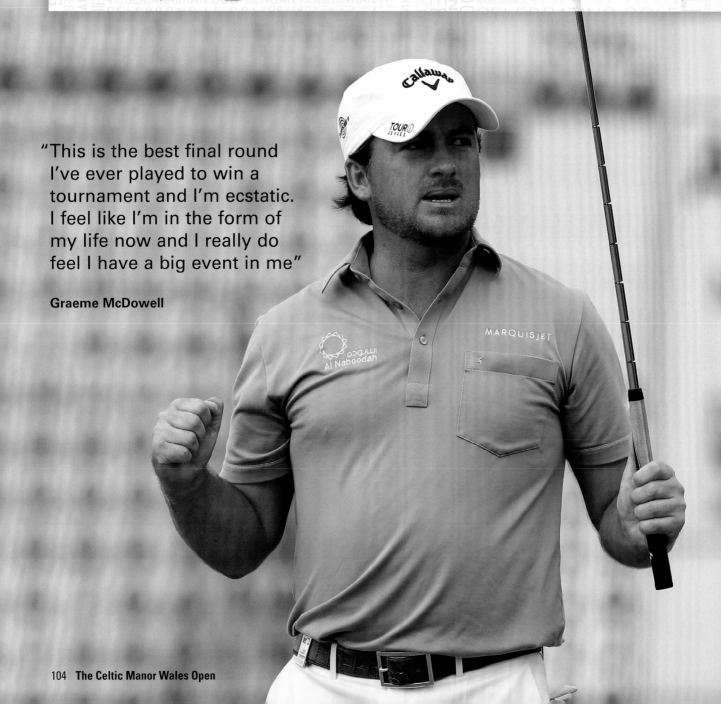

"This is the best final round I've ever played to win a tournament and I'm ecstatic. I feel like I'm in the form of my life now and I really do feel I have a big event in me"

Graeme McDowell

Luke Donald

Robert Rock

Stephen Gallacher

Rhys Davies

6, 7, 5, 6, 7, 7, 9, 7, 5, 6, 6, 7, 8, 6, 7, 6, 8, 5, but happy.

We all get those days.
Where you seriously consider packing it all in and taking up darts or something.
But even a bad round here has its positives.
Stunning championship courses.
Very reasonable green fees.
No pretentious nonsense.
A good walk through our beautiful countryside.
And best of all, in Wales tomorrow's always another day.

golfasitshouldbe.com

RYDER CUP
1927 2010
CELTIC MANOR
CITY OF NEWPORT
WALES

**Wales: Host Nation
for The 2010 Ryder Cup**

Wales
Cymru

Marcel Siem

Edoardo Molinari

Local Knowledge

Graeme McDowell has always been popular in Wales. Ever since the days he dated a local girl and lived for a while in Cardiff, the natives have harboured a soft spot for the man from Portrush. That affair of the heart may now be over but McDowell's love affair with the Principality was considerably strengthened thanks to his superb victory in The Celtic Manor Wales Open.

Along with the thousands of spectators who flocked to The Twenty Ten Course, watching Ryder Cup Captain Colin Montgomerie cannot have failed to have been impressed by McDowell's mastery of the layout where he will lead his European Team against the United States in October.

Deep in the pack after opening rounds of 72-70, there was little to suggest McDowell would be the man to watch but he put that right with stunning weekend rounds of 64-63 to eventually win by three from bone fide Welshman Rhys Davies.

The 25 year old from Bridgend closed with a course record 62, a round that saw him cover the middle 12 holes in ten under par, to put the heat on McDowell but the Ulsterman responded magnificently on a thrilling final day, matching Davies' outward half of 30 before carding further birdies at the tenth and 11th to open up a lead he did not relinquish. It left Davies second for the second week in succession, two strokes clear of the man who beat him in the previous week's Madrid Masters, England's Luke Donald.

"It is certainly a very nice feeling to win again. The final day had its ups and down but the most important thing was that I pulled it off when I needed to and closed out the tournament"

Thomas Björn

ESTORIL OPEN DE PORTUGAL
Penha Longa Hotel, Spa and Golf Resort
Linho Sintra, Estoril, Portugal
June 10–13, 2010

1	**THOMAS BJÖRN**		67	65	65	68	265	-23
2	Richard Green		67	69	64	70	270	-18
3	Mark F Haastrup		67	68	70	67	272	-16
4	Robert Rock		68	67	68	71	274	-14
5	Damien McGrane		64	70	68	73	275	-13
6	Darren Clarke		75	67	68	66	276	-12
	Robert Coles		68	66	69	73	276	-12
8	Gary Lockerbie		69	69	71	68	277	-11
	Daniel Vancsik		69	66	68	74	277	-11
	Steve Webster		67	67	70	73	277	-11

Manuel Agrellos, President of the Portuguese Golf Federation and Thomas Björn

Total Prize Fund €1,011,916   **First Prize €166,660**

estoril
OPEN DE PORTUGAL

1

366 yds - 335 mtrs
PAR 4

TURISMO DE
PORTUGAL

GREEN −16

Richard Green

Mark F Haastrup

Robert Rock

TURISMO DE
PORTUGAL

18

Björn Again

No matter how good a golfer you are – and Thomas Björn is a very good golfer – there is a direct correlation between the amount of time you spend outwith the winners' circle and the doubt in your own mind as to whether or not you will ever step back in there again.

After topping the Challenge Tour Rankings in 1995, the Dane was a consistent winner on The European Tour in the decade following 1996 but neck problems, linked to a loss of form, saw a distinct lack of silverware in his hands after his success in the Irish Open at Carton House in May 2006.

Move forward four years and 23 days to be precise and it was little wonder that Björn sported a beaming smile as he tapped in for birdie on the final green for

his fourth successive round in the 60s and a five shot victory.

Ironically, the battle with runner-up Richard Green had been closer than the final margin suggested and indeed Björn's three shot lead at the start of the final day had been cut to one by the 13th thanks to aggressive play by the left handed Australian.

But the pivotal part of the round came at the 14th and 15th where two consecutive birdies for Björn allied to back-to-back bogeys for Green saw the Dane's lead increased to five, the margin which remained until the end. It was Björn's tenth European Tour success and cemented his position as the most successful Danish golfer in history.

"In Austria golf is not that big a sport, so this win means even more because we haven't had that much success. Markus Brier changed everything when he won on The European Tour, so to follow him is fantastic"

Martin Wiegele

SAINT-OMER OPEN presented by Neuflize OBC
Aa Saint Omer Golf Club
Lumbres, France
June 17–20, 2010

#	Name		R1	R2	R3	R4	Total	Score
1	**MARTIN WIEGELE**		66	71	72	68	277	-7
2	Robert Dinwiddie		71	65	71	72	279	-5
	Pelle Edberg		70	72	70	67	279	-5
	Jamie Elson		71	67	68	73	279	-5
	Matt Haines		70	68	72	69	279	-5
	Raphaël Jacquelin		73	68	66	72	279	-5
7	Mark F Haastrup		71	67	71	72	281	-3
8	Åke Nilsson		73	68	71	70	282	-2
	Charles-Edouard Russo		68	73	72	69	282	-2
10	Lorenzo Gagli		72	71	70	70	283	-1

L-R: Jean-Jacques Durant, Tournament promoter, Martin Wiegele and Hervé de Rocquigny, Banque Neuflize OBC

Total Prize Fund €604,470   **First Prize €100,000**

Rock On

One of the beauties of golf is the fact there are no hard and fast rules about any aspect of the game. Take preparation for a tournament for example. Some coaches might suggest a sustained bout of practice to get all aspects of the swing fine-tuned to perfection while others might recommend a relaxing trip to a spa to chill out before the rigours of competition ahead.

However, it is unlikely that many coaches would propose camping on hard ground in a tent with precious little sleep for three nights thanks to a Rock Festival thundering around your ears.

Yet that is exactly what Martin Wiegele and his girlfriend did prior to the SAINT-OMER OPEN presented by Neuflize OBC and who can argue with him following

his two shot victory in the dual ranking event between The European Tour and the Challenge Tour.

The 31 year old was clearly in form following a victory in his last Challenge Tour outing two weeks previously on home soil in the Kärnten Golf Open by Markus Brier Foundation and the winner of the Qualifying School in 2007 carried that form into France.

Three shots adrift of leader Jamie Elson going into the final round and also behind the experienced duo of Robert Dinwiddie and Raphaël Jacquelin, Wiegele knew he needed a fast start and got it with birdies at the first two holes and when none of the leading trio could better 70, the Austrian's 68 was good enough to triumph.

Raphaël Jacquelin

Jamie Elson

Robert Dinwiddie

Pelle Edberg

Butterflies to Birdies

"I am very, very proud of the way I handled myself this week and to have 'Major Champion' after my name from now on is a very special feeling indeed"

Graeme McDowell

US OPEN CHAMPIONSHIP
Pebble Beach Golf Links
Pebble Beach, California, USA
June 17-20, 2010

1	**GRAEME McDOWELL**		71	68	71	74	284	0
2	Grégory Havret		73	71	69	72	285	1
3	Ernie Els		73	68	72	73	286	2
4	Phil Mickelson		75	66	73	73	287	3
	Tiger Woods		74	72	66	75	287	3
6	Matt Kuchar		74	72	74	68	288	4
	Davis Love III		75	74	68	71	288	4
8	Alex Cejka		70	72	74	73	289	5
	Dustin Johnson		71	70	66	82	289	5
	Martin Kaymer		74	71	72	72	289	5
	Brandt Snedeker		75	74	69	71	289	5

Graeme McDowell is congratulated by officials of the United States Golf Association

Total Prize Fund €6,244,276   **First Prize** €1,123,970

The Atlantic, they say, is more salty than the Pacific and where Graeme McDowell comes from on the northern coast of Ireland, the ocean is more often an angry grey than blue.

Golfers grow up tough in Portrush, where the sport is woven into the very fabric of everyday life. So it is probably not by accident that two of the three men from Ireland to win Major titles, McDowell and the late, great Fred Daly, came from this special place.

Like 1947 Open Champion Daly, McDowell is a convivial, fun-loving chap who would rather clink glasses than cross swords. Inside, however, there is a basalt core as hard as the rocks on the nearby Giant's Causeway.

Those who know McDowell, the place he comes from, and how he grew from boy to man in golf were not surprised to see him emerge from an attritional Sunday at Pebble Beach with the US Open trophy clasped to his chest.

As ever, the Championship was decided on Father's Day and McDowell's dad, Kenny, an avid amateur golfer not long retired from his job as a technician at the Academical Institute in Coleraine, followed every step and willed every shot to its target as his son became the first European since Tony Jacklin in 1970 to win America's national open championship.

It was little wonder that, as the final putt dropped, Kenny, who together with wife Marian raised three sons Gordon, Graeme and Gary, allowed his mind to wander.

Graeme first picked up a club at seven years old and could hardly wait for his tenth birthday so he could join the junior section at the local Rathmore Golf Club. From the moment he did, his gift for golf became clear and the sharp competitive instinct, which helped him ascend to the pinnacle of the game, was honed in those early years.

"The first competitive match he played was in the Fred Daly Trophy," Kenny recalled. "You need a team of seven for that but Rathmore had only five. Gary and Graeme were playing in the nearby pitch and putt so they were asked to come on over. Graeme was a 42 handicap, Gary was a 45 and the competition was played off scratch, yet Graeme took a 16 handicapper to the 16th green."

During his rise through the amateur ranks in Ulster and on to a golf scholarship in Birmingham, Alabama, he consistently won for fun. He had always been academically gifted yet his golfing

talent shone brighter and, indeed, during his final year at college in America, he won six out of 12 tournaments and broke the all-time record held jointly by Luke Donald and Tiger Woods with an average round score of 69.6.

Within weeks of turning professional in May 2002, he completed a dramatic sudden-death play-off victory in the Volvo Scandinavian Masters, only his fourth outing on The European Tour. Many 22 year olds might have spent the resulting €316,660 windfall on a Ferrari but McDowell instead bought a new house for his mum and dad in Portrush.

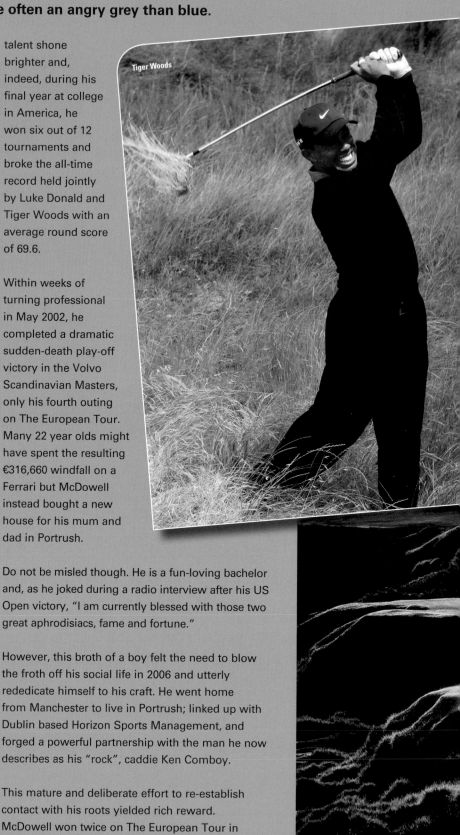
Tiger Woods

Do not be misled though. He is a fun-loving bachelor and, as he joked during a radio interview after his US Open victory, "I am currently blessed with those two great aphrodisiacs, fame and fortune."

However, this broth of a boy felt the need to blow the froth off his social life in 2006 and utterly rededicate himself to his craft. He went home from Manchester to live in Portrush; linked up with Dublin based Horizon Sports Management, and forged a powerful partnership with the man he now describes as his "rock", caddie Ken Comboy.

This mature and deliberate effort to re-establish contact with his roots yielded rich reward. McDowell won twice on The European Tour in 2008; the Ballantine's Championship in Korea and The Barclays Scottish Open, securing his Ryder Cup debut that September at Valhalla.

His fifth European Tour victory in The Celtic Manor Wales Open in May would be the springboard to his

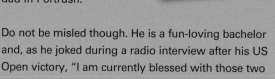

Grégory Havret

Phil Mickelson

Ernie Els

Flat, flat, flat.
So you can sleep, sleep, sleep.

Many so-called "flat" airline seats actually lie at an angle when fully reclined. Those in United's new international business class, however, lie fully, 180° flat. United is now offering their new premium product on all routes from London Heathrow to the U.S.* so it's easy to experience unrivaled comfort while travelling the world.

Visit suitedreams.united.com for exact routes and fleet progress.
To book, visit unitedairlines.co.uk or call 0845 8444 777.

A STAR ALLIANCE MEMBER  ™

UNITED
It's time to fly.®

Martin Kaymer

Alex Cejka

success at Pebble Beach. He was so relaxed and self-assured during the week in California, he even withdrew from a pre-tournament session he had planned with golfing mind-guru Dr Bob Rotella.

Though his patience was tested as his five birdies were cancelled out by five bogeys in the first round, McDowell kept his composure, shooting a superlative 68 on Friday to move into the lead on three under par 139.

Dad Kenny and manager Conor Ridge took McDowell shopping to help pass the long hours before his late tee time on Saturday, where a level par 71 sent him into the final round three behind American Dustin Johnson after the latter's outstanding 66.

With its greens playing hard and fast, Pebble Beach showed its teeth on Sunday and Johnson was badly bitten, surrendering six shots and his title hopes when a calamitous triple-bogey at the second was followed by a double at the third and a bogey at the fourth.

One by one, the leading lights; Ernie Els, Phil Mickelson and Tiger Woods, flickered out of contention. So Grégory Havret, in the group ahead, was McDowell's only rival as he played the last.

When the Frenchman missed his birdie putt on the 18th, McDowell was spared the risk of going for the green in two. After laying up, he hit a stress-free wedge to 20 feet and two putted for par, a final round 74, and a famous victory which propelled him not only to 13th on the Official World Golf Ranking and to Number One in The Race to Dubai but also into Colin Montgomerie's European Ryder Cup Team.

As a golfer, McDowell is uncannily consistent from tee to green, is a first class putter and, typically of many who have grown up on seaside links, he's blessed with imagination. Yet at Pebble Beach he proved himself a phenomenal warrior above all else, one of that special sporting breed who transform butterflies into birdies. One suspects there is much more to come from this son of Portrush.

Karl MacGinty
Irish Independent

"This has not sunk in yet because this win is what I have been trying to achieve for over a year. I felt I was good enough coming out on Tour but you never know for sure until you do it. I'm thrilled"

David Horsey

BMW Golfsport
bmw-golfsport.com
bmw.co.uk
The Ultimate Driving Machine

BMW INTERNATIONAL OPEN
Golfclub München Eichenried
Munich, Germany
June 24–27, 2010

1	**DAVID HORSEY**		69	67	67	67	270	-18
2	Ross Fisher		69	66	66	70	271	-17
3	Rafael Cabrera-Bello		71	67	66	68	272	-16
	Alex Cejka		71	67	67	67	272	-16
	Bradley Dredge		64	67	67	74	272	-16
	Kenneth Ferrie		67	67	70	68	272	-16
	Pablo Larrazábal		66	66	72	68	272	-16
8	Charl Schwartzel		67	69	68	69	273	-15
9	Alejandro Cañizares		71	67	67	69	274	-14
	Simon Thornton		67	67	67	73	274	-14

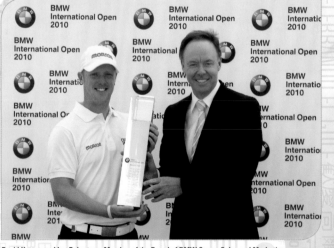

David Horsey and Ian Robertson, Member of the Board of BMW Group, Sales and Marketing

Total Prize Fund €2,017,955   **First Prize** €333,330

Bradley Dredge

Ross Fisher

Rafael Cabrera-Bello

Kenneth Ferrie

BMW

Par 5
440 m
481 yards

6

ROLEX

WELT

Emirates

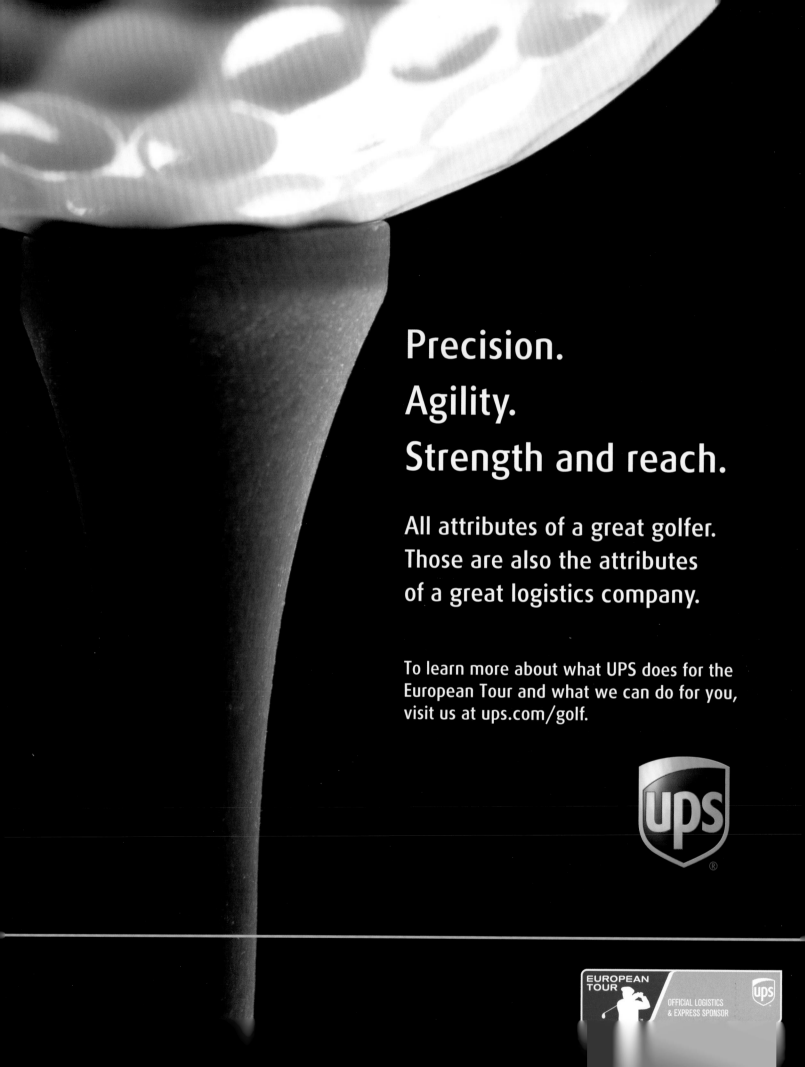

Bucking the Trend

It is fair to say that there were not many happy Englishmen in Germany on the night of Sunday June 27 although David Horsey certainly bucked that trend.

While his fellow countrymen were bemoaning the 4-1 thrashing their team suffered at German hands in the World Cup in South Africa, Horsey put a smile back on the face of English sport with a fine maiden European Tour victory.

The 25 year old had shown his pedigree when he topped the Challenge Tour Rankings in 2008 and his first season on The European Tour in 2009 had been steady if not spectacular. Now was the time to take the next step up the career ladder and he did it in considerable style.

For a while it looked like the charging Spaniard Pablo Larrazábal or Welshman Bradley Dredge – who had led since his opening round of 64 – would triumph but both came a cropper at the tricky 319 yard 16th with respective double bogey sixes.

Englishman Ross Fisher and German favourite Alex Cejka also figured in the latter stages but neither got close enough in the end to Horsey who showed how to play the 16th with a pitch and putt birdie three before putting the icing on the cake with a birdie four on the 18th.

After the presentation ceremony, he sat down to watch the World Cup match unfold on the big screen beside the 18th green, content in the knowledge that one Englishman, at least, had done his job that day.

Pablo Larrazábal

Alex Cejka

"It feels great to get another win this season and once again in a play-off. The young guys on Tour play very well nowadays but sometimes, like today, experience can be a key factor"

Miguel Angel Jiménez

ALSTOM

ALSTOM OPEN DE FRANCE
Le Golf National (Albatross Course)
Paris, France
July 1–4, 2010

1	**MIGUEL ANGEL JIMÉNEZ**		71	69	66	67	273	**-11**
2	Alejandro Cañizares		66	66	73	68	273	-11
	Francesco Molinari		69	69	68	67	273	-11
4	Rory McIlroy		68	71	69	66	274	-10
5	Danny Willett		72	67	69	68	276	-8
6	Grégory Bourdy		68	69	70	70	277	-7
	Mark Foster		76	63	70	68	277	-7
	Peter Hanson		68	69	70	70	277	-7
	Martin Kaymer		66	67	71	73	277	-7
	Oliver Wilson		68	71	71	67	277	-7

L-R: George Barbaret President of the French Golf Federation, Miguel Angel Jiménez and Patrick Kron, Chairman and CEO, Alstom

Total Prize Fund €3,040,392   **First Prize** €500,000

Rory McIlroy

Grégory Bourdy

Francesco Molinari

Alejandro Cañizares

Redemption Time

For many players, making a mistake when in sight of victory can often dent the confidence so much that any chance of redemption is slight. However, if you have the experience of a player such as Miguel Angel Jiménez, you can put it behind you to go on and lay claim to the silverware just as the Spaniard did in the Alstom Open de France.

Playing the 72nd hole with a two shot lead, the 46 year old was odds-on to claim his 17th European Tour title and his second of the 2010 season. But, inexplicably, following a fine drive, his eight iron approach to the green found the water. This mistake led to a double bogey six which saw him tie his compatriot Alejandro

Cañizares and Francesco Molinari of Italy on 11 under par 273. However, rather than see his head go down, Jiménez's famous barrel chest puffed out as he strode back to the 18th tee to right the wrong.

When Cañizares found the water from the tee, his race was run and with Molinari in sand, the advantage was firmly with Jiménez. The Italian rallied bravely and holed a testing 15 foot putt for a bogey five, forcing Jiménez to hole from 12 feet for par and the title. It saw the Spaniard become the oldest player in history to win this event at the age of 46 years and 180 days, an honour previously held by Sam Torrance at 44 and 308 days in 1998.

"It has taken a little while for me to win on Tour like Francesco so this is a dream day. The conditions were testing so I was very proud and happy the way I played"

Edoardo Molinari

 BARCLAYS
SCOTTISH OPEN

THE BARCLAYS SCOTTISH OPEN
Loch Lomond Golf Club
Glasgow, Scotland
July 8–11, 2010

1	**EDOARDO MOLINARI**		66	69	63	74	**272**	**-12**
2	Darren Clarke		65	67	67	76	275	-9
3	Raphaël Jacquelin		71	68	69	68	276	-8
4	Stephen Gallacher		67	73	69	68	277	-7
	Peter Hedblom		67	69	69	72	277	-7
	Francesco Molinari		68	69	68	72	277	-7
7	Shane Lowry		68	73	66	71	278	-6
8	Johan Edfors		67	76	68	68	279	-5
	Ross Fisher		71	73	65	70	279	-5
	Rory Sabbatini		70	69	69	71	279	-5

Edoardo Molinari and Robert E Diamond Jr, President, Barclays PLC

Total Prize Fund €3,588,941   **First Prize** €601,600

Raphaël Jacquelin

Shane Lowry

BARCLAYS
SCOTTISH OPEN
15
415 YDS 379 m PAR 4
Glen Fruin

BARCLAYS

Peter Hedblom

Darren Clarke

Stephen Gallacher

Francesco Molinari

Johan Edfors

Oh Brother!

Golfing history has a strange way of repeating itself and that facet of the sport's make-up was illustrated perfectly once again during The 2010 Barclays Scottish Open.

In 1996, the first Scottish Open to be contested at Loch Lomond was won by Thomas Björn who, the previous year, had topped the Challenge Tour Rankings. Fast forward 14 years and standing with the trophy in his hands was Edoardo Molinari who had dominated the Challenge Tour to such an extent in 2009 that he had won with record earnings for a season.

A sublime third round 63 had given the Italian a one shot lead over the vastly experienced Darren Clarke going into the final round, their threeball completed by Edoardo's younger brother Francesco. The Molinaris had won the Omega Mission Hills World Cup for Italy the previous November but had never appeared together at the business end of a regular tournament until now.

Seven shots behind his elder brother, Francesco was never really going to be a factor in the title destination and early mistakes from Clarke in the tough weather saw Edoardo five shots clear after five holes. Although the Northern Irishman battled gamely over the remaining holes he could not close the gap significantly and Edoardo eventually won by three shots. Clarke's considerable consolation was that he claimed the one remaining place on offer for The Open Championship at St Andrews the following week.

THE OPEN CHAMPIONSHIP

THE 139TH OPEN CHAMPIONSHIP
Old Course, St Andrews
Fife, Scotland
July 15-18, 2010

1	**LOUIS OOSTHUIZEN** 	65	67	69	71	272	-16
2	Lee Westwood	67	71	71	70	279	-9
3	Paul Casey	69	69	67	75	280	-8
	Rory McIlroy	63	80	69	68	280	-8
	Henrik Stenson	68	74	67	71	280	-8
6	Retief Goosen	69	70	72	70	281	-7
7	Martin Kaymer	69	71	68	74	282	-6
	Sean O'Hair	67	72	72	71	282	-6
	Robert Rock	68	78	67	69	282	-6
	Nick Watney	67	73	71	71	282	-6

Louis Oosthuizen receives the Claret Jug from Colin Brown, Captain of the Royal and Ancient Golf Club of St Andrews

Total Prize Fund €5,708,861   First Prize €1,011,840

Louis the First

"To win an Open Championship is special, but to win it here at St. Andrews is just something you dream about. Having a big lead is not easy and I'm proud of the way I held my nerve, especially on the back nine"

Louis Oosthuizen

There are Open Champions and there are St Andrews Open Champions and, on the 150th anniversary of the game's oldest Major, Louis Oosthuizen became a deserving member of both elite groups.

Some might look at a St Andrews Roll of Honour containing the likes of Sir Nick Faldo, Bobby Jones, Jack Nicklaus and Tiger Woods and conclude that Oosthuizen's name is out of place in such a list. But they were obviously elsewhere than the legendary Fife links in the third week of July. For the South African did not merely beat his rivals so much as crush them deep into the sand beneath the hallowed turf.

His 16 under par total of 272 was brilliant enough for a seven stroke triumph, the second biggest margin in The Open in 97 years. There is no prize for guessing who triumphed by eight shots - also at the Home of Golf in 2000 - and no, there is no follow up prize for saying who Oosthuizen resembled as he turned the final day into a procession. Yes, here was an impervious front-running performance of which Tiger Woods himself would have been immensely proud.

As ever, the week began with all eyes on the World Number One as he attempted to become the first golfer to win three Opens at St Andrews. In the event it was not to be with Woods finishing in a share of 23rd place, although a 67 on the first day was just the start he was chasing. By the end of the day, however, he would have peered up at the huge leaderboard and seen the damage that had been wreaked on a flat calm Thursday which, with the soft conditions

made St Andrews, in the words of defending champion Stewart Cink, "easier than it's ever been". No-one would find it any more straightforward than Rory McIlroy, who shot the lowest first round score in Open history.

We might have witnessed a brash young man mugging a defenceless old lady, but at least McIlroy left the Old Course with a shred of her dignity. The 21 year old came within a three foot putt of recording the first 62 in the history of Major Championships. Instead, after that short birdie miss on the Road Hole 17th, McIlroy birdied the last to post the 22nd 63. "There's absolutely no reason why I can't win," he said afterwards and, as the statistics sheet showed that McIlroy had now broken 70 in each of his nine competitive rounds at St Andrews, nobody was disagreeing.

Yet the links has a habit of getting its own back and how it took its vengeance on Friday. McIlroy slumped to an 80 as the gusts rose to 40 mph. So treacherous were the winds that play was suspended for an hour before the battle with the elements resumed. All this time Oosthuizen was back in his hotel room no doubt enjoying the spectacle.

Jin Jeong of Korea who finished tied 14th to win the Silver Medal as leading amateur

Retief Goosen

Henrik Stenson

The 27 year old had been second out at 6.41am and had unquestionably enjoyed the best of the day. In the McIlroy mania of Thursday few noticed that the South African himself had shot 65. Now they took notice. A 67 put on him 12 under par 132 to lie five clear of the field.

When Oosthuizen made his way back to the first tee on the Saturday the 'Shrek' headlines were everywhere. The nickname, coined due to a certain likeness to the cartoon character, was one revelation, the fact that this farmer's son was a product of The Ernie Els Foundation another. Then, there was his reputation in the locker room. Oosthuizen was clearly anything but a fluke leader. "Believe me, this boy can play, just look at his swing, it's fantastic," said Ian Poulter. "We were just surprised he took so long to win his first Tour title."

That had come four months before in the Open de Andalucia de Golf and had plainly given him the self belief he required. There was something more, however. Oosthuizen's mind had been wandering so his manager Andrew 'Chubby' Chandler put him on to the renowned mind doctor

Rory McIlroy

Lee Westwood

THE LEADER'S WATCH

No other watch is engineered quite like a Rolex. The Day-Date II, launched in 2008, enhances the legacy of the original Day-Date, which was the first watch to display the date, as well as the day in its entirety. Now in a larger, more commanding 41 mm size, the Day-Date II is a natural evolution of a classic. The Day-Date II can display the day in a wide choice of languages and is presented here in platinum.

THE DAY-DATE II

ROLEX
ROLEX.COM

Karl Morris. Together the pair came up with the red dot on his glove which Oosthuizen would stare at before each shot to get him into a zen-like state. He would need to be.

On the Saturday the roars out-muscled the gales as Paul Casey whipped the galleries into a frenzy by eating into Oosthuizen's lead. At one stage he reduced the deficit to a single shot, yet that was as close as he was ever to come. Displaying an admirable coolness, Oosthuizen finished his round birdie-par-birdie. His advantage was back to four. Casey admitted he would have to produce something very special to catch his final round playing partner.

As hard as he tried, the Englishman could not manage to become the first British Open winner of the new Millennium. In fact, he was pipped for second by his fellow countryman Lee Westwood, claiming his fourth top three finish in the last five Major Championships. Casey had to be satisfied with a share for third with Sweden's Henrik Stenson and the courageous McIlroy who shrugged off his second round nightmare with a storming weekend. With Retief Goosen one shot further back, it meant the top six were all members of The European Tour.

Like everyone, the Tour doffed its visor to Oosthuizen. After he had hugged his wife Nel-Mare and kissed his seven month old daughter Jana, Oosthuizen picked up the Claret Jug and dedicated it to his former president, Nelson Mandela, who just happened to be 92 that very day. "It felt a bit special out there," said Oosthuizen. "I was thinking about his birthday and what he's done for our country. He's unbelievable."

In a golfing sense so, most definitely, is Oosthuizen; both in the scale of his triumph and in his humbleness of the glory. He took the pot of gold back to the Rainbow Nation and bought himself a tractor to celebrate. "His life will change, he won't," said his proud mentor Ernie Els.

Louis Oosthuizen: a real champion in every sense.

James Corrigan
The Independent

Miguel Angel Jiménez extricates himself from a tight spot on the Road Hole 17th, a shot later voted European Tour Shot of the Month

Paul Casey

NORDEA SCANDINAVIAN MASTERS

Bro Hof Slott Golf Club
Stockholm, Sweden
July 22–25, 2010

1	**RICHARD S JOHNSON**		70	66	70	71	277	**-11**
2	Rafa Echenique		68	69	72	69	278	-10
3	Edoardo Molinari		68	71	71	69	279	-9
4	Mark Brown		73	69	67	71	280	-8
	Louis Oosthuizen		67	70	70	73	280	-8
	Brett Rumford		71	70	70	69	280	-8
7	Robert Karlsson		73	72	69	67	281	-7
8	Jamie Donaldson		72	68	74	68	282	-6
	Damien McGrane		73	71	69	69	282	-6
	James Morrison		71	72	72	67	282	-6

Christian Clausen, President and Group CEO of Nordea and Richard S Johnson

Total Prize Fund €1,583,950   **First Prize** €266,660

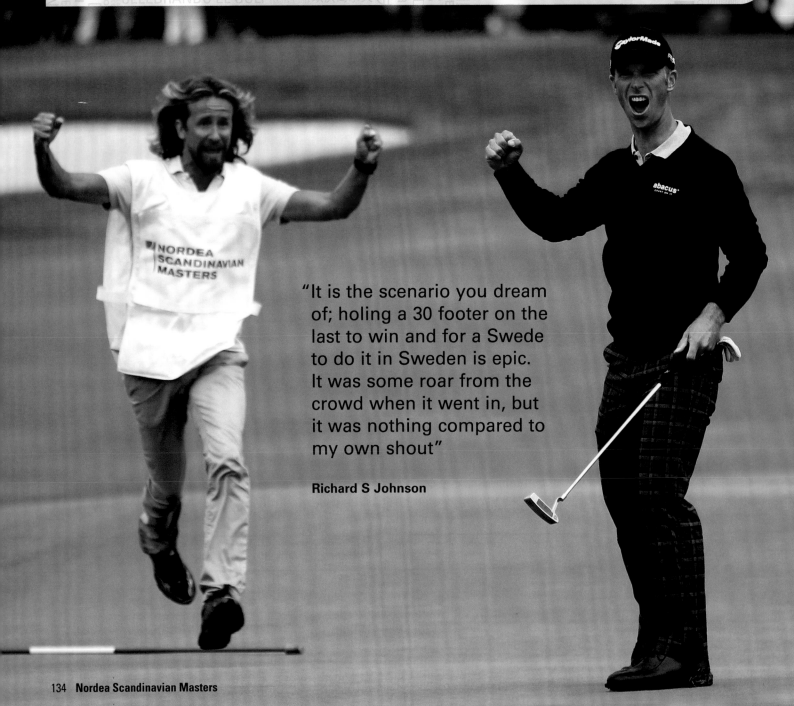

"It is the scenario you dream of; holing a 30 footer on the last to win and for a Swede to do it in Sweden is epic. It was some roar from the crowd when it went in, but it was nothing compared to my own shout"

Richard S Johnson

Brown

Rafa Echenique

Louis Oosthuizen

Damien McGrane

Magic Johnson

It is often said a change is as good as a rest and that was certainly the case for Sweden's Richard S Johnson who claimed an emotional victory in the Nordea Scandinavian Masters in his home town of Stockholm.

Johnson arrived without his usual caddie, Lance Tenbroeck, who opted instead to play in The Senior Open Championship presented by MasterCard at Carnoustie. It was a decision Tenbroeck must now regret because, as he was comfortably missing the cut in Scotland, Johnson hooked up with old family friend Anders Timell, now a successful radio talk show host in Stockholm.

The hirsute bagman drew almost as much attention from the enthusiastic galleries in the early rounds as South African Louis Oosthuizen, who was universally praised for honouring the

invitation extended to him by tournament organisers before his spectacular success in The Open Championship at St Andrews.

Oosthuizen performed admirably to finish in a share of fourth place but, in the final round, all eyes were on Johnson as he attempted to become only the fourth Swede to win his national title.

A closing 69 looked to have given Argentina's Rafa Echenique at least a spot in a play-off alongside Johnson but he had not reckoned with the Swede's astonishing finish, the winner of the 2002 ANZ Championship in Australia rolling in a stunning 30 foot birdie putt on the 18th green to win by a shot.

"I heard the roars and I knew Padraig was making a charge. But I just tried to stay patient and it feels great to come out on top against such a world class field"

Ross Fisher

3 IRISH OPEN

Killarney Golf and Fishing Club
Killarney, Co. Kerry, Ireland
July 29–August 1, 2010

1	**ROSS FISHER**		**69**	**61**	**71**	**65**	**266**	**-18**
2	Padraig Harrington		68	67	69	64	268	-16
3	Gonzalo Fernandez-Castaño		66	69	68	67	270	-14
	Chris Wood		71	65	66	68	270	-14
5	Richard Bland		69	71	66	65	271	-13
	Richard Green		65	70	69	67	271	-13
7	Michael Hoey		66	69	71	67	273	-11
8	Francesco Molinari		67	66	69	72	274	-10
9	Joost Luiten		74	65	70	66	275	-9
	Richie Ramsay		71	68	72	64	275	-9
	Brett Rumford		66	69	73	67	275	-9

L-R: George O'Grady, Chief Executive of The European Tour, Ross Fisher, Robert Finnegan, CEO of 3 and Minister Mary Hanafin TD, Minister for Tourism, Culture and Sport

Total Prize Fund €3,000,000   **First Prize €500,000**

Richard Green

Chris Wood

Gonzalo Fernandez-Castaño

King Fisher

It was a victory which left Ross Fisher thinking about opportunities to come, the whole of Ireland thinking about what might have been, and caddies everywhere thinking about their immediate future.

For not only did the 29 year old Englishman put paid to Padraig Harrington's hopes of a second victory in four years in his national Open, he did so with a new caddie on the bag – Phil 'Wobbly' Morbey – the second week in succession on The European Tour that a player had triumphed in tandem with a new bagman.

Fisher laid the groundwork for his fourth Tour triumph with a stunning ten under par 61 on the second day, a round which set a new course record and which, for a while, looked like it would also be the first 59 scored in official European Tour competition.

Three behind Fisher going into the final round, Harrington had every right to believe his closing 64 would be good enough to triumph but the Englishman responded admirably with a 65, a determined effort exemplified by his birdies at the 15th and 16th, which came immediately after Harrington had pulled level with his own eagle three at the 16th.

Fisher's 18 under par aggregate of 266 matched the record low for the tournament set by Colin Montgomerie in 2001 and, more importantly, moved him into the automatic places for a spot in Europe's Ryder Cup Team, captained by Montgomerie himself, at The Celtic Manor Resort in two months time.

Padraig Harrington

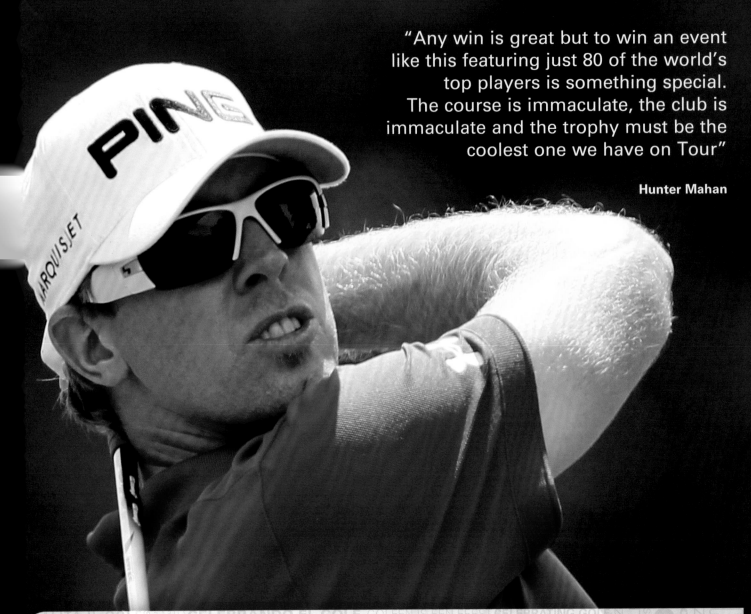

"Any win is great but to win an event like this featuring just 80 of the world's top players is something special. The course is immaculate, the club is immaculate and the trophy must be the coolest one we have on Tour"

Hunter Mahan

WGC - BRIDGESTONE INVITATIONAL
Firestone Country Club (South Course)
Akron, Ohio, USA
August 5–8, 2010

1	**HUNTER MAHAN**		**71**	**67**	**66**	**64**	**268**	**-12**
2	Ryan Palmer		70	68	63	69	270	-10
3	Retief Goosen		67	66	73	65	271	-9
	Bo Van Pelt		67	68	69	67	271	-9
5	Sean O'Hair		67	70	64	71	272	-8
6	Jeff Overton		67	70	67	69	273	-7
	Jim Furyk		72	68	69	64	273	-7
8	Peter Hanson		69	66	68	71	274	-6
9	Padraig Harrington		69	70	70	66	275	-5
	Matt Kuchar		69	67	66	73	275	-5
	Rory McIlroy		68	69	69	69	275	-5
	Louis Oosthuizen		72	70	68	65	275	-5
	Adam Scott		66	70	72	67	275	-5
	Steve Stricker		68	71	69	67	275	-5

Hunter Mahan and US PGA Tour Commissioner, Tim Finchem

Total Prize Fund €6,483,924   First Prize €1,076,840

Retief Goosen

Bounty Hunter

It is the eternal dilemma for a man who has just got engaged: do you give your betrothed a gift in addition to the ring? In Hunter Mahan's case, the situation was easy; he could simply hand over a rather nice cheque for €1,076,840 to his fiancée Kandi Harris, a former cheerleader for the Dallas Cowboys.

The bounty was reward for his stunning victory in the World Golf Championships – Bridgestone Invitational, his first WGC success and one which, aside from elevating him to 12th on the Official World Golf Ranking, also ensured his second consecutive Ryder Cup appearance having been part of the triumphant American team at Valhalla in 2008.

Mahan's champion's press conference was the first time in the week he had been invited to the Akron venue's Media Centre, proof of a victory which sneaked up on his fellow competitors; rounds of 71-67-66 seeing him enter the final round in a share of seventh place before a superb 64 saw him set the clubhouse target of 12 under par 268.

Closest challenger, fellow countryman Ryan Palmer, needed to birdie the final two holes to force a play-off but could only produce par figures at the 17th and 18th to see him finish second, one clear of Retief Goosen and Bo Van Pelt. Cue the cheerleading from the sidelines – needless to say who led that off for Hunter?

Adam Scott

Peter Hanson

Changing of the Guard

"This is just amazing. I have only been on Tour for four years and now here I am, in the top five in the world, top of The Race to Dubai and a Major winner. I have goosebumps just thinking about it"

Martin Kaymer

PGA

US PGA CHAMPIONSHIP
Whistling Straits
Kohler, Wisconsin, USA
August 12-15, 2010

1	**MARTIN KAYMER**		**72**	**68**	**67**	**70**	**277**	**-11**
2	Bubba Watson		68	71	70	68	277	-11
3	Zach Johnson		69	70	69	70	278	-10
	Rory McIlroy		71	68	67	72	278	-10
5	Jason Dufner		73	66	69	71	279	-9
	Steve Elkington		71	70	67	71	279	-9
	Dustin Johnson		71	68	67	73	279	-9
8	Wen-chong Liang		72	71	64	73	280	-8
	Camilo Villegas		71	71	70	68	280	-8
10	Jason Day		69	72	66	74	281	-7
	Matt Kuchar		67	69	73	72	281	-7

Jim Remy, President of the PGA of America and Martin Kaymer

Total Prize Fund €5,639,314 **First Prize** €1,028,877

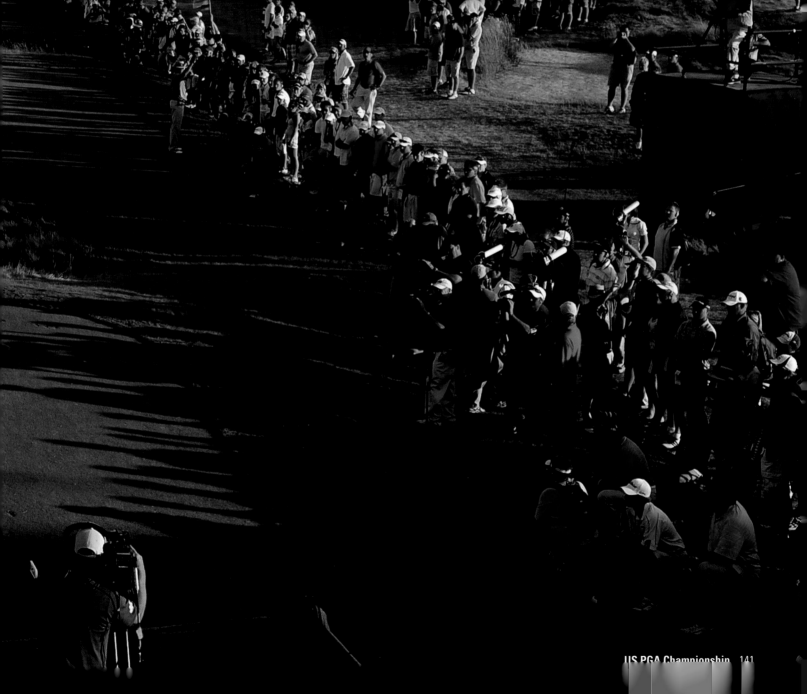

In the immediate aftermath of the 2010 US PGA Championship at Whistling Straits, it was difficult not to conclude that this was a Major Championship which would be forever discussed for one man's mistake rather than another's dramatic victory.

The mistake was Dustin Johnson's; the victory, Martin Kaymer's. In hindsight though, there is every chance we shall look back on this championship and mark it down as the first of many such triumphs for a truly outstanding player. It was the week that the 25 year old German came of age.

It was inevitable from the moment that Johnson was penalised two strokes for grounding his club in what he was unaware was a hazard at the 72nd hole - and was thus denied a place in a play-off alongside fellow American Bubba Watson and Kaymer – that some talk would centre on the rights and wrongs of a ruling that denied him the opportunity to play for his first Major trophy.

Without doubt, it provided a bizarre and traumatic finish to what turned out to be an intriguing final day - one in which several players either held, or shared, the lead. At one end of the age scale was 21 year old Rory McIlroy, who was joint leader with four holes to play, while at the other end was Steve Elkington, 26 years the Northern Irishman's senior, who made a spirited run at the title, only to come up narrowly short. Nick Watney, who started the day leading by three, went backwards almost from the off but in the end it was Kaymer who stood alone in the spotlight.

Not that that is an unusual place for the man from Düsseldorf to be, because from the moment he carded a 59 in an EPD Tour event in his native Germany in 2006, the sport of golf has recognised an exciting natural talent. Within months he was blazing a trail on the European Challenge Tour, finishing fourth in the 2006 Rankings in just eight starts, two of which he won, and that form continued with his graduation to The European Tour.

With five top tens in his first season he was announced as The Sir Henry Cotton Rookie of the Year in 2007, the first German to win the award, and his considerable talent was underlined when he won on his first appearance in 2008 with an impressive wire to wire victory in the Abu Dhabi Golf Championship.

A second win, this time in his homeland at the BMW International Open in Munich, when he became the first German to win the title, confirmed his place in the top 50 of the Official World Golf Ranking, and his rise continued in 2009 with

sensational consecutive wins at the Alstom Open de France and The Barclays Scottish Open, two of the most prestigious titles on The European Tour International Schedule, to rise to 11th in the world.

While progress was temporarily halted in August that year when he broke bones in his foot in a go-karting accident, it was not long before he resumed his winning ways, capturing the Abu Dhabi Golf Championship for the second time at the start of the 2010 season.

Top ten finishes in both the US Open Championship at Pebble Beach and The Open Championship at St Andrews hinted at the greater glory to come and he delivered in style at Whistling Straits, becoming only the second German golfer to win a Major Championship after Bernhard Langer. Indeed, the 53 year old was among the first people to call Kaymer and congratulate him.

The scale of Kaymer's achievement was measured by the fact that Bild, Germany's biggest-selling daily newspaper, carried a golf story on its front page for the first time, proclaiming that the country's "new sports superstar" had been born; likening Kaymer's ascent in golf to the rise of such iconic names as Boris Becker and Steffi Graf in tennis and Michael Schumacher in Formula One.

Of course, to achieve such adulation and in the process move both top of The Race to Dubai and up to Number Five on the Official World Golf Ranking, Kaymer had to come through the three-hole play-off against Watson, the only two left standing at 11 under par 277 following Johnson's unfortunate penalty – a direct result of the idiosyncratic layout of Whistling Straits itself.

The Kohler course is pock-marked with upwards of a thousand bunkers and spectators had been allowed to

Robert Karlsson

Bubba Watson

Dustin Johnson

Simon Dyson

Camilo Villegas

PUT YOURSELF IN HIS SHOES

EUROPEAN TOUR — OFFICIAL SUPPLIER

FJ
#1 SHOE IN GOLF

Armed with an abundance of talent, 21-year-old Rory McIlroy is already performing to high expectations. Despite the media pressure, Rory keeps a cool head on his young shoulders and lets his game do the talking. FJ ICON is the golf shoe of choice for Rory, who demands top quality equipment to play his best. The next achievement in FootJoy's iconic legacy, these shoes represent the best in style and tour inspired innovation that players have come to expect from the industry leader.

Select from the host of styles on the shelves now or create your own pair at **www.myjoys.co.uk**

Paul Casey

stand and walk in those that were outside the roped-off playing area. Players had been warned before the championship began that if they ventured into such areas, they had to treat them as normal hazards. But neither Johnson, nor his caddie, had taken proper note following his errant drive at the 72nd hole.

It meant that when he grounded his club as he prepared to play his approach shot to the green, he infringed the rules. How cruel it would have been had the six foot putt he subsequently thought he had for victory found the hole. As it was, he was soon to be told that he was being penalised two strokes for the infringement and that his tournament had run its course.

Watson started the play-off superbly with a birdie three at the tenth but Kaymer responded in

style, holing from 15 feet for a birdie two after a fine tee shot at the testing 223 yard 17th. The decisive moment, however, came moments later on the 18th when Watson hit his second shot into the water. He did hit the flag with his resultant pitch but could do no better than a double bogey six leaving Kaymer, who had sensibly laid up from the rough, to win with a five.

It crowned yet another fine week for The European Tour which, for the third Major Championship running had seen a Tour Member triumph; following Graeme McDowell's US Open victory at Pebble Beach, and Louis Oosthuizen's win at St Andrews in The Open Championship.

Without question it also added to the sense that the world of golf was witnessing a changing of the guard at the top of the game.

Peter Dixon
The Times

Rory McIlroy

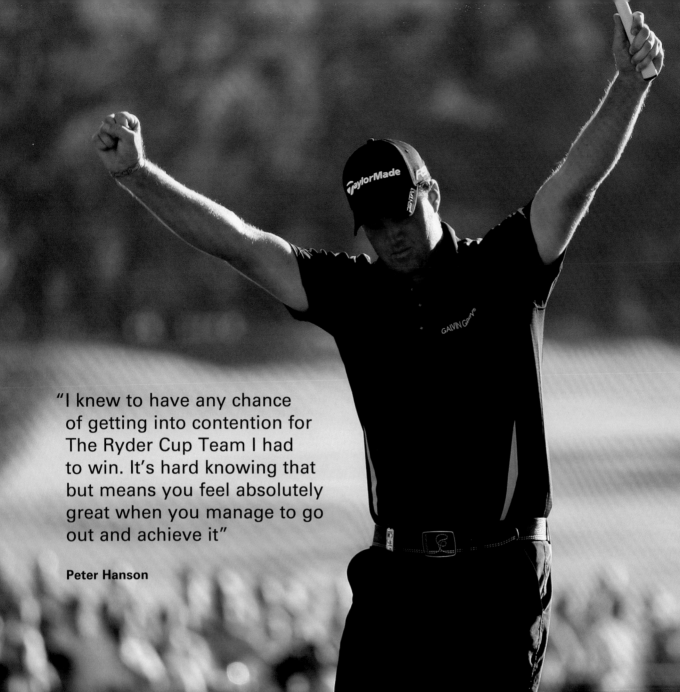

"I knew to have any chance of getting into contention for The Ryder Cup Team I had to win. It's hard knowing that but means you feel absolutely great when you manage to go out and achieve it"

Peter Hanson

CZECH OPEN 2010
Prosper Golf Resort (Old and New Courses)
Čeladná, Czech Republic
August 19–22, 2010

1	**PETER HANSON**		67	70	67	74	278	-10
2	Gary Boyd		72	70	68	68	278	-10
	Peter Lawrie		70	68	74	66	278	-10
4	Anthony Wall		70	69	73	67	279	-9
5	Simon Dyson		70	69	69	72	280	-8
	Julien Guerrier		68	72	71	69	280	-8
7	Fredrik Andersson Hed		70	68	73	70	281	-7
	Miguel Angel Jiménez		71	70	67	73	281	-7
9	Tano Goya		67	72	74	69	282	-6
	Maarten Lafeber		72	72	70	68	282	-6

Peter Hanson and Pavel Drobil, Minister of Environment of the Czech Republic

Total Prize Fund €2,026,892   **First Prize** €333,330

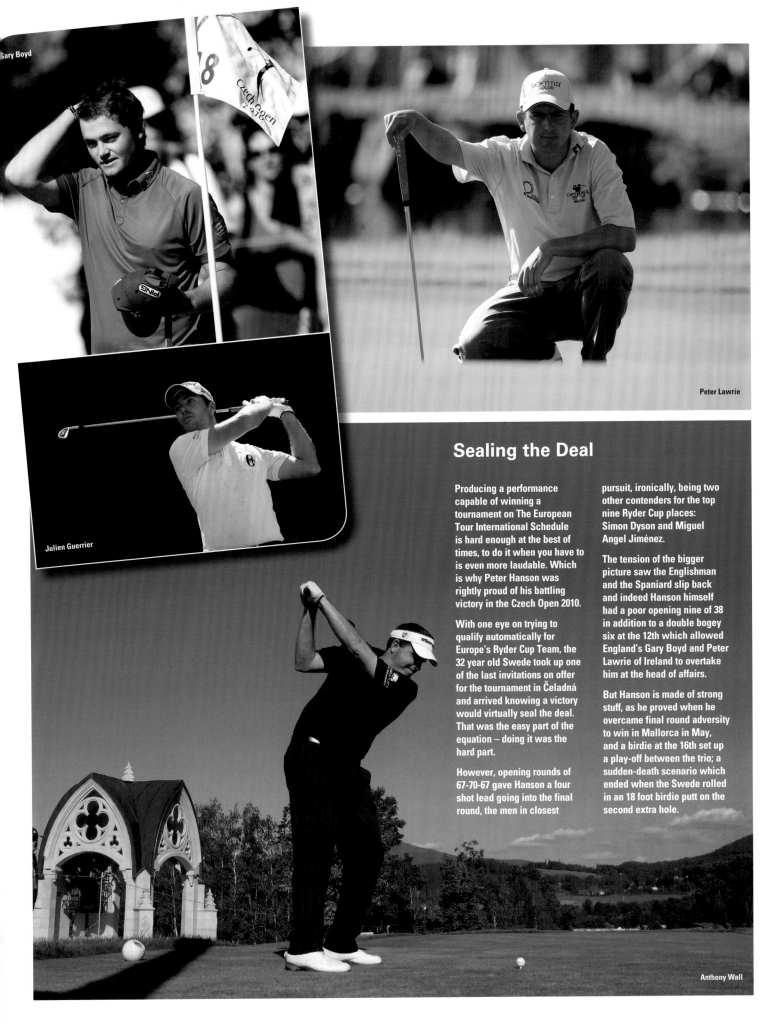

Gary Boyd

Peter Lawrie

Julien Guerrier

Sealing the Deal

Producing a performance capable of winning a tournament on The European Tour International Schedule is hard enough at the best of times, to do it when you have to is even more laudable. Which is why Peter Hanson was rightly proud of his battling victory in the Czech Open 2010.

With one eye on trying to qualify automatically for Europe's Ryder Cup Team, the 32 year old Swede took up one of the last invitations on offer for the tournament in Čeladná and arrived knowing a victory would virtually seal the deal. That was the easy part of the equation – doing it was the hard part.

However, opening rounds of 67-70-67 gave Hanson a four shot lead going into the final round, the men in closest pursuit, ironically, being two other contenders for the top nine Ryder Cup places: Simon Dyson and Miguel Angel Jiménez.

The tension of the bigger picture saw the Englishman and the Spaniard slip back and indeed Hanson himself had a poor opening nine of 38 in addition to a double bogey six at the 12th which allowed England's Gary Boyd and Peter Lawrie of Ireland to overtake him at the head of affairs.

But Hanson is made of strong stuff, as he proved when he overcame final round adversity to win in Mallorca in May, and a birdie at the 16th set up a play-off between the trio; a sudden-death scenario which ended when the Swede rolled in an 18 foot birdie putt on the second extra hole.

Anthony Wall

"This is hugely emotional for me. Not only the way I won the tournament, but then to be given the chance to play with my brother Francesco in The Ryder Cup. It is just unreal"

Edoardo Molinari

JOHNNIE WALKER CHAMPIONSHIP AT GLENEAGLES
The Gleneagles Hotel (PGA Centenary Course)
Perthshire, Scotland
August 26–29, 2010

1	**EDOARDO MOLINARI**		70	68	69	71	278	-10
2	Brett Rumford		71	70	68	70	279	-9
3	Jamie Donaldson		69	74	69	69	281	-7
	Miguel Angel Jiménez		70	68	71	72	281	-7
	Francesco Molinari		68	70	68	75	281	-7
6	Simon Dyson		68	70	70	74	282	-6
7	Bradley Dredge		71	68	74	70	283	-5
	Damien McGrane		72	67	70	74	283	-5
	Marcel Siem		71	71	71	70	283	-5
10	Phillip Archer		70	73	69	72	284	-4
	Grégory Bourdy		68	70	70	76	284	-4
	George Coetzee		69	68	74	73	284	-4
	Jyoti Randhawa		70	70	69	75	284	-4

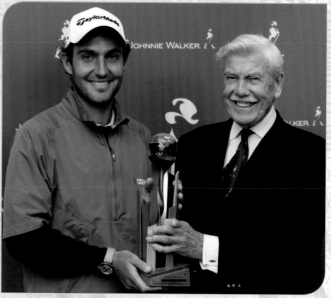

Edoardo Molinari and Lord Macfarlane of Bearsden, Honorary Life President of Diageo Scotland

Total Prize Fund €1,683,378   **First Prize €282,773**

Brett Rumford

Francesco Molinari

Miguel Angel Jiménez

JOHNNIE WALKER
15
463 YDS 423 M
PAR 4

JOHNNIE WALKER

Simon Dyson

The PGA Centenary Course, Gleneagles.
Host Venue for The Ryder Cup 2014.

Scotland™
The Home of Golf

We're the next European host to The Ryder Cup in 2014.
But you don't need to wait that long to visit us...

Scotland is The Home of Golf. It's packed full of memories of this ancient game; after all,
it's been played here for centuries.

And with over 550 golf courses to choose from, wherever you play, you'll find a truly
warm welcome and an authentic golfing experience.

Find out more at www.RyderCup2014.com

RYDER CUP
1927   2014
GLENEAGLES SCOTLAND

Something Special

It takes a lot to impress Colin Montgomerie. Having graced The European Tour since 1988 it is fair to say the 2010 European Ryder Cup Captain has seen it all in his time so, when he admitted that the finish produced by Edoardo Molinari to win the Johnnie Walker Championship at Gleneagles was the best he had witnessed in his time on Tour, you knew the Italian had done something special.

Two behind Australian Brett Rumford with three holes to play, by no means was Molinari favourite for the title but he changed all that with a truly stunning ending to the tournament. Two putts for a birdie four on the long 16th set the ball rolling before he sank a curling 30 footer for a birdie two on the 17th to move level with Rumford who was on the practice putting green bracing himself for a play-off.

That, however, was not required as Molinari, short of the par five 18th in two, produced an exquisite chip shot to within 18 inches of the hole before tapping in for a title clinching birdie four.

Being able to produce such quality under pressure finally convinced the watching Montgomerie to select Edoardo as one of his three wild picks for The Ryder Cup an hour after play finished, the others going to Luke Donald and Padraig Harrington. After his sterling show in the Czech Republic the previous week and his share of 19th place at Gleneagles, Peter Hanson held onto the ninth automatic qualifying place while Miguel Angel Jiménez's share of third in Perthshire saw him finish one place higher to book his fourth Ryder Cup appearance.

Jamie Donaldson

Bradley Dredge

Captain Colin Montgomerie with Vice Captains Thomas Björn, Darren Clarke and Paul McGinley following the official announcement of Europe's 2010 Ryder Cup Team

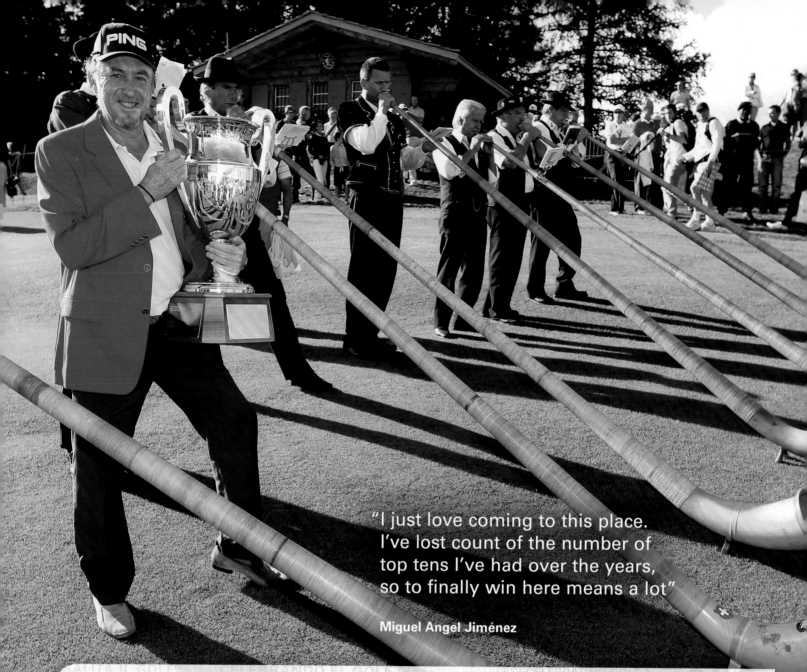

"I just love coming to this place. I've lost count of the number of top tens I've had over the years, so to finally win here means a lot"

Miguel Angel Jiménez

1	**MIGUEL ANGEL JIMÉNEZ**		67	61	68	67	263	-21
2	Edoardo Molinari		66	65	68	67	266	-18
3	Matteo Manassero		64	67	69	68	268	-16
4	Noh Seung-yul		71	66	67	67	271	-13
5	Robert Coles		66	71	67	68	272	-12
	Robert-Jan Derksen		67	68	70	67	272	-12
	Charl Schwartzel		68	66	70	68	272	-12
	Oliver Wilson		68	68	67	69	272	-12
9	Mikko Ilonen		65	67	75	66	273	-11
	Peter Lawrie		72	69	63	69	273	-11
	Marc Warren		69	69	68	67	273	-11
	Steve Webster		66	70	64	73	273	-11

L-R: Stephen Urquhart, President of Omega, Miguel Angel Jiménez and Gaston Barras, President of the Organising Committee for the Omega European Masters

Total Prize Fund €2,000,000   **First Prize** €333,330

Matteo Manassero

Robert-Jan Derksen

Noh Seung-yul

Mountain High

To succeed in professional golf you have to have many attributes but high on that list is perseverance as Miguel Angel Jiménez perfectly illustrated with his victory in the Omega European Masters.

For 21 years, the Spaniard had made the trek up the Alps to the beautiful town of Crans Montana to compete in the tournament and on 21 occasions had made the return journey back down the mountains empty handed. Not this time though.

A course record 61 in the second round laid the foundations for his 21 under par total of 263 with Italy's Edoardo Molinari and Matteo Manassero in second and third place respectively.

At 46 years and 243 days old, Jiménez became the oldest player to win three tournaments in a single season since Sam Torrance won three times in 1995 at the age of 42, and the first player to win three times in a year since both Paul Casey and Johan Edfors gathered three titles each during the 2006 season.

Like the fine wine he loves to savour at his leisure, Jiménez is improving with age; a point proved conclusively by the fact that now 11 of his 18 European Tour titles have come since he turned 40.

Also delighted by the victory was Ryder Cup Captain Colin Montgomerie who had now seen five of his team bound for The Celtic Manor Resort win over the past six weeks; Ross Fisher, Martin Kaymer, Peter Hanson, Edoardo Molinari and Jiménez.

Edoardo Molinari

"When you win a Major Championship it gives you the biggest confidence boost possible and the belief you can go on and win again. I thought I could do well here and I'm delighted to have come out on top"

Martin Kaymer

KLM OPEN

KLM OPEN
Hilversumsche Golf Club
Hilversum, The Netherlands
September 9–12, 2010

1	**MARTIN KAYMER**		**67**	**67**	**66**	**66**	**266**	**-14**
2	Christian Nilsson		68	65	68	69	270	-10
	Fabrizio Zanotti		68	68	65	69	270	-10
4	Gonzalo Fernandez-Castaño		66	69	67	69	271	-9
	David Horsey		67	67	69	68	271	-9
	José Manuel Lara		67	68	71	65	271	-9
	Louis Oosthuizen		73	67	66	65	271	-9
8	Felipe Aguilar		69	69	68	66	272	-8
	Nicolas Colsaerts		62	70	70	70	272	-8
	Francesco Molinari		68	71	67	66	272	-8

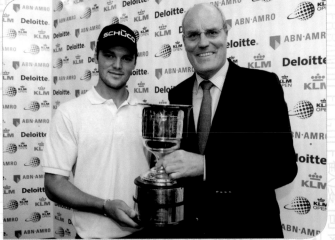

Martin Kaymer and Peter Hartman, CEO KLM

Total Prize Fund €1,821,516   **First Prize** €300,000

Unerring Accuracy

For those people who witnessed his stunning US PGA Championship triumph at Whistling Straits four weeks previously there was little doubt, but anyone still questioning Martin Kaymer's pedigree as a truly outstanding golfer had such misgivings emphatically answered by his fine victory in the KLM Open.

The trip to the Netherlands was the 25 year old German's first competitive action since his Wisconsin win but no semblance of rustiness was apparent as two opening rounds of 67 followed by matching weekend rounds of 66 gave Kaymer a four shot winning margin over his nearest challengers, Sweden's Christian Nilsson and Fabrizio Zanotti of Paraguay.

After birdieing the final two holes of his third round to take a one shot lead into the final day, Kaymer quickly extended his lead over Nilsson and Zanotti and an unerring display of accuracy – which saw him hit 17 out of 18 greens in regulation – left the chasing pack needing something special to mount a challenge that never seriously materialised.

The German phenomenon is well used to seeing his name in golf's record books and this latest victory added yet another entry as he joined Spain's Miguel Angel Jiménez as the only two players to have won on three occasions on The 2010 European Tour International Schedule. It also, of course, significantly strengthened his position at the top of The Race to Dubai.

Christian Nilsson

Fabrizio Zanotti

Gonzalo Fernandez-Castaño

AUSTRIAN GOLFOPEN PRESENTED BY BOTARIN

Diamond Country Club
Atzenbrugg, Austria
September 16–19, 2010

José Manuel Lara and Christian Guzy, owner of the Diamond Country Club

1	**JOSÉ MANUEL LARA**		66	71	70	64	**271**	**-17**
2	David Lynn		68	71	64	68	271	-17
3	Graeme McDowell		69	68	68	69	274	-14
	Alexander Noren		69	70	67	68	274	-14
	Danny Willett		69	69	65	71	274	-14
6	Chris Gane		69	70	66	70	275	-13
	Damien McGrane		67	76	67	65	275	-13
8	Clodomiro Carranza		68	70	68	70	276	-12
9	Luis Claverie		71	71	66	69	277	-11
	Raphaël Jacquelin		69	69	70	69	277	-11

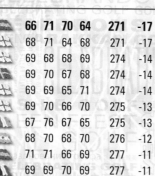

Total Prize Fund €753,366   **First Prize €125,000**

"I saved my card today which is fantastic and I can now look forward. I played well last week and I wanted to win this week – I just can't believe that my dream came true"

José Manuel Lara

David Lynn

botarin

die Schönheitsformel

Alex Noren

Graeme McDowell

Danny Willett

Change of Fortune

One of the beauties of professional golf is that a change in fortune can be just around the corner – a fact perfectly illustrated by José Manuel Lara with his victory in the Austrian GolfOpen presented by Botarin.

Prior to the previous week's KLM Open in the Netherlands, where he finished in a share of fourth place, the Spaniard's form had been wretched with a run of nine missed cuts in a row stretching all the way back to the BMW International Open in Munich in June.

But the Dutch performance gave the 33 year old from Valencia hope and he built on that, confidence which ended with him beating England's David Lynn at the first hole of a sudden-death play-off to claim

his second European Tour title, almost four years after his first triumph in the UBS Hong Kong Open.

Going into the final round four shots off the pace set by Lynn and another Englishman Danny Willett, Lara set the clubhouse target with a superb closing 64. Willett could not match it and had to settle for a share of third with Graeme McDowell and Alex Noren, but Lynn did. However, a bogey five at the first play-off hole from the Englishman, saw Lara triumph with a par four.

More importantly it moved the Spaniard, who had been harbouring genuine fears about losing his Tour card for the first time since 2002, from 130th up to the safety of 93rd on The Race to Dubai.

"I felt I was good enough to win on The European Tour, it was just a case of putting it all together. I was nervous trying to control my emotions but I'm proud of the way I handled it all"

John Parry

1	**JOHN PARRY**		64	67	70	70	**271**	**-17**
2	Johan Edfors		61	74	67	71	273	-15
3	François Delamontagne		66	69	68	71	274	-14
	Robert-Jan Derksen		66	69	68	71	274	-14
	Mark F Haastrup		66	70	66	72	274	-14
	Søren Kjeldsen		65	70	69	70	274	-14
	Jarmo Sandelin		65	66	72	71	274	-14
8	Richard Green		68	66	69	72	275	-13
	Padraig Harrington		68	74	69	64	275	-13
	Pablo Larrazábal		69	67	68	71	275	-13
	James Morrison		66	68	73	68	275	-13

John Parry and Simon Gillham, Executive Vice President, Communications, Vivendi

Total Prize Fund €1,232,330   **First Prize €204,160**

Padraig Harrington

Rising to the Challenge

There is little doubt about the importance of the Challenge Tour in preparing golfers for life on The European Tour and that facet of the game was proved once again by John Parry's success in the Vivendi Cup 2010.

The 23 year old Englishman became the fourth Challenge Tour graduate of 2009 to triumph on The 2010 European Tour – following in the footsteps of Rhys Davies, James Morrison and Edoardo Molinari – and indeed it is the second year in succession that four Challenge Tour graduates have gone on to triumph the following season at European golf's top table.

One shot in front going into the final round, early jitters saw Parry caught by former Ryder Cup player Jarmo Sandelin but after three birdies on the front nine, the Englishman turned two shots in front.

Another birdie at the tenth, in addition to solid play from there to the finishing line, saw him maintain the two shot advantage to pick up the €204,160 first prize and a one year European Tour exemption as none of the chasing pack were able to mount a sustained challenge.

Sandelin ended in a group of five players tied for third while his fellow Swede Johan Edfors took second on his own with a closing 71. Elsewhere, Padraig Harrington cheered watching Ryder Cup Captain Colin Montgomerie with a best of day final round 64 to finish in a tie for eighth place.

Søren Kjeldsen

François Delamontagne

Johan Edfors

ALFRED DUNHILL LINKS CHAMPIONSHIP
Old Course St Andrews, Carnoustie and Kingsbarns
Scotland
October 7–10, 2010

1	**MARTIN KAYMER**		68	69	68	66	271	-17
2	Danny Willett		67	73	67	67	274	-14
3	John Parry		67	65	71	72	275	-13
4	Gary Boyd		69	72	67	68	276	-12
5	Simon Dyson		69	70	72	66	277	-11
	Martin Laird		66	75	69	67	277	-11
	Alvaro Quiros		68	69	68	72	277	-11
8	David Howell		69	73	71	67	280	-8
	Richard McEvoy		72	71	69	68	280	-8
	Phillip Price		70	70	68	72	280	-8

Champion Martin Kaymer on the Swilcan Bridge

Total Prize Fund €3,467,322   **First Prize** €580,046

ALFRED DUNHILL
LINKS CHAMPIONSHIP

ALFRED DUNHILL
LINKS CHAMPIONSHIP

"I can still remember coming here for the first time as an amateur, walking down the first and over the Swilcan Bridge. It was always one of my dreams to win at St Andrews – it's a very special place"

Martin Kaymer

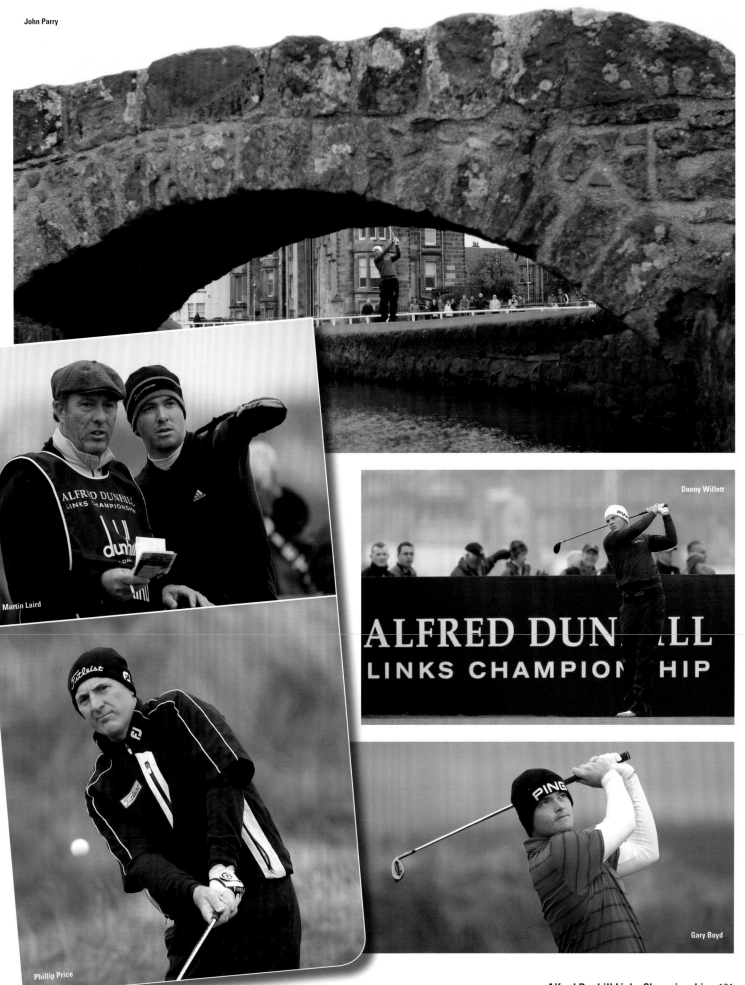

John Parry

Martin Laird

Danny Willett

Phillip Price

Gary Boyd

Dream Victory

When you equal a golfing record set by Tiger Woods you know your game is in pretty decent shape which is exactly what Martin Kaymer achieved with his victory in the Alfred Dunhill Links Championship at St Andrews.

The 25 year old German continued a remarkable recent run of form to notch his third consecutive stroke play success on The European Tour, following victories in his last two outings in the US PGA Championship and the KLM Open.

In doing so, he became the first player to achieve such a feat since Woods in 2006 when the American won The Open Championship, the US PGA Championship and the WGC – Bridgestone Invitational and the first European player to do so since Nick Faldo won the PGA Championship,

the British Masters and the Open de France in 1989.

Nine players from the previous week's successful European Ryder Cup Team teed up in Scotland and it was therefore appropriate that one of them triumphed, rounds of 68-69-68-66 giving Kaymer a three shot victory over England's Danny Willett with Vivendi Cup winner John Parry a further shot adrift in third.

It ensured Kaymer became only the ninth player in history to win four times in a single season on The European Tour. It also saw him climb to number four on the Official World Golf Ranking and move the small matter of €995,580 clear of Graeme McDowell in The 2010 Race to Dubai.

Kieran McManus and Søren Hansen

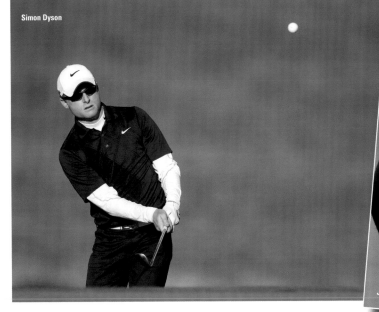

Simon Dyson

Johann Rupert and Lee Westwood

TEAM RESULTS

1	**ROBERT KARLSSON AND DERMOT DESMOND**	68	60	64	66	258
2	Søren Hansen and Kieran McManus	67	66	65	62	260
3	Richard McEvoy and Rick Quinn	65	66	65	65	261
	John Parry and Simon Andrews	66	61	70	64	261
	Lee Westwood and Johann Rupert	67	66	64	64	261

Robert Karlsson and Dermot Desmond, winners of the Amateur Team competition

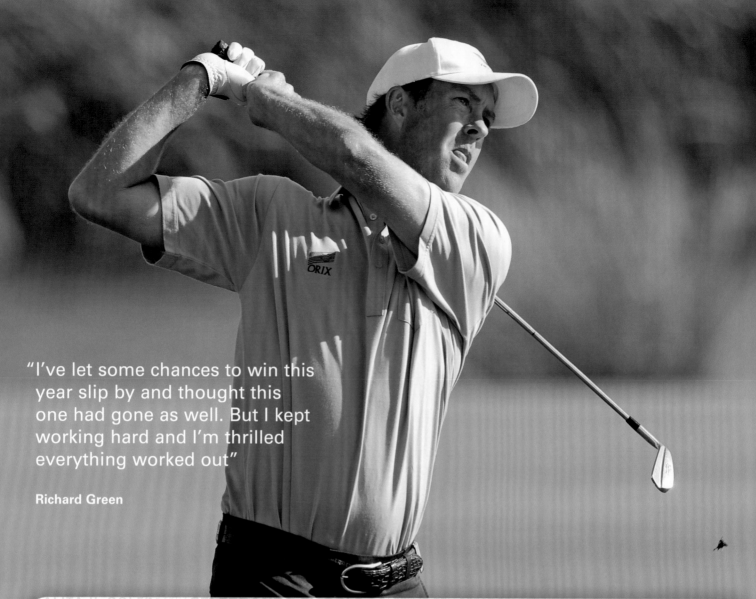

"I've let some chances to win this year slip by and thought this one had gone as well. But I kept working hard and I'm thrilled everything worked out"

Richard Green

PORTUGAL MASTERS
Oceânico Victoria Golf Course
Vilamoura, Portugal
October 14–17, 2010

1	**RICHARD GREEN**		**70**	**66**	**69**	**65**	**270**	**-18**
2	Gonzalo Fernandez-Castaño		69	67	68	68	272	-16
	Robert Karlsson		64	71	70	67	272	-16
	Joost Luiten		70	68	65	69	272	-16
	Francesco Molinari		74	62	74	62	272	-16
6	David Dixon		68	67	71	67	273	-15
	Peter Lawrie		68	68	68	69	273	-15
	Pablo Martin		67	68	63	75	273	-15
9	Fredrik Andersson Hed		71	66	70	67	274	-14
	Gary Boyd		68	68	69	69	274	-14
	Ignacio Garrido		71	68	66	69	274	-14
	Mikko Ilonen		65	68	69	72	274	-14
	Thongchai Jaidee		70	66	68	70	274	-14
	Steven O'Hara		68	71	66	69	274	-14
	Charl Schwartzel		67	71	66	70	274	-14
	Oliver Wilson		70	66	65	73	274	-14

Bernardo Trindade, Portuguese Secretary of State for Tourism and Richard Green

Total Prize Fund €3,000,000   **First Prize** €500,000

Gonzalo Fernandez-Castaño

Joost Luiten

14
424 Yds 388 Mtrs
PAR 4

PORTUGAL
20 18
RYDER CUP
CANDIDATE

PORTUGAL
MASTERS

oceanico · TURISMO DE PORTUGAL · TIVOLI

TURISMO DE
PORTUGAL

PORTUGAL
MASTERS

PORTUGAL
MASTERS

Francesco Molinari

Golf All Year Round.

Imagine to be able to golf from January to December.
Portugal offers the perfect combination of high standard
golf courses and great weather. So if you're a fan of golf,
come and visit us. And you'll simply become a fan of
everything else we have to offer.

P RTUGAL
The beauty of simplicity

visitportugal.com

TURISMO 2015

COMPETE

QREN
QUADRO DE REFERÊNCIA
ESTRATÉGICO
NACIONAL

UNIÃO EUROPEIA
Fundo Europeu
de Desenvolvimento Regional

TURISMO DE
PORTUGAL

Robert Karlsson

Pablo Martin

David Dixon

Green Day

There must be something about the Portuguese air which particularly appeals to Richard Green because, four months after finishing runner-up to Thomas Björn in the Estoril Open de Portugal at Penha Longa Golf Club, he returned to the country to triumph in the Portugal Masters at the Oceânico Victoria Golf Course in Vilamoura.

While he had a realistic chance of beating Björn in June before the Dane's strong finish took the title, it was fair to say that beginning the final round of the Portugal Masters seven shots adrift of leader Pablo Martin of Spain led not many people to believe the left handed Australian would be standing with the trophy in his hands come the end of play.

In the 2010 season, only Simon Khan had recovered a seven shot final round deficit to triumph – in the BMW PGA Championship at Wentworth Club – but Green's best of day 65 for an 18 under par total of 270, allied with Martin's uncertain closing 75, saw him match the Englishman's achievement.

Green's two previous European Tour triumphs – the 1997 Dubai Desert Classic and the 2007 BA-CA Golf Open in Austria – had both come as the result of play-offs but none of the chasing pack could get close enough to force him into extra time again; Gonzalo Fernandez-Castaño, Robert Karlsson, Joost Luiten and Francesco Molinari all sharing second place on 16 under par 272, two shots adrift of the Australian.

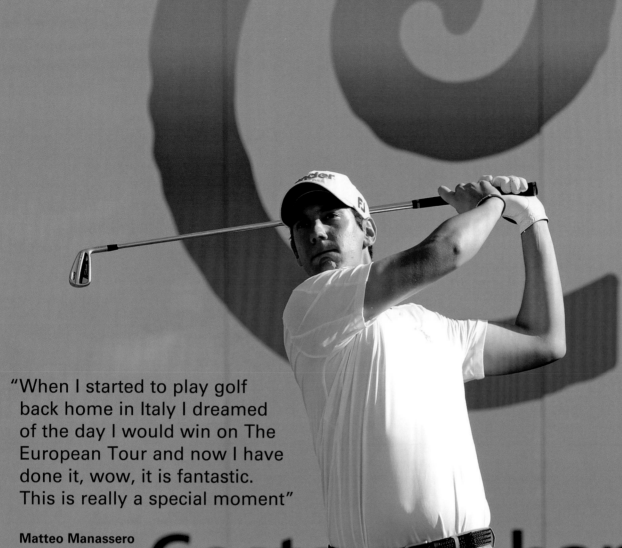

"When I started to play golf back home in Italy I dreamed of the day I would win on The European Tour and now I have done it, wow, it is fantastic. This is really a special moment"

Matteo Manassero

CASTELLÓ MASTERS COSTA AZAHAR
Club de Campo del Mediterráneo
Castellón, Spain
October 21–24, 2010

1	**MATTEO MANASSERO**		68	66	67	67	**268**	**-16**
2	Ignacio Garrido		70	66	68	68	272	-12
3	Gary Boyd		68	68	63	74	273	-11
	Peter Lawrie		72	64	67	70	273	-11
	Joost Luiten		68	72	65	68	273	-11
	Christian Nilsson		68	67	66	72	273	-11
7	Gonzalo Fernandez-Castaño		68	66	70	70	274	-10
8	Nicolas Colsaerts		70	67	69	69	275	-9
	Jean-Baptiste Gonnet		66	71	71	67	275	-9
	Peter Hedblom		69	64	71	71	275	-9
	Carl Suneson		68	69	67	71	275	-9
	Martin Wiegele		71	66	69	69	275	-9

Vicente Rambla, Vice President of the Generalitat Valenciana and Matteo Manassero

Total Prize Fund €2,011,982   **First Prize €333,330**

Peter Lawrie

Gary Boyd

Christian Nilsson

Ignacio Garrido

Record Breaker

Given the consistently high standards, it takes a performance of considerable magnitude to set new records on The European Tour which is exactly what Matteo Manassero produced as he stormed to victory at the CASTELLÓ MASTERS Costa Azahar.

At 17 years and 188 days, the Italian teenage sensation became the youngest winner in European Tour history, beating the previous record set by New Zealand's Danny Lee, who was 18 years and 213 days old when he won the 2009 Johnnie Walker Classic.

Furthermore, he also became the youngest person to become a full European Tour Member, eclipsing the legendary Severiano Ballesteros who was 17 years and 200 days when he became a full member at the end of the 1974 season and who wrote Manassero a congratulatory letter in the wake of his achievement.

Manassero, the former British Amateur Champion who shot to prominence when he won the Silver Medal by finishing tied 13th at The Open Championship in 2009, carded a four under par final round of 67 – the only player in the field to card all four rounds in the 60s – to finish at 16 under par 268, four shots clear of his nearest challenger, the host nation's Ignacio Garrido.

Having started the final round two shots behind England's Gary Boyd, whose final round 74 saw him finish tied third with Peter Lawrie, Joost Luiten and Christian Nilsson, Manassero applied early pressure before a superb run of three birdies in a row from the 13th left the destination of the title in no doubt.

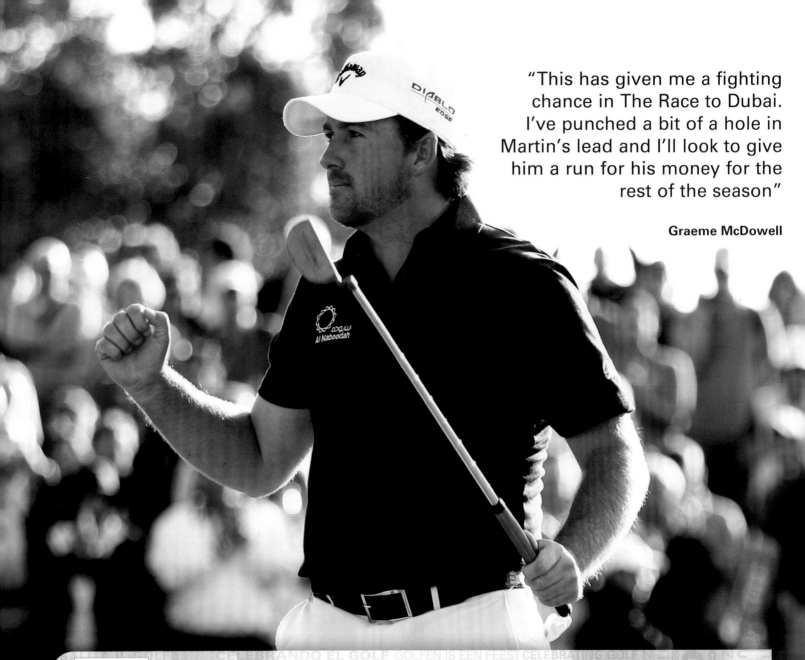

> "This has given me a fighting chance in The Race to Dubai. I've punched a bit of a hole in Martin's lead and I'll look to give him a run for his money for the rest of the season"
>
> **Graeme McDowell**

ANDALUCIA VALDERRAMA MASTERS

Club de Golf Valderrama
Sotogrande, Spain
October 28–31, 2010

1	**GRAEME McDOWELL**		68	67	72	74	**281**	**-3**
2	Søren Kjeldsen		71	75	68	69	283	-1
	Gareth Maybin		69	68	70	76	283	-1
	Damien McGrane		68	73	70	72	283	-1
5	Thomas Björn		72	69	71	72	284	0
	Joost Luiten		74	69	72	69	284	0
7	Raphaël Jacquelin		71	70	73	71	285	1
	Miguel Angel Jiménez		70	70	71	74	285	1
9	S S P Chowrasia		71	73	72	71	287	3
10	Sergio Garcia		70	73	69	76	288	4
	José Maria Olazábal		73	72	73	70	288	4
	Anthony Wall		72	73	71	72	288	4
	Steve Webster		73	74	69	72	288	4

L-R: Manuel Jiménez Barrios, Secretary of Sports for the Junta de Andalucía, Graeme McDowell and Felipe Ortiz-Patiño, President Club de Golf Valderrama

Total Prize Fund €3,000,000   **First Prize** €500,000

Søren Kjeldsen

Gareth Maybin

Joost Luiten

Game On

Graeme McDowell not only continued to illustrate his position as one of the world's top players, he also re-ignited The Race to Dubai with his victory in the Andalucia Valderrama Masters – his third triumph of an already superb 2010 European Tour season and one which moved him into the top ten on the Official World Golf Ranking.

Prior to events in the south of Spain, Martin Kaymer had begun to develop somewhat of a stranglehold on The Race, successive victories in America, the Netherlands and Scotland seeing the German move almost €1 million ahead.

But with Kaymer unable to finish inside the top 20 in Andalucia, McDowell took advantage in clinical fashion, battling the tough conditions and the demanding Valderrama layout to post a winning total of three under

par 281 to win by two shots from Denmark's Søren Kjeldsen and the Irish duo of Gareth Maybin and Damien McGrane.

McDowell and Maybin had begun the day with a four shot lead over the field but it was McGrane who moved into pole position as proceedings neared a conclusion. However a stuttering finish allowed the chasing pack back into affairs and McDowell took full advantage, holding his nerve to seal a fine win.

The €500,000 first prize saw the Northern Irishman cut Kaymer's lead at the top of The Race to Dubai by almost half to €528,580 and with more than €16 million available in prizemoney for the last four events of the season, it was game on.

Damien McGrane

.2
PAR 4
421 yards
385 metres

WGC - HSBC CHAMPIONS
Sheshan International Golf Club
Shanghai, China
November 4–7, 2010

1	**FRANCESCO MOLINARI**		65	70	67	67	**269**	**-19**
2	Lee Westwood		66	70	67	67	270	-18
3	Luke Donald		68	70	68	73	279	-9
	Richie Ramsay		69	68	71	71	279	-9
5	Rory McIlroy		71	71	71	67	280	-8
6	Fredrik Andersson Hed		69	71	71	70	281	-7
	Paul Casey		73	71	67	70	281	-7
	Ernie Els		72	65	71	73	281	-7
	Retief Goosen		70	74	69	68	281	-7
	Richard Green		72	68	73	68	281	-7
	Peter Hanson		73	69	70	69	281	-7
	Tiger Woods		68	72	73	68	281	-7

Francesco Molinari and Peter Wong, CEO of HSBC, Asia-Pacific

Total Prize Fund €5,017,561   **First Prize** €860,153

"To have the World Number One chasing you all the way is pretty demanding. I've been in the position of trying to catch a leader a few times so I know it's not easy, but finally it was my time to win. It was the perfect week"

Francesco Molinari

Battle Royal

Francesco Molinari not only made Italian golfing history with his superb wire-to-wire victory in the WGC-HSBC Champions, he also crowned a truly sensational season on the world stage for European Tour Members.

The man from Turin, who turned 28 the day after his victory, became the third Italian winner on Tour in 2010 after his brother Edoardo and Matteo Manassero and also the third European Tour Member to win a World Golf Championship event in the one season, following Ian Poulter and Ernie Els. Add both those notable firsts to the Major Championships won by Graeme McDowell, Louis Oosthuizen and Martin Kaymer and it is little wonder that many commentators rate this the best season ever for European Tour golf.

Another factor in that observation was the rise of Lee Westwood to World Number One on the eve of the event and the Englishman arrived in Shanghai determined to produce a performance to complement his new standing in the game.

That he certainly achieved and his 18 under par total of 270 left the majority of the field trailing miles adrift and was a score which would have won each of the four previous stagings of the tournament. However, he had reckoned without Molinari.

The duo engaged in a battle royal all week, matching each other stride for stride from Friday to Sunday with rounds of 70-67-67. When the dust had settled, it was Molinari's 65 in the first round to Westwood's 66 that was the only thing which separated them.

Lee Westwood

Luke Donald

Richie Ramsay

L-R: Phil Mickelson, Tiger Woods, Lee Westwood and Martin Kaymer practise Tai Chi in downtown Shanghai prior to the tournament

Graeme McDowell's caddie, Ken Comboy - HSBC Caddie of the Year

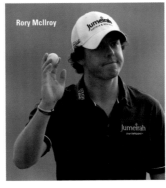

Rory McIlroy

"To see this event grow to the stature it now enjoys and to be able to come back and win again is thrilling for me. National Opens are the kind of events you dream about winning as a kid"

Adam Scott

BARCLAYS SINGAPORE OPEN
Sentosa Golf Club (Tanjong and Serapong Courses)
Singapore
November 11–15, 2010

1	**ADAM SCOTT**		65	65	69	68	267	-17
2	Anders Hansen		71	66	65	68	270	-14
3	Rikard Karlberg		64	70	70	67	271	-13
	Graeme McDowell		65	68	68	70	271	-13
5	Kyung-nam Kang		66	67	67	72	272	-12
6	Jamie Donaldson		66	69	68	70	273	-11
	Ian Poulter		69	63	68	73	273	-11
8	Keith Horne		65	72	69	68	274	-10
	Miguel Angel Jiménez		66	71	71	66	274	-10
10	Martin Kaymer		68	68	70	69	275	-9
	Wen-chong Liang		69	65	71	70	275	-9
	Prayad Marksaeng		69	65	70	71	275	-9
	Chris Wood		63	73	71	68	275	-9

Robert Morrice, Chairman and Chief Executive Asia-Pacific, Barclays PLC and Adam Scott

Total Prize Fund €4,291,823   **First Prize €713,165**

Bob Diamond, President of Barclays PLC, former US President Bill Clinton and George O'Grady, European Tour Chief Executive at the Barclays Asia Forum

Kang Kyung-nam and Graeme McDowell

Anders Hansen

569 YDS

Ian Poulter

Jamie Donaldson

Horses for Courses

The phrase 'horses for courses' is a term used widely across sport but perhaps nowhere is it more appropriate than when used in conjunction with Adam Scott and the Barclays Singapore Open at Sentosa Golf Club.

The 30 year old took the title in both 2005 and 2006 when it was purely an Asian Tour event but returned to the Lion City in this, its second year as a co-sanctioned event with The European Tour, to win for a third time to take his tally of European Tour International Schedule titles to seven.

The Australian overcame not only a high quality field over the venue's Serapong and Tanjong Courses but also adverse weather conditions over the course of the week which forced the tournament's denouement into Monday.

With the leaders requiring to finish ten holes on the additional day, Scott began three shots clear of defending champion Ian Poulter who was looking to emulate the Australian's back-to-back triumphs. An uncertain resumption from the Englishman, however, saw him lose ground to leave the charging Anders Hansen as Scott's main challenger.

Only two behind, the Dane stood over a 20 foot birdie putt on the 15th green to reduce the deficit to only one shot but when the ball stayed above ground and Scott, in the group behind, birdied the hole himself moments later, the destiny of the title was assured.

"The last two weeks I was really disappointed so this feels more than good. I don't think I've hit as many good golf shots as consistently as I did today in a very long time, so this is very pleasing indeed"

Ian Poulter

UBS HONG KONG OPEN
Hong Kong Golf Club (New and Eden Courses)
Fanling, Hong Kong
November 18–21, 2010

1	**IAN POULTER**		67	60	64	67	258	-22
2	Simon Dyson		64	65	65	65	259	-21
	Matteo Manassero		67	63	67	62	259	-21
4	Anthony Kang		67	61	67	65	260	-20
5	Graeme McDowell		65	65	63	68	261	-19
6	Rory McIlroy		63	66	66	67	262	-18
7	Jamie Donaldson		66	66	65	66	263	-17
	Gareth Maybin		67	67	68	61	263	-17
	Jeev Milkha Singh		63	67	66	67	263	-17
10	Marcus Fraser		68	63	67	66	264	-16

Allen Lo, Country Head & Chief Executive, UBS Hong Kong and Ian Poulter

Total Prize Fund €1,794,552   **First Prize €301,447**

Grégory Bourdy

Matteo Manassero

Anthony Kang

"Trench"
1
468 YDS (428m) PAR

UBS
Hong Kong
Open
Championship 2010

Simon Dyson

L-R: Kathryn Shih (UBS), Rory McIlroy, Graeme McDowell and Allen Lo (UBS) mark the start of the 2010 UBS Hong Kong Open at a special ceremony held in the International Finance Centre in the heart of Hong Kong's business district

Third Time Lucky

Ian Poulter ensured he made it third time lucky with an impressive triumph in the UBS Hong Kong Open, the Englishman's tenth success on The European Tour International Schedule.

In the previous two weeks the 34 year old had victory in his sights only to let others overtake him on the home straight, but he made no mistake in Fanling after a scintillating second round 60 put him in pole position at the halfway stage of the tournament and gave him a lead he was not to relinquish.

Indeed Poulter's dominance was such that he did not drop a shot until the third hole of the final round with his only other bogey being at the 72nd hole where he allowed himself the luxury of playing conservatively on the tricky 410 yard 18th to ensure the title was his.

Italian teenager Matteo Manassero continued to underline his vast potential with a closing 62 to share second with the 2000 champion Simon Dyson who threatened Poulter in the early stages of the final round but whose level par figures for the final 11 holes were insufficient to mount a serious challenge.

Elsewhere, Graeme McDowell knocked €76,689 off Martin Kaymer's lead in The Race to Dubai going into the season's final week with his fifth place finish, while Anthony Kang's reward for finishing fourth was to move into the top 117 on The Race to Dubai – and among those who keep their playing privileges for next season by rights.

"This has been a great day and a great week. If you look at the quality of the field we had here with all the top European players at the top of the world rankings, this is a fantastic victory"

Robert Karlsson

True Colours

DUBAI
WORLD CHAMPIONSHIP
PRESENTED BY: DP WORLD

DUBAI WORLD CHAMPIONSHIP PRESENTED BY: DP WORLD

Jumeirah Golf Estates (Earth Course)

Dubai, UAE

November 25-28, 2010

1	**ROBERT KARLSSON**		65	75	67	67	274	-14
2	Ian Poulter		69	66	69	70	274	-14
3	Alvaro Quiros		72	67	69	67	275	-13
	Lee Westwood		69	67	71	68	275	-13
5	Rory McIlroy		71	72	66	67	276	-12
6	Paul Casey		70	67	71	69	277	-11
	Francesco Molinari		71	67	68	71	277	-11
8	Thongchai Jaidee		68	69	69	73	279	-9
9	Luke Donald		74	67	69	70	280	-8
	Noh Seung-yul		66	73	74	67	280	-8

L-R: George O'Grady, Chief Executive of The European Tour, Robert Karlsson and His Highness Sheikh Majid bin Mohammed bin Rashid al Maktoum Chairman of Dubai Arts & Culture Authority

Total Prize Fund €5,446,799   **First Prize €910,349**

It was not a prerequisite but was certainly quite a coincidence and will give those in contention going into the final round of next year's Dubai World Championship something to consider when pondering their wardrobes. For it appears that those who wear a red shirt and white trousers on a Sunday always win at Jumeirah Golf Estates.

Twelve months ago Lee Westwood donned the attire as he strode to victory and this year it was Robert Karlsson's turn to wear the combination and show his true colours as he beat Ian Poulter at the second hole of a sudden-death play-off to take the prestigious title and the €910,349 first prize after the pair had tied on 14 under par 274 on the Earth Course.

Poulter might not have been the winner but golf certainly was following a bizarre ending to proceedings although one which proved once again why the game stands on its own in terms of integrity in the world of sport. After both men had made birdie four on their first return to the 18th hole, the Englishman prepared to face a 30 foot putt for birdie four at the second time of asking when, inexplicably as he bent down, the ball slipped from his grasp, hit the front edge of his marker and flipped the coin over.

Of the thousands of people surrounding the green, Poulter was the only man to see what happened but his immediate response was to call European Tour Senior Referee Andy McFee over who informed him of the one shot penalty. It meant Poulter's putt for birdie suddenly became a putt for par and it was little surprise that it stayed above ground. The Englishman garnered some small consolation when Karlsson proceeded to hole his own birdie putt moments later to put the seal on the win.

For the towering Swede, though, it was a triumph which confirmed once and for all his return to the top of a game that he graced so memorably in 2008 when ten top ten finishes and two victories saw him become the first Scandinavian golfer to win The Harry Vardon Trophy as European Number One.

It also confirmed that he was back to full fitness following an injury blighted 2009 season. A debilitating complaint,

Lee Westwood

which saw fluid gather behind the retina in his left eye leading to blurred vision and dizziness, saw him miss almost five months of competition in the middle of the season. Although he returned this year to win the Commercialbank Qatar Masters in January, Karlsson admitted it was not until June that he felt completely back to 100 per cent.

There was certainly no doubting his committed start to the final round, however. Beginning the day three shots behind Poulter, the Swede, incredibly, turned that into a one shot lead within three holes thanks to a birdie-birdie-eagle start, the latter courtesy of a holed eight iron from 172 yards down the middle of the third fairway.

From there, until the closing stages, the final round of The 2010 European Tour International Schedule became a cagey affair with the leading contenders jockeying for position like a group of 1500 metre runners on the penultimate lap, waiting for the bell to sound before making a break for the tape. When it did eventually clang as the field turned

Alvaro Quiros

Ian Poulter

for home it was Karlsson and Poulter who kicked on, the Swede's birdies at the tenth and 11th holes matched by the Englishman's own gains at the 11th and 12th to take them clear of the pack.

Defending champion Lee Westwood made a late run with three birdies in a row from the 14th but came up one shot short as did Spaniard Alvaro Quiros who would have also featured in the play-off had he holed his eagle putt from 15 feet on the 72nd hole. But it stayed out leaving centre stage clear for Karlsson and Poulter to act out their thrilling denouement.

Going into the week at Jumeirah Golf Estates there were three stories which gripped the attention of the golfing world. Robert Karlsson answered the question of who would become the second Dubai World Championship winner, which left the destiny of The Race to Dubai and possession of the Number One position in the Official World Golf Ranking up for grabs.

That the latter scenario unfolded in The European Tour's final event of the season, showed precisely how far the European game has progressed in recent years and the fact that the two men in competition for the top spot – Lee Westwood and Martin Kaymer – have both committed themselves fully to The European Tour for 2011 augurs well for the future of the game on this side of the Pond.

Kaymer needed to finish in the top two to have a chance of dislodging Westwood from Number One but his tie for 13th place on six under par 282 saw the Englishman deservedly end the season in a position his unerringly consistent golf over the past 24 months has thoroughly merited.

Then again there was good news for Kaymer. Entering the tournament in pole position in The Race to Dubai, the 25 year old from Dusseldorf knew the only man who could catch him was Northern Ireland's Graeme McDowell, with whom he had shared the joy of Major Championship and Ryder Cup success this season and who needed to finish third at worst, with Kaymer outside the top 20, to erode his €290,901 lead.

Paul Casey

Francesco Molinari

Rory McIlroy works with Sebastian Nohse, Executive Chef Al Qasr at MJ's Steakhouse in the Madinat Jumeirah

Martin Kaymer, The 2010 Race to Dubai Champion

In truth, McDowell's opening rounds of 72-73 to leave him in a share of 42nd place at the halfway stage finished the contest there and then but the Ulsterman's famed resilience – which had seen him knock some €700,000 off the German's lead in the past month – resurfaced and closing rounds of 69-68 saw him rise to finish alongside Kaymer on 282. For a pair who had been neck and neck for most of the year, it was highly appropriate that they finished the last tournament side by side.

Kaymer ended the year with a new record season earnings tally of €4,461,011, outstripping the €4,237,762 earned by Lee Westwood in 2009 – figures which look pretty impressive in black and white. For Robert Karlsson however, the colours which mattered most were red and white.

Scott Crockett

George O'Grady (right), Chief Executive of The European Tour presents Honorary Life Membership of The European Tour to (L-R) Martin Kaymer, Graeme McDowell and Louis Oosthuizen in honour of their Major Championship victories in 2010

THE RACE TO DUBAI ON THE 2010 EUROPEAN TOUR INTERNATIONAL SCHEDULE

Pos	Name	Country	Played	€	Pos	Name	Country	Played	€	Pos	Name	Country	Played	€
1	Martin KAYMER	(GER)	(22)	4461010.84	51	John PARRY	(ENG)	(35)	706107.54	101	Richard McEVOY	(ENG)	(28)	261196.00
2	Graeme McDOWELL	(NIR)	(24)	3896995.62	52	Marcus FRASER	(AUS)	(24)	696772.77	102	Mark BROWN	(NZL)	(34)	255985.03
3	Lee WESTWOOD	(ENG)	(14)	3222422.67	53	Chris WOOD	(ENG)	(27)	694465.40	103	Martin LAIRD	(SCO)	(5)	242991.98
4	Ian POULTER	(ENG)	(15)	3027008.01	54	Robert-Jan DERKSEN	(NED)	(28)	690480.39	104	Niclas FASTH	(SWE)	(29)	238923.55
5	Francesco MOLINARI	(ITA)	(27)	2799692.17	55	Grégory BOURDY	(FRA)	(30)	639563.71	105	Alex CEJKA	(GER)	(3)	235809.51
6	Robert KARLSSON	(SWE)	(21)	2296485.76	56	Thomas BJÖRN	(DEN)	(31)	634441.17	106	Kenneth FERRIE	(ENG)	(33)	235302.69
7	Ernie ELS	(RSA)	(15)	2261606.91	57	Robert ROCK	(ENG)	(33)	629314.66	107	Robert COLES	(ENG)	(29)	233213.51
8	Charl SCHWARTZEL	(RSA)	(24)	2207965.44	58	Thomas AIKEN	(RSA)	(28)	628041.04	108	Hennie OTTO	(RSA)	(26)	229218.28
9	Miguel Angel JIMÉNEZ	(ESP)	(29)	2179418.31	59	Johan EDFORS	(SWE)	(26)	623759.75	109	Jean-Baptiste GONNET	(FRA)	(26)	224634.50
10	Louis OOSTHUIZEN	(RSA)	(23)	2070763.10	60	Søren HANSEN	(DEN)	(31)	610703.67	110	Thomas LEVET	(FRA)	(24)	217256.15
11	Edoardo MOLINARI	(ITA)	(28)	2009336.88	61	James MORRISON	(ENG)	(28)	518750.44	111	Anthony KANG	(USA)	(28)	216420.41
12	Paul CASEY	(ENG)	(14)	1888850.34	62	Shane LOWRY	(IRL)	(31)	501727.73	112	Jeppe HULDAHL	(DEN)	(29)	215027.40
13	Rory McILROY	(NIR)	(16)	1821050.07	63	Bradley DREDGE	(WAL)	(26)	494369.88	113	Steven O'HARA	(SCO)	(27)	213769.49
14	Alvaro QUIROS	(ESP)	(25)	1750255.33	64	Richard FINCH	(ENG)	(31)	474851.69	114	David DIXON	(ENG)	(30)	213598.54
15	Luke DONALD	(ENG)	(13)	1678072.07	65	Richard BLAND	(ENG)	(28)	451270.64	115	Ricardo GONZALEZ	(ARG)	(27)	211962.23
16	Ross FISHER	(ENG)	(22)	1393686.26	66	Pablo MARTIN	(ESP)	(26)	440294.16	116	Felipe AGUILAR	(CHI)	(30)	207829.66
17	Peter HANSON	(SWE)	(22)	1322390.85	67	Nicolas COLSAERTS	(BEL)	(27)	423512.54	117	Mark F HAASTRUP	(DEN)	(26)	203322.40
18	Rhys DAVIES	(WAL)	(31)	1218635.57	68	Mikko ILONEN	(FIN)	(25)	418587.03	118	Sam HUTSBY	(ENG)	(27)	197809.34
19	Anders HANSEN	(DEN)	(27)	1166040.67	69	Paul LAWRIE	(SCO)	(25)	412292.77	119	Pelle EDBERG	(SWE)	(19)	196217.81
20	Padraig HARRINGTON	(IRL)	(14)	1145016.83	70	Andrew DODT	(AUS)	(21)	405080.72	120	Martin WIEGELE	(AUT)	(17)	190973.69
21	Richard GREEN	(AUS)	(26)	1128465.29	71	Christian NILSSON	(SWE)	(24)	403625.60	121	Nick DOUGHERTY	(ENG)	(28)	179411.07
22	Fredrik ANDERSSON HED	(SWE)	(27)	1110525.20	72	Wen-chong LIANG	(CHN)	(13)	400896.52	122	Julien GUERRIER	(FRA)	(22)	172304.91
23	Danny WILLETT	(ENG)	(25)	1062416.18	73	David DRYSDALE	(SCO)	(33)	394699.28	123	Paul McGINLEY	(IRL)	(23)	159769.60
24	Retief GOOSEN	(RSA)	(12)	994342.34	74	Jeev Milkha SINGH	(IND)	(15)	393448.87	124	Marc WARREN	(SCO)	(29)	153043.46
25	Simon KHAN	(ENG)	(28)	972685.88	75	Fabrizio ZANOTTI	(PAR)	(30)	385587.28	125	Mikael LUNDBERG	(SWE)	(28)	152542.72
26	Stephen GALLACHER	(SCO)	(30)	931930.79	76	Anthony WALL	(ENG)	(24)	384606.36	126	George COETZEE	(RSA)	(25)	152302.24
27	Grégory HAVRET	(FRA)	(28)	928672.06	77	Ross McGOWAN	(ENG)	(28)	383392.13	127	Alastair FORSYTH	(SCO)	(32)	149175.77
28	Joost LUITEN	(NED)	(28)	905440.57	78	Rafael CABRERA-BELLO	(ESP)	(30)	380946.53	128	Clodomiro CARRANZA	(ARG)	(25)	148908.26
29	Thongchai JAIDEE	(THA)	(23)	892417.70	79	James KINGSTON	(RSA)	(24)	380526.95	129	Colin MONTGOMERIE	(SCO)	(18)	148215.94
30	Darren CLARKE	(NIR)	(28)	892388.25	80	Marcel SIEM	(GER)	(28)	370556.17	130	Christian CÉVAËR	(FRA)	(28)	146564.27
31	Matteo MANASSERO	(ITA)	(19)	890401.87	81	Oliver FISHER	(ENG)	(29)	352209.23	131	Marco RUIZ	(PAR)	(26)	146482.96
32	David HORSEY	(ENG)	(30)	882339.33	82	Rafa ECHENIQUE	(ARG)	(30)	349986.58	132	Jamie ELSON	(ENG)	(26)	146021.12
33	Simon DYSON	(ENG)	(28)	873818.37	83	Graeme STORM	(ENG)	(30)	346774.48	133	Ariel CANETE	(ARG)	(30)	145222.00
34	Seung-yul NOH	(KOR)	(20)	869921.25	84	David LYNN	(ENG)	(27)	341124.60	134	Rick KULACZ	(AUS)	(25)	144948.75
35	Gonzalo FDEZ-CASTAÑO	(ESP)	(29)	860106.38	85	Alexander NOREN	(SWE)	(26)	339828.54	135	S S P CHOWRASIA	(IND)	(25)	138206.25
36	Peter LAWRIE	(IRL)	(32)	845717.63	86	Peter WHITEFORD	(SCO)	(29)	334270.68	136	Mardan MAMAT	(SIN)	(10)	136459.95
37	Y E YANG	(KOR)	(14)	845034.40	87	Stephen DODD	(WAL)	(24)	333758.53	137	Markus BRIER	(AUT)	(29)	130287.67
38	Alejandro CAÑIZARES	(ESP)	(28)	806509.55	88	Pablo LARRAZÁBAL	(ESP)	(31)	332500.49	138	Jarmo SANDELIN	(SWE)	(24)	128824.77
39	Raphaël JACQUELIN	(FRA)	(32)	789148.12	89	Peter HEDBLOM	(SWE)	(27)	326856.35	139	Jean-François LUCQUIN	(FRA)	(32)	123608.01
40	Gareth MAYBIN	(NIR)	(27)	784076.09	90	Michael HOEY	(NIR)	(27)	322120.30	140	Daniel VANCSIK	(ARG)	(32)	117414.88
41	Damien McGRANE	(IRL)	(31)	782719.18	91	Mark FOSTER	(ENG)	(28)	321032.58	141	Simon THORNTON	(IRL)	(22)	116954.05
42	Sergio GARCIA	(ESP)	(14)	771156.42	92	Steve WEBSTER	(ENG)	(29)	319417.95	142	Benjamin HEBERT	(FRA)	(21)	116834.21
43	Søren KJELDSEN	(DEN)	(28)	757512.77	93	José Manuel LARA	(ESP)	(32)	295191.14	143	Andrew COLTART	(SCO)	(25)	116089.98
44	Ignacio GARRIDO	(ESP)	(32)	754387.97	94	Keith HORNE	(RSA)	(18)	292494.70	144	Tetsuji HIRATSUKA	(JPN)	(7)	114392.94
45	Brett RUMFORD	(AUS)	(24)	753673.07	95	Paul WARING	(ENG)	(25)	289758.08	145	Scott HEND	(AUS)	(19)	112913.93
46	Jamie DONALDSON	(WAL)	(27)	748458.81	96	David HOWELL	(ENG)	(32)	285160.91	146	François DELAMONTAGNE	(FRA)	(29)	107968.68
47	Richie RAMSAY	(SCO)	(32)	740693.98	97	Shiv KAPUR	(IND)	(32)	277160.58	147	Prayad MARKSAENG	(THA)	(12)	107552.24
48	Oliver WILSON	(ENG)	(27)	738597.93	98	Maarten LAFEBER	(NED)	(24)	276660.21	148	Scott STRANGE	(AUS)	(22)	105155.18
49	Henrik STENSON	(SWE)	(15)	718403.77	99	Tano GOYA	(ARG)	(31)	274857.26	149	Kiradech APHIBARNRAT	(THA)	(6)	99904.37
50	Gary BOYD	(ENG)	(28)	715105.86	100	Phillip PRICE	(WAL)	(29)	264558.40	150	Michael JONZON	(SWE)	(29)	99662.92

Pos	Name	Country	Played	€
151	Phillip ARCHER	(ENG)	(25)	99210.50
152	Barry LANE	(ENG)	(20)	99037.32
153	Anton HAIG	(RSA)	(19)	95532.62
154	Chapchai NIRAT	(THA)	(15)	95100.57
155	Darren FICHARDT	(RSA)	(8)	93676.92
156	Julien QUESNE	(FRA)	(32)	93302.56
157	James KAMTE	(RSA)	(18)	92870.88
158	Sion E BEBB	(WAL)	(20)	90739.97
159	Danny LEE	(NZL)	(22)	88257.36
160	Paul BROADHURST	(ENG)	(21)	84668.18
161	José-Filipe LIMA	(POR)	(29)	83603.82
162	Oskar HENNINGSSON	(SWE)	(24)	83069.17
163	Gary LOCKERBIE	(ENG)	(33)	82011.23
164	Jyoti RANDHAWA	(IND)	(24)	81461.49
165	Eirik Tage JOHANSEN	(NOR)	(22)	79001.17
166	Peter GUSTAFSSON	(SWE)	(6)	78986.67
167	Carl SUNESON	(ESP)	(25)	77277.00
168	Darren BECK	(AUS)	(6)	76691.14
169	Martin ERLANDSSON	(SWE)	(29)	72758.53
170	Robert DINWIDDIE	(ENG)	(9)	65847.63
171	Patrik SJÖLAND	(SWE)	(22)	65819.03
172	Miles TUNNICLIFF	(ENG)	(17)	61215.38
173	Carlos DEL MORAL	(ESP)	(12)	60950.00
174	Alvaro VELASCO	(ESP)	(8)	60742.73
175	Marcus BOTH	(AUS)	(11)	60359.37
176	Todd HAMILTON	(USA)	(12)	58446.02
177	Charles-Edouard RUSSO	(FRA)	(4)	57540.00
178	Chris GANE	(ENG)	(20)	57366.84
179	George MURRAY	(SCO)	(5)	55920.00
180	John DALY	(USA)	(5)	55012.13
181	Santiago LUNA	(ESP)	(11)	54680.00
182	Sam LITTLE	(ENG)	(33)	53789.75
183	José Maria OLAZÁBAL	(ESP)	(3)	53775.00
184	Michiel BOTHMA	(RSA)	(13)	53432.50
185	Arjun ATWAL	(IND)	(7)	52508.92
186	Steven JEPPESEN	(SWE)	(24)	51581.50
187	Thaworn WIRATCHANT	(THA)	(9)	51387.99
188	Michael LORENZO-VERA	(FRA)	(15)	51060.51
189	Adilson DA SILVA	(BRA)	(6)	50327.61
190	Benn BARHAM	(ENG)	(15)	49595.29
191	Scott DRUMMOND	(SCO)	(21)	49040.00
192	Peter O'MALLEY	(AUS)	(17)	47615.39
193	Gary CLARK	(ENG)	(18)	47084.80
194	Colm MORIARTY	(IRL)	(5)	43769.60
195	Wen-tang LIN	(TPE)	(6)	41297.32
196	Dale WHITNELL	(ENG)	(7)	40975.00
197	Alessandro TADINI	(ITA)	(4)	39860.00
198	Andrew McARTHUR	(SCO)	(19)	39235.00
199	Branden GRACE	(RSA)	(8)	37462.50
200	Jean-François REMESY	(FRA)	(3)	37032.50

FLAGS OF THE WORLD

	Abu Dhabi		Kazakhstan
	Argentina		Kenya
	Australia		Malaysia
	Austria		Morocco
	Barbados		Netherlands
	Belgium		New Zealand
	Brunei		Northern Ireland
	Chile		Norway
	China		Paraguay
	Chinese Taipei		Phillipines
	Colombia		Poland
	Czech Republic		Portugal
	Denmark		Qatar
	Dubai		Russia
	England		Scotland
	Estonia		Singapore
	Fiji		South Africa
	Finland		South Korea
	France		Spain
	Germany		Sweden
	Hong Kong		Switzerland
	Iceland		Taiwan
	India		Thailand
	Indonesia		Trinidad & Tobago
	Ireland		United Arab Emirates
	Italy		USA
	Jamaica		Wales
	Japan		Zimbabwe

Stroke Average

Pos	Name	Stroke Average	Total Strokes	Total Rounds	Pos	Name	Stroke Average	Total Strokes	Total Rounds	Pos	Name	Stroke Average	Total Strokes	Total Rounds
1	**Martin KAYMER**	**70.04**	**5463**	**78**	51	Simon DYSON	71.17	6334	89	76	Maarten LAFEBER	71.46	5574	78
2	Graeme McDOWELL	70.07	5956	85	52	Robert KARLSSON	71.20	5055	71	77	Paul WARING	71.51	6150	86
3	Charl SCHWARTZEL	70.13	6171	88	53	Michael HOEY	71.22	6267	88	78	Jean-Baptiste GONNET	71.54	5795	81
4	Lee WESTWOOD	70.17	3368	48	54	Søren KJELDSEN	71.22	6623	93	79	Steven O'HARA	71.55	6368	89
5	Francesco MOLINARI	70.20	6809	97	55	Rhys DAVIES	71.24	7551	106	80	Tano GOYA	71.55	6296	88
6	Rory McILROY	70.23	3933	56	56	Shane LOWRY	71.25	7339	103	81	Oliver WILSON	71.57	5940	83
7	Louis OOSTHUIZEN	70.31	5203	74	57	Pablo LARRAZÁBAL	71.28	6700	94	82	Jeppe HULDAHL	71.59	6228	87
8	Jeev Milkha SINGH	70.34	3095	44	58	Richie RAMSAY	71.28	6914	97	83	Julien GUERRIER	71.61	4726	66
9	Matteo MANASSERO	70.41	4647	66	59	Steve WEBSTER	71.28	6130	86	84	David HOWELL	71.63	6447	90
10	Joost LUITEN	70.49	7331	104	60	Gary BOYD	71.33	6134	86	85	Peter WHITEFORD	71.63	6518	91
11	Luke DONALD	70.52	3103	44	61	Robert DINWIDDIE	71.33	1712	24	86	James KINGSTON	71.64	5588	78
12	Ian POULTER	70.53	3597	51	62	Søren HANSEN	71.33	7062	99	87	Fabrizio ZANOTTI	71.65	6090	85
13	Darren CLARKE	70.61	6567	93	63	Nicolas COLSAERTS	71.34	5850	82	88	Carlos DEL MORAL	71.66	2293	32
14	Alvaro QUIROS	70.62	6073	86	64	John PARRY	71.35	7848	110	89	Marcel SIEM	71.66	6091	85
15	Grégory BOURDY	70.65	7630	108	65	Keith HORNE	71.35	3924	55	90	Mark F HAASTRUP	71.66	5016	70
16	Richard GREEN	70.66	5794	82	66	Wen-chong LIANG	71.36	3354	47	91	Benjamin HEBERT	71.67	4730	66
17	Padraig HARRINGTON	70.68	3110	44	67	Robert ROCK	71.37	7422	104	92	Phillip PRICE	71.67	6594	92
18	Peter LAWRIE	70.70	7353	104	68	Richard FINCH	71.38	6496	91	93	Mark BROWN	71.68	7025	98
19	Damien McGRANE	70.74	7711	109	69	Robert COLES	71.38	5782	81	94	Richard McEVOY	71.68	5878	82
20	Pelle EDBERG	70.75	4033	57	70	Anthony WALL	71.42	5571	78	95	Jamie ELSON	71.70	5306	74
21	Jamie DONALDSON	70.81	6373	90	71	Brett RUMFORD	71.43	4857	68	96	Alexander NOREN	71.71	5952	83
22	Gonzalo FDEZ-CASTAÑO	70.82	6728	95	72	Graeme STORM	71.44	6358	89	97	Benn BARHAM	71.71	3227	45
23	Ignacio GARRIDO	70.82	7719	109	73	Mikko ILONEN	71.45	5073	71	98	Niclas FASTH	71.72	5881	82
24	Paul CASEY	70.82	3541	50	74	Christian NILSSON	71.46	5145	72	99	Sam HUTSBY	71.72	6455	90
25	Robert-Jan DERKSEN	70.83	6658	94	75	David DRYSDALE	71.46	7217	101	100	Grégory HAVRET	71.73	6025	84
26	Ernie ELS	70.84	3471	49										
27	Anders HANSEN	70.85	6518	92										
28	Miguel Angel JIMÉNEZ	70.85	6943	98										
29	Raphaël JACQUELIN	70.85	7227	102										
30	Thongchai JAIDEE	70.85	5243	74										
31	Ross FISHER	70.86	5244	74										
32	Edoardo MOLINARI	70.90	7161	101										
33	Chris WOOD	70.91	6098	86										
34	Paul LAWRIE	70.91	5531	78										
35	Thomas AIKEN	70.91	6666	94										
36	Alejandro CAÑIZARES	70.92	6950	98										
37	Danny WILLETT	70.96	5748	81										
38	Peter HANSON	70.96	5677	80										
39	Richard BLAND	70.97	6458	91										
40	Stephen GALLACHER	70.97	7452	105										
41	David HORSEY	71.00	6603	93										
42	Bradley DREDGE	71.01	6249	88										
43	Fredrik ANDERSSON HED	71.02	6463	91										
44	Gareth MAYBIN	71.06	6964	98										
45	Marcus FRASER	71.10	5475	77										
46	David LYNN	71.14	5976	84										
47	Seung-yul NOH	71.14	5051	71										
48	Thomas BJÖRN	71.14	6118	86										
49	Y E YANG	71.16	3131	44										
50	Johan EDFORS	71.17	5480	77										

Genworth Financial Brand Ambassador Ross Fisher (second right), European Tour professionals Ian Poulter (left) and Luke Donald (second left) and European Tour Financial Director Jonathan Orr (right) received a cheque for $50,000 towards the Tour Players Foundation from Genworth Financial Managing Director Peter Barrett (centre). The cheque was in recognition of the Tour professionals' part in Genworth Financial's Putts4Charity campaign at seven designated tournaments across the year. At these tournaments, for every one putt holed on the course, Genworth Financial donated $2 while the players also took part in special one-putt appearances in the Genworth stands in the various Tented Villages

Driving Distance (yds)

Pos	Name	Average Yards	Stats Rounds
1	Nicolas COLSAERTS	307.7	76
2	Scott HEND	306.5	59
3	Alvaro QUIROS	305.7	64
4	Anton HAIG	305.2	33
5	George COETZEE	302.9	62
6	James KAMTE	302.7	47
7	Daniel VANCSIK	302.5	64
8	Pelle EDBERG	301.3	49
9	Rory McILROY	301.3	35
10	Paul WARING	300.4	74
11	Seung-yul NOH	299.8	53
12	Julien GUERRIER	299.7	56
13	Paul CASEY	299.1	28
14	Johan EDFORS	298.9	71
15	Ricardo GONZALEZ	298.8	68
16	Danny WILLETT	298.7	67
17	Carl SUNESON	298.1	54
18	Stephen GALLACHER	296.7	87
19	Clodomiro CARRANZA	295.8	67
20	Andrew MCARTHUR	295.5	36
21	Gary BOYD	295.4	73
22	Eirik Tage JOHANSEN	295.2	55
23	Phillip ARCHER	295.1	49
24	Charl SCHWARTZEL	294.9	60
25	Lee WESTWOOD	294.7	30

Driving Accuracy (%)

Pos	Name	%	Stats Rounds
1	Peter O'MALLEY	75.0	44
2	David HORSEY	73.5	75
3	Richie RAMSAY	73.1	89
4	Matteo MANASSERO	72.7	52
5	Francesco MOLINARI	72.1	69
6	Colin MONTGOMERIE	71.9	48
7	Peter LAWRIE	71.7	92
8	Marcus FRASER	70.7	73
9	Steven O'HARA	70.7	80
10	Ignacio GARRIDO	70.6	92
11	Lee WESTWOOD	69.9	30
12	Felipe AGUILAR	69.4	75
13	Grégory BOURDY	69.2	87
14	Ian POULTER	69.1	28
15	Edoardo MOLINARI	68.9	74
16	Graeme McDOWELL	68.6	65
17	Gareth MAYBIN	68.5	84
18	Richard GREEN	68.5	78
19	Graeme STORM	68.3	82
20	Anders HANSEN	68.0	80
21	Henrik STENSON	68.0	31
22	Luke DONALD	67.8	24
23	Miguel Angel JIMÉNEZ	67.8	72
24	Fabrizio ZANOTTI	67.7	79
25	James MORRISON	67.7	67

Average Putts Per Round

Pos	Name	Putts per Round	Stats Rounds
1	Fredrik ANDERSSON HED	28.1	77
2	George COETZEE	28.3	62
3	Luke DONALD	28.3	24
4	Marcus FRASER	28.3	73
5	Pelle EDBERG	28.4	49
6	Christian CÉVAËR	28.5	62
7	Miguel Angel JIMÉNEZ	28.5	72
8	David HOWELL	28.7	77
9	James MORRISON	28.7	67
10	Lee WESTWOOD	28.7	30
11	Søren KJELDSEN	28.7	66
12	David HORSEY	28.8	75
13	Michael LORENZO-VERA	28.8	32
14	Paul BROADHURST	28.8	45
15	Thongchai JAIDEE	28.8	61
16	Brett RUMFORD	28.9	69
17	Damien McGRANE	28.9	105
18	Jamie ELSON	28.9	58
19	Nick DOUGHERTY	28.9	71
20	Prayad MARKSAENG	28.9	29
21	Rhys DAVIES	28.9	81
22	Robert KARLSSON	28.9	47
23	Mark F HAASTRUP	29.0	58
24	Simon DYSON	29.0	69
25	Stephen DODD	29.0	63

Greens In Regulation (%)

Pos	Name	%	Stats Rounds
1	Ian POULTER	77.4	28
2	Steven O'HARA	76.6	80
3	Graeme McDOWELL	75.5	65
4	Nicolas COLSAERTS	74.3	76
5	Richie RAMSAY	74.0	89
6	Søren HANSEN	73.8	75
7	Edoardo MOLINARI	73.7	74
8	Rory McILROY	73.5	35
9	Francesco MOLINARI	73.1	69
10	Clodomiro CARRANZA	73.1	67
11	Luke DONALD	72.7	24
12	Charl SCHWARTZEL	72.6	60
13	Chris WOOD	72.4	73
14	Matteo MANASSERO	72.3	52
15	Michael HOEY	72.2	77
16	Peter LAWRIE	72.0	92
17	Gary BOYD	71.9	73
18	Stephen GALLACHER	71.9	87
19	Thomas BJÖRN	71.8	76
20	Anders HANSEN	71.7	80
21	Simon KHAN	71.7	64
22	Ernie ELS	71.6	26
23	Ross McGOWAN	71.5	62
24	Keith HORNE	71.4	27
25	Paul CASEY	71.2	28

Sand Saves (%)

Pos	Name	%	Stats Rounds
1	Luke DONALD	73.9	24
2	Ian POULTER	73.7	28
3	Jeev Milkha SINGH	71.4	44
4	Robert KARLSSON	68.4	47
5	Fredrik ANDERSSON HED	67.0	77
6	Hennie OTTO	63.6	63
7	Robert-Jan DERKSEN	63.5	84
8	Mikael LUNDBERG	63.2	73
9	Pablo MARTIN	63.2	66
10	Pelle EDBERG	63.0	49
11	James RUTH	62.9	31
12	Louis OOSTHUIZEN	62.5	48
13	Paul CASEY	62.2	28
14	Rhys DAVIES	62.0	81
15	Martin WIEGELE	61.9	41
16	Charl SCHWARTZEL	61.6	60
17	Shane LOWRY	61.4	90
18	Ross FISHER	61.2	56
19	Gary BOYD	60.7	73
20	Richard GREEN	60.5	78
21	Anthony WALL	60.2	70
22	Anders HANSEN	60.0	80
23	Stephen GALLACHER	59.8	87
24	Thongchai JAIDEE	59.8	61
25	Jeppe HULDAHL	59.4	73

Putts Per Green In Regulation

Pos	Name	Putts per GIR	Stats Rounds
1	Luke DONALD	1.704	24
2	Pelle EDBERG	1.722	49
3	Miguel Angel JIMÉNEZ	1.723	72
4	Lee WESTWOOD	1.725	30
5	Ian POULTER	1.726	28
6	Fredrik ANDERSSON HED	1.731	77
7	George COETZEE	1.733	62
8	Robert KARLSSON	1.733	47
9	Rhys DAVIES	1.737	81
10	Marcus FRASER	1.743	73
11	Rory McILROY	1.747	35
12	Thongchai JAIDEE	1.747	61
13	Graeme McDOWELL	1.755	65
14	Martin KAYMER	1.756	56
15	Damien McGRANE	1.758	105
16	Matteo MANASSERO	1.759	52
17	Nick DOUGHERTY	1.760	71
18	Søren KJELDSEN	1.760	66
19	Christian CÉVAËR	1.762	62
20	Mark F HAASTRUP	1.762	58
21	Pablo MARTIN	1.763	66
22	Richard GREEN	1.763	78
23	Patrik SJÖLAND	1.764	56
24	Brett RUMFORD	1.765	69
25	Jamie ELSON	1.765	58

Scrambles

Pos	Name	%	AVE SPR	AVE Missed GPR	Total Missed GIR	Total Scrambles	Stats Rounds
1	Luke DONALD	70.3	3.5	5	118	83	24
2	Paul CASEY	64.8	3.4	5	145	94	28
3	Thongchai JAIDEE	64.6	3.6	6	336	217	61
4	Martin KAYMER	63.5	3.4	5	299	190	56
5	Marcus FRASER	62.4	4.3	7	502	313	73
6	Ian POULTER	62.3	2.5	4	114	71	28
7	Lee WESTWOOD	62.0	3.3	5	158	98	30
8	Oliver WILSON	61.8	3.7	6	400	247	67
9	David HORSEY	61.6	3.9	6	471	290	75
10	Fredrik ANDERSSON HED	61.3	3.9	6	493	302	77
11	Louis OOSTHUIZEN	60.8	3.5	6	278	169	48
12	Jeev Milkha SINGH	60.5	3.4	6	248	150	44
13	Richard GREEN	60.5	3.5	6	446	270	78
14	Robert-Jan DERKSEN	60.1	3.4	6	471	283	84
15	Søren KJELDSEN	59.9	3.7	6	406	243	66
16	Miguel Angel JIMÉNEZ	59.7	3.7	6	447	267	72
17	Charl SCHWARTZEL	59.5	2.9	5	296	176	60
18	Damien McGRANE	59.5	3.5	6	625	372	105
19	Prayad MARKSAENG	59.2	4.2	7	206	122	29
20	Joost LUITEN	58.8	3.1	5	459	270	87
21	Henrik STENSON	58.5	3.5	6	183	107	31
22	Colin MONTGOMERIE	58.4	3.6	6	293	171	48
23	Pelle EDBERG	58.4	3.5	6	296	173	49
24	Simon DYSON	58.4	3.5	6	409	239	69
25	Raphaël JACQUELIN	58.3	3.4	6	487	284	84

Average One Putts Per Round

Pos	Name	One Putts Average	Stats Rounds
1	Luke DONALD	7.13	24
2	Prayad MARKSAENG	6.66	29
3	Henrik STENSON	6.61	31
4	Oliver WILSON	6.57	67
5	Michael LORENZO-VERA	6.44	32
6	Richard GREEN	6.41	78
7	Stephen DODD	6.38	63
8	Robert ROCK	6.26	85
9	Wen-chong LIANG	6.23	35
10	Miguel Angel JIMÉNEZ	6.18	72
11	Patrik SJÖLAND	6.16	56
12	Peter WHITEFORD	6.16	75
13	Jarmo SANDELIN	6.14	59
14	Søren KJELDSEN	6.14	66
15	Lee WESTWOOD	6.10	30
16	Julien QUESNE	6.05	77
17	Eirik Tage JOHANSEN	6.00	55
18	Ian POULTER	6.00	28
19	Shiv KAPUR	5.98	81
20	Christian CÉVAËR	5.97	62
21	Mikael LUNDBERG	5.96	73
22	Hennie OTTO	5.95	63
23	Scott HEND	5.95	59
24	Thomas BJÖRN	5.95	76
25	Grégory BOURDY	5.94	87

THE 2010 EUROPEAN TOUR INTERNATIONAL SCHEDULE

	Date	Event	Venue
Dec '09	10-13	**Alfred Dunhill Championship**	Leopard Creek CC, Malelane, South Africa
	17-20	**South African Open Championship**	Pearl Valley Golf Estates, Paarl, Western Cape, South Africa
Jan 10	7-10	**Africa Open**	East London GC, East London, Eastern Cape, South Africa
	14-17	**Joburg Open**	Royal Johannesburg & Kensington GC, Johannesburg, South Africa
	21-24	**Abu Dhabi Golf Championship**	Abu Dhabi GC, Abu Dhabi, UAE
	28-31	**Commercialbank Qatar Masters presented by Dolphin Energy**	Doha GC, Doha, Qatar
Feb	4-7	**Omega Dubai Desert Classic**	Emirates GC, Dubai, UAE
	11-14	**Avantha Masters**	DLF G&CC, New Delhi, India
	17-21	**WGC – Accenture Match Play**	Ritz-Carlton GC, Dove Mountain, Marana, Arizona, USA
Mar	4-7	**Maybank Malaysian Open**	Kuala Lumpur G&CC, Kuala Lumpur, Malaysia
	11-14	**WGC – CA Championship**	Doral Golf Resort & Spa, Doral, Florida, USA
	18-21	**Trophée Hassan II**	Royal Golf Dar Es Salam, Rabat, Morocco
	25-28	**Open de Andalucia de Golf**	Parador de Málaga Golf, Málaga, Spain
Apr	8-11	**Madeira Islands Open BPI - Portugal**	Porto Santo Golfe, Madeira, Portugal
	8-11	MASTERS TOURNAMENT	Augusta National GC, Georgia, USA
	15-18	**Volvo China Open**	Suzhou Jinji Lake International GC, Suzhou, China
	22-25	**Ballantine's Championship**	Pinx GC, Jeju Island, South Korea
	29-2 May	**Open de España**	Real Club de Golf de Sevilla, Seville, Spain
May	6-9	**BMW Italian Open**	Royal Park I Roveri, Turin, Italy
	13-16	**Iberdrola Open Cala Millor Mallorca**	Pula GC, Son Servera, Mallorca, Spain
	20-23	**BMW PGA CHAMPIONSHIP**	Wentworth Club, Surrey, England
	27-30	**Madrid Masters**	Real Sociedad Hípica Española Club de Campo, Madrid, Spain
Jun	3-6	**The Celtic Manor Wales Open**	The Celtic Manor Resort, City of Newport, Wales
	10-13	**Estoril Open de Portugal**	Penha Longa Hotel, Spa & Golf Resort, Linho Sintra, Estoril, Portugal
	17-20	**SAINT-OMER OPEN presented by Neuflize OBC**	Aa Saint Omer GC, Lumbres, France
	17-20	US OPEN CHAMPIONSHIP	Pebble Beach Golf Links, Pebble Beach, California, USA
	24-27	**BMW International Open**	Golfclub München Eichenried, Munich, Germany
Jul	1-4	**Alstom Open de France**	Le Golf National, Paris, France
	8-11	**The Barclays Scottish Open**	Loch Lomond GC, Glasgow, Scotland
	15-18	THE 139th OPEN CHAMPIONSHIP	Old Course, St Andrews, Fife, Scotland
	22-25	**Nordea Scandinavian Masters**	Bro Hof Slott GC, Stockholm, Sweden
	29-1 Aug	**3 Irish Open**	Killarney Golf & Fishing Club, Killarney, Co. Kerry, Ireland
Aug	5-8	**WGC - Bridgestone Invitational**	Firestone CC, Akron, Ohio, USA
	12-15	US PGA CHAMPIONSHIP	Whistling Straits, Kohler, Wisconsin, USA
	19-22	**Czech Open 2010**	Prosper Golf Resort, Čeladná, Czech Republic
	26-29	**Johnnie Walker Championship at Gleneagles**	The Gleneagles Hotel, Perthshire, Scotland
Sep	2-5	**Omega European Masters**	Crans-sur-Sierre, Crans Montana, Switzerland
	9-12	**KLM Open**	Hilversumsche GC, Hilversum, The Netherlands
	16-19	**Austrian GolfOpen presented by Botarin**	Diamond CC, Atzenbrugg, Austria
	23-26	**Vivendi Cup 2010**	Golf de Joyenval, Chambourcy, Paris, France
Oct	1-4	THE RYDER CUP*	The Celtic Manor Resort, City of Newport, Wales
	7-10	**Alfred Dunhill Links Championship**	Old Course, St Andrews, Carnoustie & Kingsbarns, Scotland
	14-17	**Portugal Masters**	Oceânico Victoria GC, Vilamoura, Portugal
	21-24	**CASTELLÓ MASTERS Costa Azahar**	Club de Campo del Mediterráneo, Castellón, Valencia, Spain
	28-31	**Andalucia Valderrama Masters**	Club de Golf Valderrama, Sotogrande, Spain
Nov	4-7	**WGC - HSBC Champions**	Sheshan International GC, Shanghai, China
	11-15	**Barclays Singapore Open**	The Tanjong & The Serapong, Sentosa GC, Singapore
	18-21	**UBS Hong Kong Open**	Hong Kong GC, Fanling, Hong Kong
	25-28	**DUBAI WORLD CHAMPIONSHIP presented by: DP World**	Jumeirah Golf Estates, Dubai, UAE

* Denotes Approved Special Event

** Denotes Play-off

^ Reduced to 54 holes because of inclement weather

Winner	Score	First prize / Prize fund
Pablo Martin, ESP	68-63-71-69=271 (-17)	€158,500 / €1,000,000
Richie Ramsay, SCO**	67-75-68-65=275 (-13)	€158,500 / €1,010,637
Charl Schwartzel, RSA	67-70-68-67=272 (-20)	€158,500 / €1,000,000
Charl Schwartzel, RSA	63-68-64-66=261 (-23)	€206,050 / €1,313,847
Martin Kaymer, GER	67-67-67-66=267 (-21)	€250,000 / €1,504,497
Robert Karlsson, SWE	68-70-70-65=273 (-15)	€294,584 / €1,760,945
Miguel Angel Jiménez, ESP**	70-67-68-72=277 (-11)	€296,500 / €1,765,104
Andrew Dodt, AUS	67-68-71-68=274 (-14)	€250,000 / €1,488,260
Ian Poulter, ENG	def Paul Casey ENG 4 and 2	€1,019,635 / €6,190,643
Noh Seung-yul, KOR	69-70-67-68=274 (-14)	€246,291 / €1,497,605
Ernie Els, RSA	68-66-70-66=270 (-18)	€1,022,353 / €6,207,143
Rhys Davies, WAL	68-64-68-66=266 (-25)	€229,160 / €1,361,205
Louis Oosthuizen, RSA	67-63-66-67=263 (-17)	€166,660 / €1,017,802
James Morrison, ENG	67-65-66-70=268 (-20)	€116,660 / €700,000
Phil Mickelson, USA	67-71-67-67=272 (-16)	€1,002,904/€5,595,094
Y E Yang, KOR	68-66-68-71=273 (-15)	€311,708 / €1,881,480
Marcus Fraser, AUS	65-70-69=204 (-12)^	€367,500 / €2,196,793
Alvaro Quiros, ESP**	68-72-67-70=277 (-11)	€333,330 / €2,038,766
Fredrik Andersson Hed, SWE	70-66-63-73=272 (-16)	€216,660 / €1,300,000
Peter Hanson, SWE**	72-69-67-66=274 (-6)	€133,330 / €800,000
Simon Khan, ENG	72-69-71-66=278 (-6)	€750,000 / €4,553,916
Luke Donald, ENG	65-67-68-67=267 (-21)	€250,000 / €1,515,687
Graeme McDowell, NIR	72-70-64-63=269 (-15)	€350,940 / €2,118,254
Thomas Björn, DEN	67-65-65-68=265 (-23)	€166,660 / €1,011,916
Martin Wiegele, AUT	66-71-72-68=277 (-7)	€100,000 / €604,470
Graeme McDowell, NIR	71-68-71-74=284 (L)	€1,123,970 / €6,244,276
David Horsey, ENG	69-67-67-67=270 (-18)	€333,330 / €2,017,955
Miguel Angel Jiménez, ESP**	71-69-66-67=273 (-11)	€500,000 / €3,040,392
Edoardo Molinari, ITA	66-69-63-74=272 (-12)	€601,600 / €3,588,941
Louis Oosthuizen, RSA	65-67-69-71=272 (-16)	€1,011,840 / €5,708,861
Richard S Johnson, SWE	70-66-70-71=277 (-11)	€266,660 / €1,583,950
Ross Fisher, ENG	69-61-71-65=266 (-18)	€500,000 / €3,000,000
Hunter Mahan, USA	71-67-66-64=268 (-12)	€1,076,840 / €6,483,924
Martin Kaymer, GER**	72-68-67-70=277 (-11)	€1,028,877 / €5,639,314
Peter Hanson, SWE **	67-70-67-74=278 (-10)	€333,330 / €2,026,892
Edoardo Molinari, ITA	70-68-69-71=278 (-10)	€282,773 / €1,683,378
Miguel Angel Jiménez, ESP	67-61-68-67=263 (-21)	€333,330 / €2,000,000
Martin Kaymer, GER	67-67-66-66=266 (-14)	€300,000 / €1,821,516
José Manuel Lara, ESP**	66-71-70-64=271 (-17)	€125,000 / €753,366
John Parry, ENG	64-67-70-70= 271 (-17)	€204,160 / €1,232,330
EUROPE 14½ - USA 13½		
Martin Kaymer, GER	68-69-68-66= 271 (-17)	€580,046 / €3,467,322
Richard Green, AUS	70-66-69-65= 270 (-18)	€500,000 / €3,000,000
Matteo Manassero, ITA	68-66-67-67= 268 (-16)	€333,330 / €2,011,970
Graeme McDowell, NIR	68-67-72-74=281 (-3)	€500,000 / €3,000,000
Francesco Molinari, ITA	65-70-67-67=269 (-19)	€860,153 / €5,017,561
Adam Scott, AUS	65-65-69-68=267 (-17)	€713,165 / €4,291,823
Ian Poulter, ENG	67-60-64-67=258 (-22)	€301,447 / €1,794,552
Robert Karlsson, SWE**	65-75-67-67=274 (-14)	€910,349 / €5,446,799

Live the
Dream

THE EUROPEAN TOUR QUALIFYING SCHOOL
PGA Catalunya Resort, Girona, Spain

L-R: Mike Stewart, Qualifying School Director, Simon Khan and Angel Gallardo, Vice-Chairman of The PGA European Tour Board of Directors

There has possibly been no more unusual entry into golf's record books than that achieved by Simon Khan in 2010. His success in The European Tour's flagship event, the BMW PGA Championship, only six months after winning The European Tour Qualifying School – Final Stage, ranks as one of the most memorable accomplishments seen on the fairways in the history of the game. Khan confessed: "When I won at Wentworth it was a shock – a total shock!"

There has possibly been no more unusual entry into golf's record books than that achieved by Simon Khan in 2010. His success in The European Tour's flagship event, the BMW PGA Championship, only six months after winning The European Tour Qualifying School – Final Stage, ranks as one of the most memorable accomplishments seen on the fairways in the history of the game. Khan confessed: "When I won at Wentworth it was a shock – a total shock!"

With his win Khan became the fourth player in history – following Gordon Brand Jnr, José Maria Olazábal and Oskar Henningsson – to triumph the following season having won the Qualifying School itself. Yet the story of his return from the wings to the centre stage spotlight was made all the more extraordinary by the fact that his place in the BMW PGA Championship came about through an eleventh hour invitation.

The Englishman explained: "The Tour used to invite the winner of the School to play in the PGA Championship, but that stopped a few years back. I wrote to Chief Executive George O'Grady and I was delighted when I heard on the Monday of the Championship that I was in. I was ready mentally for it because I have always felt comfortable playing at Wentworth."

Nevertheless Khan would be the first to acknowledge that the Lazarus-like resurrection of his career owed much not only to his own determination and skill but also the Qualifying School. In fact he was no stranger to the School having made no fewer than nine appearances. Even so his return in 2009 surprised most observers as he had elevated his status on the Tour by capturing The 2004 Celtic Manor Wales Open, finishing as high as 25th on The Race to Dubai (formerly the Order of Merit) in 2006 and earning career winnings of approximately €4 million.

Khan, who was inspired to take up golf as a 12 year old after watching Seve Ballesteros win The Open Championship at St Andrews in 1984, arrived at PGA Catalunya Resort, situated in the north east of Spain in the town of Caldas between Barcelona and Girona, intent on passing with flying colours. He did not let himself down. Khan compiled scores of 68-63-67-66-70-74 to finish the 108-hole Qualifying School on 20 under par 408, one stroke clear of compatriot Sam Hutsby and two in front of Scotland's Stephen Gallacher.

What the 2009 Qualifying School demonstrated perhaps more than any previous one was the sheer quality and strength in depth of The European Tour. The competition was immense with Khan feeling the pressure of the final day as he led a group of 31 graduates onto The 2010 Race to Dubai. The tension stretched through the field with Scotland's Scott Drummond, winner of the 2004 BMW PGA Championship, chipping in from 25 yards on the 18th to pass the examination and Australia's Rick Kulacz surging to his first European Tour card by holing a nerve-defying 40 foot putt on the last hole to complete a stunning closing 64.

Moreover Sweden's Fredrik Andersson Hed, who finished 12th at the School, showed the importance of such success when, like Khan, he also won on The 2010 European Tour International Schedule – securing the BMW Italian Open title prior to finishing tied second with Luke Donald behind Khan in the BMW PGA Championship, a tournament in which Gallacher finished fourth.

Andersson Hed's achievement was all the more remarkable as he has made no fewer than 14 appearances at the Qualifying School. There was, of course, no need for him to return in 2010 when the Final Stage again unfolded at PGA Catalunya Resort following the playing of Stage One at Ribagolfe (Portugal), The London Club (England), Ebreichsdorf (Austria), Barbaroux (France), Dundonald Links (Scotland), Fleesensee (Germany), Wychwood Park (England) and Circolo Golf Bogogno (Italy), and Stage Two at four Spanish venues: Costa Ballena Ocean Club, Arcos Gardens, Hacienda del Alamo and El Valle Golf Resort.

Similarly Gallacher, third at the Qualifying School in 2009, turned his career around with a brilliant sequence of results on The 2010 European Tour International Schedule. He finished tied fourth in not only the BMW PGA Championship but also The Celtic Manor Wales Open and The Barclays Scottish Open

Fredrik Andersson Hed

and with a top 25 finish in The Open Championship climbed, at that time, to 19th place on The Race to Dubai. Indeed it was interesting to note that following The Open, won by Louis Oosthuizen who emerged from the School in 2003 and again in 2005, Khan (15th), Andersson Hed (16th) and Gallacher (19th) held places in the top 20 in The Race to Dubai with Spain's Alejandro Cañizares in 21st place.

Cañizares, who won the Russian Open in 2006 on The European Tour, regained his playing rights with a fifth place finish at the 2009 School – then came within a whisker of a second Tour win in both the Iberdrola Open Cala Millor Mallorca and Alstom Open de France, losing both in play-offs, and a third place in the Open de España before making a glorious challenge for The Open Championship itself for three rounds.

All of which once again underlined how The European Tour Qualifying School can allow players to live the dream.

Stephen Gallacher

Alejandro Cañizares

Historic Moments

OMEGA MISSION HILLS WORLD CUP
Mission Hills Golf Club, China

L-R: Dr David Chu, Group Chairman, Mission Hills Group, Francesco Molinari, Edoardo Molinari and Stephen Urquhart, President of Omega

The Omega Mission Hills World Cup returns to the international calendar in 2011 as a biennial event – staged in every odd year – and with a tradition to continue creating historic moments which have been celebrated since the event was first played in 1953.

Canada Cup 1953

Italians Edoardo and Francesco Molinari were responsible for weaving the latest momentous chapter when, in 2009, they became the first brothers to capture this prestigious title. In so doing Italy became the 15th country to triumph – following the first winners Argentina, Australia, Canada, England, Germany, Ireland, Japan, Scotland, South Africa, Spain, Sweden, Taiwan, the United States and Wales.

Now, in 2011, the Mission Hills Resort on Hainan Island in Southern China will become the 46th course to host an event which, since its birth, has fulfilled the dream of popularising the game internationally.

The event was the brainchild of John Jay Hopkins, a wealthy Canadian industrialist, visionary and keen golfer, who formed the International Golf Association. Initially known as the Canada Cup – seven nations competed in the inaugural contest won by the Argentine team of Antonio Cerda and Roberto de Vicenzo.

The philosophy of playing in faraway places and uniting nations in friendship proved a winning formula with the event re-titled the World Cup of Golf in 1967, and with the growth of the game so the two-man team format produced exciting competition in addition to revolutionary results.

Hsieh Min Nan and Lu Liang Huan gained a famous win for Taiwan at Royal Melbourne in Australia in 1972 and although the United States were the dominant force throughout the formative years so Spain, first through Seve Ballesteros and Manuel Piñero at Palm Springs in California in 1976, won four times in eight events.

David Llewellyn and Ian Woosnam brought glory for Wales at Kapalua, Hawaii, in 1987 and other much celebrated victories were achieved by Germany (Torsten Giedeon and Bernhard Langer) at Grand Cypress in Florida in 1990 and Sweden (Anders Forsbrand and Per-Ulrik Johansson) at La Querce in Rome a year later.

The United States returned to centre stage with Fred Couples and Davis Love winning four times in

Ian Woosnam (left) and David Llewellyn, Hawaii 1987

succession from 1992 although since David Duval and Tiger Woods won at Buenos Aires Golf Club in Argentina in 2000, the winning nations have been England, Germany, Japan, Scotland, South Africa (twice), Sweden, Wales and, most recently, Italy.

Edoardo and Francesco had good reason to be delighted with their performance at the Mission Hills Golf Club in China because they were compelled to produce excellent golf down the stretch to win with a 25 under par score of 259 – one ahead of Ireland (Graeme McDowell and Rory McIlroy) and Sweden (Robert Karlsson and Henrik Stenson) and three in front of England (Ross Fisher and Ian Poulter).

The re-positioning of the Omega Mission Hills World Cup, which had been played four times at Mission Hills, Shenzhen, China, to the Mission Hills Resort on Hainan Island as a biennial event followed the decision by the International Olympic Committee to re-introduce golf to the Olympic movement from 2016. By playing the event in alternate years the World Cup is aligned with many of the major sports in the Olympic movement, such as the World Athletics Championships, which are contested biennially and are not in any potential conflict with the summer and winter Olympic Games.

In 2011 the Omega Mission Hills World Cup will be among the richest events in world golf with prize money for the 28 team competition increasing to a record US$7,500,000. The winning team will earn US$2,400,000 – US$1,200,000 to each player – and the format will remain unchanged with two series of foursomes and two series of fourballs.

The Omega Mission Hills World Cup will be hosted on the Blackstone course, a spectacular, 350-acre layout that weaves through a striking landscape of mature trees, expansive wetlands, ancient town ruins and ever-present lava rock. The course – 7,777 yards in length – features a myriad of risk and reward holes through the inward half and is set in front of the 525-room, five-star resort complex.

David Duval (left) and Tiger Woods, Argentina 2000

Ireland: Rory McIlory (left) and Graeme McDowell

Sweden: Henrik Stenson (left) and Robert Karlsson

Wins Around the World

The 2010 season saw European Tour Members triumph in all four corners of the globe. Once again the United States provided a bountiful harvest with particular praise going to Ernie Els who not only won on the US PGA Tour, but who also captured the PGA Grand Slam of Golf in Bermuda. Indeed, European Tour Members dominated America's mid-season and particularly during a glorious 11 week spell from May to July which yielded seven victories – Tim Clark, Rory McIlroy, Justin Rose (twice), Adam Scott and Lee Westwood on the regular US PGA Tour – in addition to Graeme McDowell's US Open triumph. Furthermore, Bernhard Langer continued to monopolise the US Champions Tour with three titles to claim both Player of the Year and Money List honours for the third consecutive season. It was not only in America that trophies were garnered however. Tour Members triumphed six times in Asia and on a total of 13 occasions in South Africa with pride of place going to Jean Hugo who won three times.

Take a bow, one and all.

Ernie Els - PGA Grand Slam of Golf (below) and Arnold Palmer Invitational presented by MasterCard

Sergio Garcia and John Cook – Gary Player Invitational presented by Coca-Cola

Adam Scott - Valero Texas Open

David Frost - 3M Championship

Geoff Ogilvy - SBS Championship

Lee Westwood - St Jude Classic presented by Smith & Nephew

Padraig Harrington - Iskandar Johor Open

Darren Fichardt - Dimension Data Pro-Am

Y E Yang - Kolon Korean Open

Anthony Kim - Shell Houston Open

Mike Harwood - Queensland Senior PGA Championship

Arjun Atwal - Wyndham Championship

Bernhard Langer - Outback Steakhouse Pro-Am (above), Allianz Championship and Boeing Classic

Rory McIlroy - Quail Hollow Championship

Liang Wen-chong - Thailand Open

Adilson Da Silva -
Suncoast Classic (below)
and Zambia Open

James Kingston - Vodacom Business Origins of Golf Selborne

Lin Wen-tang - Ballantine's Taiwan Championship

Justin Rose - AT&T National (below) and the
Memorial Tournament presented by Morgan Stanley

Brandon Grace – Coca-Cola Championship
hosted by Gary Player

Michiel Bothma - Telkom PGA Championship (below)
and SAA Pro-Am Invitational

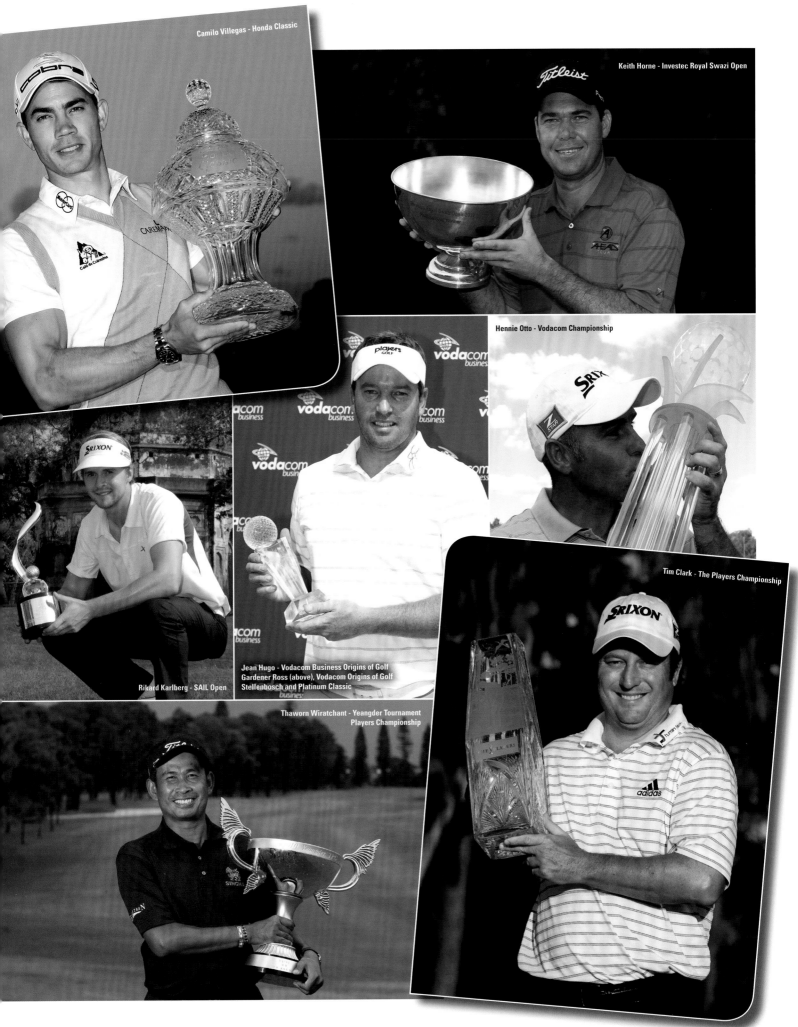

Camilo Villegas - Honda Classic

Keith Horne - Investec Royal Swazi Open

Hennie Otto - Vodacom Championship

Jean Hugo - Vodacom Business Origins of Golf
Gardener Ross (above), Vodacom Origins of Golf
Stellenbosch and Platinum Classic

Rikard Karlberg - SAIL Open

Thaworn Wiratchant - Yeangder Tournament
Players Championship

Tim Clark - The Players Championship

Knockout
Performance

Andy Stubbs, Managing Director of the European Senior Tour, presents the 2010 John Jacobs Trophy to Boonchu Ruangkit

He might have begun the 2010 season as a relative unknown outside Asia but by the time he was crowned as the new European Senior Tour Number One, Boonchu Ruangkit was no longer in need of an introduction.

Four victories and a host of records ensured that the player considered to be 'The Godfather' of Thai golf won not only the Senior Tour Order of Merit, but also the respect and admiration of his illustrious peers.

Never without a smile on his face, Ruangkit's relentless birdie charges came to define the 2010 season, as he succeeded two former Ryder Cup Captains, Ian Woosnam (2008) and Sam Torrance (2009) as recipient of the coveted John Jacobs Trophy with season earnings of €266,609.

"I'm so proud to follow great players like Ian and Sam," he said. "This is a big moment for me in my career. They are household names and it's great that a Thai player can come and win like this on the European Senior Tour. Hopefully

this win will help inspire other Thai players. I'm the first Asian golfer to do this but I think there will be more over the next few years."

Given the dominance that Torrance, Woosnam and all-time leading Senior Tour money winner Carl Mason exerted on the Order of Merit over the previous seven campaigns, few observers would have foreseen their stranglehold being broken so spectacularly. Fewer still could have predicted that it would be the unheralded Ruangkit, a former kickboxer, who would knock down the Senior Tour heavyweights.

Not even a member of the Tour when he took his place in the field for the second event of the season, The Aberdeen Brunei Senior Masters presented by The Stapleford Forum, the 54 year old

Sam Torrance

announced himself on the scene in dramatic fashion, defeating Frankie Minoza of the Philippines on the second extra hole of a play-off.

If that was an auspicious start, better still was to follow in the next event as, buoyed by his maiden triumph, Ruangkit bulldozed his way to a second title by a Senior Tour record margin of 11 shots in front of his home supporters in the inaugural Chang Thailand Senior Masters presented by ISPS.

His 21 under par total of 195 was also the lowest in Senior Tour history as he hit the top of the Order of Merit for the first time, given that his Brunei victory as a non-member did not count towards the money list.

Ruangkit did not have to wait long for his next record, however, becoming the quickest player to win three times on the Senior Tour when he recovered from a second round 78 to complete his hat-trick, two weeks later, in the Berenberg Bank Masters in South Africa.

A perceived adversity to playing in the colder climes brought some self-doubt as to his Order of Merit credentials, but a share of second place finish in the Handa Senior Masters presented by The Stapleford Forum, the first event of the season on European soil, hinted that Ruangkit would also be a durable, as well as a potent force.

Further top ten finishes came in the Bad Ragaz PGA Seniors Open

Andrew Oldcorn

Gordon Brand Jnr

David J Russell

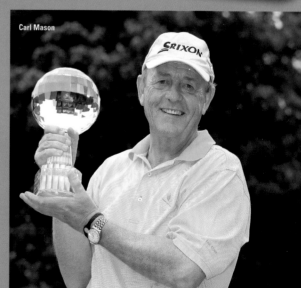
Carl Mason

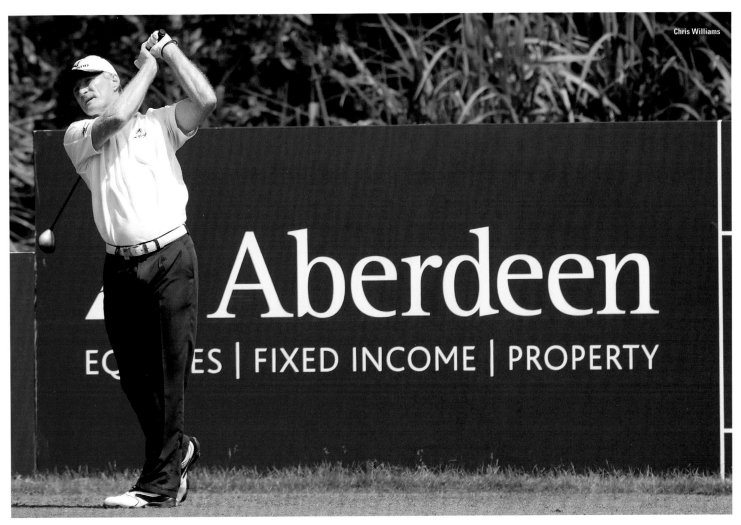

Chris Williams

and the Travis Perkins plc Senior Masters, before he placed one hand on the Order of Merit crown with his first career victory in Europe, and fourth win of the season, in the Benahavis Senior Masters in Marbella in October.

The Thai player then returned to Spain to grasp the John Jacobs Trophy with both hands in the OKI Castellón Senior Tour Championship, producing another characteristic birdie flurry in a final round 65 to finish in a share of eighth place in the season's final event. He ended the campaign €39,259 clear of South African Chris Williams – a margin that would have been even greater had his prize money of €44,332 from Brunei counted.

"I had no expectations at all coming into this season," he said. "I just wanted to play well. I thought I could maybe win once but I never thought I could do it four times. This has been the best year of my career."

Williams did not enjoy a victory in 2010 but showed a remarkable level of consistency during the season, finishing in the top ten 12 times from his 19 outings to amass €227,350 in earnings, while third placed Angel Franco of Paraguay garnered €217,308, helped largely by nine top ten finishes from his 18 tournaments.

The season, however, belonged to Ruangkit. He took up the sport as a teenager and, after joining the services, honed his game at the Royal Army Course. A brief flirtation with a career in kickboxing followed but that ended abruptly when he was knocked out cold in just his third bout, convincing him to concentrate on golf, and he turned professional at the age of 30.

Des Smyth

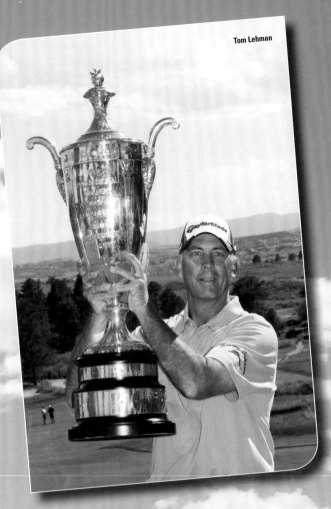

Tom Lehman

Kickboxing's loss was undoubtedly golf's gain. Ruangkit flourished with age and experience and he soon learned how to deliver knockout blows of his own on the fairways, winning five times on the Asian Tour - including the Thailand Open for the second time in his career at the age of 47 – and finishing runner-up on the Asian Tour Order of Merit in 1997.

Having won the US Champions Tour Qualifying School in 2006, Ruangkit appeared destined for a Senior career on the other side of the Pond but he struggled to adapt to life in America, while he was also hampered by a finger injury.

Surgery rectified the latter problem and enabled him, at 53 years and 82 days, to almost become the oldest winner in Asian Tour history, losing in a play-off to Australian Darren Beck at the Brunei Open in 2009.

He was, however, to get his hands on a trophy when he returned to the Empire Hotel and Country Club in Brunei in March, landing the killer punch in the play-off with Minoza to claim a maiden Senior Tour victory that sparked his most memorable of years.

Unsurprisingly Ruangkit, who is also Chairman of the Thailand PGA, picked up the Senior Tour Rookie of the Year Award too and, after Kevin Spurgeon had claimed his own maiden title in the season opening Mauritius Commercial Bank Open, the pair set something of a trend for first time winners in 2010.

Former Ryder Cup players Gordon Brand Jnr and Barry Lane captured their respective first titles in the Matrix Jersey Classic and Cleveland Golf/Srixon Scottish Senior Open, the former success helping Brand Jnr reach a career high of fourth on the Order of Merit, while Marc Farry also made the transition from European Tour winner to Senior Tour

Angel Franco

Domingo Hospital

Mike Cunning

George Ryall

THE SENIOR OPEN CHAMPIONSHIP
Carnoustie 2010

459 yds
420 mts
Par 4

MasterCard

Bernhard Langer

HANDA SENIOR MASTERS
THE STAPLEFORD FORUM

ISPS
PRESENTED BY THE STAPLE

Bill Longmuir

champion, claiming both the Handa Irish Senior Open presented by Fáilte Ireland and the Cannes Mougins Masters – an event the Frenchman helped promote.

Other first time champions included George Ryall and Domingo Hospital, winners of two events which appeared on the schedule for the first time in 2010 – the Van Lanschot Senior Open and Sicilian Senior Open respectively; David J Russell, who after nine runner up finishes captured the De Vere Collection PGA Seniors Championship; and Gary Wolstenholme, one of Great Britain and Ireland's most successful amateurs who triumphed on just his second Senior Tour appearance in the lucrative Casa Serena Open.

Elsewhere, several players continued their winning ways, none more so than Bernhard Langer, the two time Masters Tournament winner and former Ryder Cup Captain, who ended his search for a Senior Major in spectacular style, winning The Senior Open Championship presented by MasterCard at Carnoustie, holding off Corey Pavin in the process, before crossing the Atlantic to win the US Senior Open in Seattle the following week. It was the highlight of an exceptional year for the German who also continued his domination of the US Champions Tour, not only topping the Schwab Cup points race for the first time but also winning Player of the Year and Money List honours for the third consecutive season.

Another former Ryder Cup Captain, Tom Lehman, landed the season's first Senior Major when he edged out Fred Couples and David Frost in a play-off to win the US Senior PGA Championship in Colorado, while other men to enjoy the feel of silverware in their hands on a Sunday night were Bill Longmuir (Handa Senior Masters presented by The Stapleford Forum), John Bland (Ryder Cup Wales Seniors Open), Des Smyth (Travis Perkins plc Senior Masters) and Mike Cunning, who brought the curtain down on the season with his victory in the OKI Castellón Senior Tour Championship.

There was also an historic 23rd Senior Tour title for the prolific Carl Mason in the Bad Ragaz PGA Seniors Open, as the Englishman equalled Tommy Horton's ten year old record for the most victories on Tour, on his way to completing the top five on the 2010 Order of Merit.

While that remarkable benchmark might be out of Boonchu Ruangkit's reach for the foreseeable future, the Thai's own achievements would imply that his defence of the John Jacobs Trophy in 2011 might be somewhat harder to breach than his guard in the boxing ring.

Steve Todd

Kevin Spurgeon

Barry Lane

John Bland

Gary Wolstenholme

	Date	Event	Venue	Winner	Score	First prize / Prize fund
Dec 09	11-13	The Mauritius Commercial Bank Open	Constance Belle Mare Plage, Mauritius	**Kevin Spurgeon ENG**	71-67-72=210 (-6)	€34,500 / €230,000
Mar 10	5-7	The Aberdeen Brunei Senior Masters presented by The Stapleford Forum	The Empire Hotel & Country Club, Brunei	**Boonchu Ruangkit THA****	64-69-66=199 (-14)	€44,333 / €295,552
	12-14	Chang Thailand Senior Masters presented by ISPS	Royal Gems Golf and Sports Club, Thailand	**Boonchu Ruangkit THA**	64-66-65=195 (-21)	€43,815 / €292,101
	26-28	Berenberg Bank Masters	The Links, Fancourt, South Africa	**Boonchu Ruangkit THA**	69-78-69=216 (-3)	€75,000 / €499,650
May	12-14	Handa Senior Masters presented by The Stapleford Forum	Stapleford Park, Leicestershire, England	**Bill Longmuir, SCO**	64-68-66=199 (-20)	€71,381 / €476,185
	27-30	US SENIOR PGA CHAMPIONSHIP	Colorado GC, Denver, Colorado, USA	**Tom Lehman, USA ****	68-71-71-71=281 (-7)	€292,730 / €1,631,363
Jun	4-6	Matrix Jersey Classic	La Moye GC, Jersey	**Gordon Brand Jnr, SCO**	63-66-72=201 (-15)	€25,081 / €163,772
	11-13	Handa Irish Senior Open presented by Fáilte Ireland	Carton House, Maynooth, Co Kildare, Ireland	**Marc Farry, FRA**	67-70-69=206 (-10)	€37,500 / €250,000
	18-20	Ryder Cup Wales Seniors Open	Royal Porthcawl GC, Porthcawl, Wales	**John Bland, RSA**	69-68-71=208 (-8)	€90,090 / €600,600
	24-27	De Vere Collection PGA Seniors Championship	Hunting Course, De Vere Slaley Hall, Hexham, England	**David J Russell, ENG**	71-67-70-75=283 (-5)	€47,732 / €298,325
Jul	2-4	Bad Ragaz PGA Seniors Open	Golf Club Bad Ragaz, Switzerland	**Carl Mason, ENG**	64-67-68=199 (-11)	€37,500 / €250,000
	9-11	Van Lanschot Senior Open	Royal Haagsche Golf & Country Club, The Hague, The Netherlands	**George Ryall, ENG**	72-68-66= 206 (-10)	€37,500 / €250,312
	22-25	THE SENIOR OPEN CHAMPIONSHIP PRESENTED BY MASTERCARD	Championship Course, Carnoustie, Scotland	**Bernhard Langer, GER**	67-71-69-72 = 279 (-5)	€242,639 / €1,538,187
	29-1 Aug	US SENIOR OPEN*	Sahalee CC, Seattle, Washington, USA	**Bernhard Langer, GER**	69-68-68-67=272 (-8)	US$470,000/$2,600,000
Aug	20-22	Cleveland Golf / Srixon Scottish Senior Open	Fairmont St. Andrews, Fife, Scotland	**Barry Lane, ENG**	69-71-72=212 (-4)	€45,847 / €305,650
Sep	3-5	Travis Perkins plc Senior Masters	Duke's Course, Woburn GC, England	**Des Smyth, IRL**	66-71-69=206 (-10)	€47,853 / €318,797
	17-19	Casa Serena Open	Casa Serena Golf, Kutna Hora, Czech Republic	**Gary Wolstenholme, ENG**	66-67-67=200 (-13)	€90,000 / €600,000
Oct	9-11 (Sat - Mon)	Cannes Mougins Masters	Cannes Mougins, Cannes, France	**Marc Farry, FRA**	69-65-73=207 (-9)	€38,287 / €250,000
	15-17	Benahavis Senior Masters	La Quinta G&CC, Marbella, Spain	**Boonchu Ruangkit, THA**	68-65-64 =197 (-16)	€27,000 / €180,000
	22-24	Sicilian Senior Open	Il Picciolo Golf Club, Castiglione di Sicilia, Italy	**Domingo Hospital, ESP****	70-67-74= 211 (-5)	€37,500 / €250,000
Nov	5-7	OKI Castellón Senior Tour Championship	Club de Campo del Mediterráneo, Castellón, Valencia, Spain	**Mike Cunning, USA**	69-69-64=202 (-14)	€64,433 / € 400,000

** Denotes play-off

* Money won does not count towards the 2010 European Senior Tour Order of Merit

THE 2010 EUROPEAN SENIOR TOUR ORDER OF MERIT

Pos	Name	Country	Played	€	Pos	Name	Country	Played	€
+ 1	**Boonchu RUANGKIT**	(THA)	(17)	266609.00	55	Stephen BENNETT	(ENG)	(16)	30248.06
2	**Chris WILLIAMS**	(RSA)	(19)	227350.02	+ 56	Steve CIPA	(ENG)	(9)	30177.99
3	**Angel FRANCO**	(PAR)	(18)	217308.16	57	Torsten GIEDEON	(GER)	(12)	29188.46
4	**Gordon BRAND JNR**	(SCO)	(13)	197017.33	58	Eamonn DARCY	(IRL)	(10)	28378.29
5	**Carl MASON**	(ENG)	(16)	190007.67	59	Emilio RODRIGUEZ	(ESP)	(12)	26056.27
6	**David J RUSSELL**	(ENG)	(19)	165722.45	60	Graham BANISTER	(AUS)	(10)	26024.07
+ 7	**Andrew OLDCORN**	(SCO)	(15)	163114.41	61	Martin GRAY	(SCO)	(15)	25952.75
8	**Marc FARRY**	(FRA)	(18)	146570.17	62	Mike WILLIAMS	(ZIM)	(16)	24834.72
9	**Des SMYTH**	(IRL)	(15)	142748.71	63	Simon OWEN	(NZL)	(10)	24542.96
10	**Sam TORRANCE**	(SCO)	(16)	141046.95	+ 64	Fraser MANN	(SCO)	(16)	21194.91
11	**Bill LONGMUIR**	(SCO)	(18)	138180.49	+ 65	Graham GUNN	(CAN)	(5)	20356.27
12	**Jerry BRUNER**	(USA)	(19)	130778.62	66	Sandy LYLE	(SCO)	(6)	18995.56
13	**Roger CHAPMAN**	(ENG)	(17)	127427.75	67	Noel RATCLIFFE	(AUS)	(12)	18366.71
14	**Mike CUNNING**	(USA)	(17)	123430.99	+ 68	Ricky WILLISON	(ENG)	(5)	18038.92
15	**Gordon J BRAND**	(ENG)	(19)	122757.85	69	Martin POXON	(ENG)	(13)	16574.95
16	**Ross DRUMMOND**	(SCO)	(18)	122012.75	70	Peter DAHLBERG	(SWE)	(8)	16206.03
** 17	**Gary WOLSTENHOLME**	(ENG)	(6)	120013.65	71	Jeff HALL	(ENG)	(14)	15920.31
18	**Juan QUIROS**	(ESP)	(18)	118051.61	72	Pete OAKLEY	(USA)	(14)	15895.93
19	**David MERRIMAN**	(AUS)	(19)	111942.16	73	Ian MOSEY	(ENG)	(17)	15425.41
+ 20	**Barry LANE**	(ENG)	(7)	110894.92	74	Denis DURNIAN	(ENG)	(10)	15211.08
21	**John BLAND**	(RSA)	(6)	104285.67	75	Manuel PIÑERO	(ESP)	(13)	12829.08
22	**Glenn RALPH**	(ENG)	(20)	102954.85	76	Maurice BEMBRIDGE	(ENG)	(14)	12256.15
23	**Bobby LINCOLN**	(RSA)	(19)	99590.71	** 77	Steve VAN VUUREN	(RSA)	(6)	12108.42
24	**Bob CAMERON**	(ENG)	(20)	95205.96	78	Tony ALLEN	(ENG)	(6)	11510.97
+ 25	**Mark BELSHAM**	(ENG)	(15)	93686.11	79	Anders JOHNSSON	(SWE)	(17)	11036.52
26	**Kevin SPURGEON**	(ENG)	(20)	89492.97	80	Mike MILLER	(SCO)	(18)	9175.10
27	**George RYALL**	(ENG)	(16)	87211.04	81	Tony CHARNLEY	(ENG)	(13)	8694.18
28	**Ian WOOSNAM**	(WAL)	(13)	85425.63	82	Jean Pierre SALLAT	(FRA)	(7)	7022.49
29	**Peter FOWLER**	(AUS)	(15)	84331.06	83	José Maria CAÑIZARES	(ESP)	(5)	6747.45
30	**Bob BOYD**	(USA)	(13)	81502.88	84	Antonio GARRIDO	(ESP)	(15)	6364.68
31	Luis CARBONETTI	(ARG)	(17)	81388.70	85	Eddie POLLAND	(NIR)	(11)	5828.41
32	Nick JOB	(ENG)	(20)	80366.44	86	John BENDA	(USA)	(5)	5604.21
33	Peter MITCHELL	(ENG)	(16)	79856.57	87	Victor GARCIA	(ESP)	(10)	5489.60
34	Tony JOHNSTONE	(ZIM)	(16)	79480.63	88	Bill HARDWICK	(CAN)	(11)	5162.02
35	Adan SOWA	(ARG)	(18)	77665.81	89	Gery WATINE	(FRA)	(5)	4115.25
36	Katsuyoshi TOMORI	(JPN)	(12)	74902.26	** 90	Mitch KIERSTENSON	(ENG)	(3)	4108.50
37	Domingo HOSPITAL	(ESP)	(13)	68501.08	** 91	Jeb STUART	(USA)	(4)	4096.28
38	Mike HARWOOD	(AUS)	(15)	68359.38	+ 92	Terry BURGOYNE	(SCO)	(7)	3507.51
39	Jim RHODES	(ENG)	(19)	66727.65	93	Peter ALLAN	(ENG)	(7)	3177.91
40	Horacio CARBONETTI	(ARG)	(17)	65034.47	94	Peter TERAVAINEN	(USA)	(5)	3026.74
+ 41	John HARRISON	(ENG)	(15)	63791.01	95	Greg HOPKINS	(USA)	(6)	2985.97
42	Mike CLAYTON	(AUS)	(15)	62906.90	96	Matt BRIGGS	(ENG)	(5)	2927.57
43	Denis O'SULLIVAN	(IRL)	(19)	62784.89	97	Jeff HAWKES	(RSA)	(7)	2923.12
44	José RIVERO	(ESP)	(13)	62740.88	** 98	Barrie STEVENS	(ENG)	(5)	2422.68
45	Bertus SMIT	(RSA)	(19)	54564.09	99	Terry GALE	(AUS)	(8)	2353.85
46	Costantino ROCCA	(ITA)	(14)	49965.06	100	Glyn DAVIES	(WAL)	(5)	1703.41
+ 47	John GOULD	(ENG)	(14)	46083.69	101	Bill McCOLL	(SCO)	(4)	1533.00
48	John CHILLAS	(SCO)	(16)	45281.46	** 102	Neville CLARKE	(RSA)	(4)	1456.00
49	Doug JOHNSON	(USA)	(16)	44137.84	103	Christy O'CONNOR JNR	(IRL)	(6)	1402.86
50	Jimmy HEGGARTY	(NIR)	(18)	40482.35	** 104	Doug YOUNG	(ENG)	(3)	692.00
51	Delroy CAMBRIDGE	(JAM)	(18)	39179.27	** 105	Stephen SHIELDS	(ENG)	(2)	675.00
52	Angel FERNANDEZ	(CHI)	(12)	37143.54	** 106	Chris LINSTEAD	(ENG)	(2)	480.00
53	Giuseppe CALI	(ITA)	(16)	35910.90	** 107	Jannie ACKERMAN	(RSA)	(1)	425.00
54	Andrew MURRAY	(ENG)	(10)	34546.13	** 108	Trevor FISHER SNR	(RSA)	(2)	375.00

+ Denotes rookie

** Denotes affiliate member

Consummate
Professional

Alain de Soultrait, Challenge Tour Director, congratulates Rankings winner Alvaro Velasco

If 2009 was a bittersweet year for Spaniard Alvaro Velasco, as he married his long-term partner Marta but lost his playing privileges on The European Tour, then 2010 was unquestionably an annus mirabilis.

For not only did his native Spain lift the World Cup for the first time in their history, he also ended the 2010 Challenge Tour campaign clutching a European Tour card as the Number One graduate, putting the seal on the most satisfying season of his career to date.

His professional career, which started in 2005, has been marked by peaks and troughs, but the 29 year old hardly put a foot wrong in a season which saw him – like Edoardo Molinari, his predecessor as the winner of the Rankings – capture two titles, on home soil at the Fred Olsen Challenge de España in June and then at the lucrative Kazakhstan Open in September.

The Spaniard thus showed some serious signs of fulfilling the potential he first displayed in 2006 when, having developed his game first as an amateur at the University of South Carolina in the

United States and then as a professional on the Spanish national Tour, he got his debut Challenge Tour campaign underway in noteworthy fashion, with three top ten finishes.

Velasco, who studied Marketing and Management, recalled: "My first tournament on the Challenge Tour was in Estoril in 2006, and I played really well to finish fourth, which meant I got into the next tournament, in Kenya, where I finished in the top ten.

"That gave me a lot of confidence, and also made it easier to get sponsors' invitations. I finished the season 50th in the Rankings, which meant I had a good category for the next season and so didn't need any sponsors' invitations. Fortunately I made the most of it, as I ended up finishing inside the top 20 to make it onto The European Tour in 2008. It had always been a dream of mine to

Matt Haines

Floris de Vries

Oscar Floren

Daniel Gaunt

play on The European Tour since I first started playing golf, and now I had finally arrived."

Up until that point the professional game had come easily to Velasco, who first picked up a club aged six when his whole family decided to take up golf, was down to scratch by the age of 16, and finished second in his first appearance as a professional on Spain's domestic Tour.

But suddenly the softly-spoken Spaniard was now competing against seasoned campaigners and at first he struggled to find his feet in 2008, earning just over €15,000 from his first five events, with a tie for 28th place at the Alfred Dunhill Championship in South Africa his best effort.

At the Madeira Islands Open BPI – Portugal, however, his rhythm returned, and courtesy of matching rounds of 68 at

the weekend, he secured the first of what he hoped would be many top ten finishes on The European Tour.

With confidence fully restored, Velasco repeated the feat in three of his next seven events to go some way towards retaining his card, which he confirmed with a top 15 finish on home turf at the CASTELLÓ MASTERS Costa Azahar in October.

If that was a peak, however, a trough was soon to follow, as he made another sluggish start in 2009. This time he failed to recover and for the first time in his career he was forced to deal with a serious setback.

"Sometimes though, you learn more about yourself and your game from playing badly than you do from playing well," he acknowledged with admirable wisdom and his customary humility. "My feet were still on the ground and I knew I would have to play very well on the Challenge Tour in 2010, because the level

Robert Dinwiddie

Mark Tullo

George Murray

Thorbjørn Olesen

Bernd Wiesberger

BORN FOR GREATNESS

SAN DOMENICO GOLF - SAVELLETRI DI FASANO - PUGLIA

A LAND THAT NURTURES ANCIENT HISTORY, A TIME HONORED CUISINE, NATURE'S FINEST INGREDIENTS AND A SUN BLESSED CLIMATE IS NOW A DESTINATION FOR GREAT GOLF.

Sitting on the edge of the sea whilst it winds through a grove of timeless olive trees, San Domenico championship golf course (home to the European Challenge Tour Grand Final) together with its fine hotels Borgo Egnazia and Masseria Cimino offer a golfing experience to remember.

San Domenico Golf

WWW.SANDOMENICOGOLF.COM

San Domenico Hotels

WWW.SANDOMENICOHOTELS.COM

of competition is very high. My main goal was just to finish in the top ten and get my card back, but I never believed I would win the Rankings."

That he managed to do so was due largely to those two victories, secured in the contrasting countries – and conditions – of the Canary Islands and Kazakhstan.

He said: "It was a fantastic week in La Gomera – I'd played well at times in the weeks running up to the tournament, just hadn't managed to put four good rounds together. But that week I kept it going for all four days, so it was special to win my first event on the Challenge Tour, and made even more special by the fact that it was in my home country. A lot of the Spanish players stayed together that week so there was a really good atmosphere."

Another night of celebration would follow a fortnight later, as Velasco – whose beloved Barcelona supplied over half of the team – watched

Vicente Del Bosque's Spanish side overcome their Dutch counterparts in South Africa to win the World Cup.

Velasco, a consummate professional whose affable nature hides a steely determination, soon returned to the day job and, after finishing in a tie for second place behind French amateur sensation Romain Wattel at the ALLIANZ EurOpen Strasbourg–Golf de la Wantzenau, went one better in Almaty a week later.

"It was great to get my first win in Spain but my win in Kazakhstan was probably more important because it meant I had my card back," he said. "I practiced really well leading up to the tournament so my game felt good, and the week couldn't have gone any better. It meant I could relax and enjoy the rest of the season, because the only pressure was whether I was going to finish top of the Rankings, which is a very nice position to be in."

Had Austrian Bernd Wiesberger, winner of the ALLIANZ Golf Open

David Vanegas

Lee Slattery

Joel Sjöholm

Julio Zapata

de Lyon and the ALLIANZ Golf Open du Grand Toulouse, been able to maintain his early momentum on the final day of the season-ending Apulia San Domenico Grand Final, Velasco might have been denied at the death.

But as the Austrian's challenge faded down the stretch and victory went instead to England's Matt Haines, Velasco was able to savour the finest achievement of his career.

The Spaniard can now look forward to renewing acquaintances with his compatriots on The European Tour in 2011 and beyond, when his mission is to follow Molinari not only into the winners' enclosure, but also the top 50 of the Official World Golf Ranking.

He said: "I know the other Spanish guys on the Tour very well – people like Alvaro Quiros, Gonzalo Fernandez-Castaño, Pablo Martin, Alejandro Cañizares and Pablo Larrazabal. We normally all go out together whenever we're on Tour,

and we always try to stay in the same hotels. We have a lot of fun, especially with Alvaro – whenever we go out for dinner, nobody else can get a word in because he's always talking so much!

"He's a great guy, and also a great player. Hopefully I can reach the same levels as him but my aim now is to win on The European Tour. Obviously I've still got a long way to go, but Edoardo has shown what is possible. European golf is strong at the moment and I want to be a part of it."

Velasco will be joined in The 2011 Race to Dubai by ten of the 20 winners from the 2010 Challenge Tour Schedule, namely: Matt Haines, who graduated in second place in the Rankings; Denmark's Thorbjørn Olesen, who won The Princess en route to finishing third; his fellow rookie Floris de Vries of the Netherlands, who took fourth thanks largely to his victory at the Mugello-Tuscany Open; two-time winner Bernd Wiesberger, who finished fifth; and

Matthew Zions

Marius Thorp (right) talks with Challenge Tour Press Officer Paul Symes

Martin Wiegele

Lorenzo Gagli

Raymond Russell

TURKISH AIRLINES

Carlos Del Moral

Magnus A Carlsson

Alexandre Kaleka

Scott Jamieson

Alessandro Tadini

abacus
COUNT ON IT

Sam Walker

Charlie Ford

Sweden's Oscar Floren, winner of the SWALEC Wales Challenge and the sixth graduate.

Also making the step up are Australian Daniel Gaunt, who owed his seventh place finish largely to his victory at the English Challenge; England's Robert Dinwiddie, who finished one place below thanks in part to his victory early on in the season at the Kenya Open; Chile's Mark Tullo, who saw off Matteo Manassero at the Rolex Trophy and Rory McIlroy at the Egyptian Open 2010 presented by SODIC en route to finishing ninth; Scotland's George Murray, the tenth graduate who captured his maiden title on home soil at the Scottish Hydro Challenge; and England's Lee Slattery, who returns to The European Tour as the 13th graduate after winning the Telenet Trophy.

A further nine players – Argentina's Julio Zapata (who finished 11th in the Rankings), the Swedish duo of Joel Sjöholm (12th) and Magnus A Carlsson (18th), the Scottish pair of Scott Jamieson (14th) and Raymond Russell (19th), Australian Matthew Zions (15th), Norwegian Marius Thorp (16th), Italian Lorenzo Gagli (17th)

and Frenchman Alexandre Kaleka (20th) – owe their places on The 2011 European Tour International Schedule to the admirable consistency they displayed throughout the season.

Finally, in a season where standards continued to rise on the European Challenge Tour, nowhere was that more evident than in the fact that eight players – Christopher Ryan Baker, Carlos Del Moral, Charlie Ford, Andreas Hartø, Alessandro Tadini, David Vanegas, Sam Walker and Romain Wattel – all won during the course of the year but could not force their way into the top 20 come the final curtain call.

Particularly unfortunate was Velasco's compatriot Del Moral whose victory in the M2M Russian Challenge Cup 2010, allied to four other top 20 finishes saw him finish in 21st place in the Rankings, a mere €558 behind 20th placed Alexandre Kaleka. It can be a cruel game at times but Del Moral, just like Velasco before him, will be back to try again next season.

Paul Symes

Christopher Ryan Baker

Andreas Hartø

Romain Wattel

CT Graduates line-up, back row (l-r): Alexandre Kaleka, Daniel Gaunt, Robert Dinwiddie, Raymond Russell, Magnus Carlsson, Marius Thorp, Matthew Zions, Scott Jamieson, Lee Slattery, Floris de Vries, George Murray, Bernd Wiesberger. Front row (l-r): Julio Zapata, Lorenzo Gagli, Oscar Floren, Mark Tullo, Alvaro Velasco, Matt Haines, Joel Sjöholm, Thorbjørn Olesen.

THE 2010 EUROPEAN CHALLENGE TOUR

	Date	Event	Venue	Winner	Score	First prize / Prize fund
Feb	18-21	Abierto Internacional de Golf "II Copa Antioquia"	Club Deportivo El Rodeo, Sede La Macarena, Medellin, Colombia	David Vanegas, COL	67-69-69-67=272 (-12)	€25,636 / €165,500
Mar	25-28	Kenya Open	Muthaiga GC, Nairobi, Kenya	Robert Dinwiddie, ENG	68-69-70-65=272 (-12)	€30,400 / €192,166
Apr	29-2 May	Turkish Airlines Challenge hosted by Carya Golf Club	Carya GC, Belek, Antalya, Turkey	Charlie Ford, ENG**	73-68-66-70=277 (-11)	€28,000 / €178,710
May	6-9	ALLIANZ Open Côtes d'Armor Bretagne	Golf Blue Green de Pléneuf Val André, Le Val André, France	Sam Walker, ENG	63-70-70-69=272 (-8)	€24,000 / €152,475
	20-23	Mugello – Tuscany Open	Poggio dei Medici GC, Scarperia, Florence, Italy	Floris de Vries, NED**	67-68-71-68=274 (-10)	€24,000 / €155,175
	27-30	Telenet Trophy	Rinkven GC, Anvers, Belgium	Lee Slattery, ENG	64-68-68-67=267 (-21)	€24,000 / €153,180
Jun	3-6	Kärnten Golf Open by Markus Brier Foundation	GC Klagenfurt-Seltenheim, Klagenfurt, Austria	Martin Wiegele, AUT	62-76-71-66=275 (-13)	€25,600 / €161,824
	10-13	Scottish Hydro Challenge	Macdonald Spey Valley GC, Aviemore, Scotland	George Murray, SCO	67-67-67-66=267 (-17)	€32,000 / €203,300
	17-20	Moroccan Golf Classic^	Pullman El Jadida Royal Golf and Spa, El Jadida, Morocco	Christopher Ryan Baker, USA	69-66-72-68=275 (-13)	€24,000 / €153,825
	17-20	SAINT-OMER OPEN presented by Neuflize OBC*	Aa St Omer GC, Lumbres, France	Martin Wiegele, AUT	66-71-72-68=277 (-7)	€83,333 / €604,470*
	24-27	Fred Olsen Challenge de España	Tecina Golf, La Gomera, Canary Islands, Spain	Alvaro Velasco, ESP	70-63-68-65=266 (-18)	€24,000 / €153,180
Jul	1-4	The Princess	Båstad GK, Båstad, Sweden	Thorbjørn Olesen, DEN	69-66-65-70=270 (-14)	€24,000 / €153,825
	8-11	ALLIANZ Golf Open de Lyon	Golf du Gouverneur, Monthieux, France	Bernd Wiesberger, AUT	67-67-71-62=267 (-17)	€24,000 / €152,100
	15-18	Credit Suisse Challenge	Golf Sempachersee, Hildisrieden, Switzerland	Alessandro Tadini, ITA	69-68-64-65=266 (-22)	€24,000 / €151,305
	22-25	English Challenge	Stoke by Nayland Hotel, Golf & Spa, Colchester, England	Daniel Gaunt, AUS	64-69-70-68=271 (-17)	€24,000 / €152,100
Aug	11-14 (Wed-Sat)	Rolex Trophy	Golf Club de Genève, Geneva, Switzerland	Mark Tullo, CHI	69-66-66-65=266 (-22)	€24,400 / €190,240
	19-22	ECCO Tour Championship	Green Eagle GC (North Course), Winsen, Germany	Andreas Hartø (AM), DEN	68-72-70-74=284 (-8)	N/A / €181,062
	25-28 (Wed-Sat)	SWALEC Wales Challenge	Vale Hotel Golf & Spa Resort, Cardiff, Wales	Oscar Floren, SWE	69-65-71-75=280 (-8)	€24,400 / €152,100
Sep	2-5	ALLIANZ Europen Strasbourg Golf de la Wantzenau	Golf de la Wantzenau, La Wantzenau, France	Romain Wattel (AM), FRA	67-69-68-67=271 (-17)	N/A / €150,000
	9-12	Kazakhstan Open	Zhailjau Golf Resort, Almaty, Kazakhstan	Alvaro Velasco ESP	67-66-65-69=267 (-21)	€64,000 / €407,560
	16-19	M2M Russian Challenge Cup 2010	Tseleevo Park & Polo Club, Moscow, Russia	Carlos del Moral ESP	72-68-71-66 = 277 (-11)	€28,000 / €176,995
Oct	7-10	ALLIANZ Golf Open du Grand Toulouse	Golf de Toulouse-Seilh, Seilh, France	Bernd Wiesberger AUT	70-70-67-68 = 275 (-9)	€24,000 / €154,125
	13-16 (Wed-Sat)	Roma Golf Open 2010 presented by REZZA	Olgiata GC, Rome, Italy	Andreas Hartø, DEN**	66-65-65-69 = 265 (-19)	€24,000 / €152,100
	20-23 (Wed-Sat)	Egyptian Open 2010 presented by SODIC	JW Marriott Mirage City GC, Cairo, Egypt	Mark Tullo, CHI	71-68-70-66=275 (-13)	€28,612 / €179,882
	27-30 (Wed-Sat)	Apulia San Domenico Grand Final	San Domenico Golf, Puglia, Italy	Matt Haines, ENG	69-72-69-66=276 (-8)	€51,500/ €300,000

* Dual ranking event, for Ranking point purposes the prize fund will be capped at €500,000

** Denotes play-off

^ Rearranged from original date of April 21-24, 2010

THE 2010 EUROPEAN CHALLENGE TOUR RANKINGS

Pos	Name	Country	Played	€	Pos	Name	Country	Played	€
1	Alvaro VELASCO	(ESP)	(16)	134296.83	51	Wade ORMSBY	(AUS)	(17)	24160.83
2	Matt HAINES	(ENG)	(16)	107152.18	52	Elliot SALTMAN	(SCO)	(11)	24105.00
3	Thorbjorn OLESEN	(DEN)	(21)	104754.10	53	Andrew WILLEY	(ENG)	(17)	23411.61
4	Floris DE VRIES	(NED)	(23)	101288.18	54	Åke NILSSON	(SWE)	(13)	22851.75
5	Bernd WIESBERGER	(AUT)	(22)	99988.71	55	Branden GRACE	(RSA)	(17)	22251.42
6	Oscar FLOREN	(SWE)	(21)	98948.00	56	Lloyd SALTMAN	(SCO)	(18)	21998.57
7	Daniel GAUNT	(AUS)	(11)	97520.63	57	Lloyd KENNEDY	(ENG)	(19)	21779.43
8	Robert DINWIDDIE	(ENG)	(18)	95650.17	58	Craig LEE	(SCO)	(6)	21686.36
9	Mark TULLO	(CHI)	(18)	92582.89	59	Matt FORD	(ENG)	(5)	21435.00
10	George MURRAY	(SCO)	(20)	92339.34	60	Klas ERIKSSON	(SWE)	(15)	21425.80
11	Julio ZAPATA	(ARG)	(21)	86960.95	61	Daniel BROOKS	(ENG)	(17)	20648.53
12	Joel SJÖHOLM	(SWE)	(21)	83907.19	62	Anders Schmidt HANSEN	(DEN)	(19)	19988.66
13	Lee SLATTERY	(ENG)	(16)	78358.45	63	Simon WAKEFIELD	(ENG)	(18)	19707.40
14	Scott JAMIESON	(SCO)	(22)	67413.07	64	Callum MACAULAY	(SCO)	(18)	18654.55
15	Matthew ZIONS	(AUS)	(19)	63176.45	65	Garry HOUSTON	(WAL)	(20)	18513.00
16	Marius THORP	(NOR)	(15)	63126.54	66	Fredrik HENGE	(SWE)	(11)	18429.38
17	Lorenzo GAGLI	(ITA)	(14)	62545.29	67	Paul DWYER	(ENG)	(18)	17570.67
18	Magnus A CARLSSON	(SWE)	(19)	60469.42	68	Wil BESSELING	(NED)	(19)	17543.97
19	Raymond RUSSELL	(SCO)	(19)	59376.38	69	Nicolas MEITINGER	(GER)	(19)	17149.50
20	Alexandre KALEKA	(FRA)	(23)	58887.89	70	Christophe BRAZILLIER	(FRA)	(21)	17140.50
21	Carlos DEL MORAL	(ESP)	(16)	58329.90	71	Anthony SNOBECK	(FRA)	(21)	17065.15
22	Charlie FORD	(ENG)	(20)	57196.57	72	Benn BARHAM	(ENG)	(10)	16589.77
23	Stuart MANLEY	(WAL)	(19)	57115.89	73	Tom WHITEHOUSE	(ENG)	(14)	16357.33
24	Charles-Edouard RUSSO	(FRA)	(22)	56921.70	74	Richard KIND	(NED)	(20)	16116.33
25	Alessandro TADINI	(ITA)	(21)	56195.72	75	Marcus HIGLEY	(ENG)	(18)	15982.05
26	Steven TILEY	(ENG)	(19)	52666.24	76	Bernd RITTHAMMER	(GER)	(17)	15766.67
27	Pelle EDBERG	(SWE)	(9)	52300.00	77	Michiel BOTHMA	(RSA)	(13)	15629.34
28	Sam WALKER	(ENG)	(18)	49500.46	78	Niklas LEMKE	(SWE)	(11)	15209.61
29	Peter GUSTAFSSON	(SWE)	(13)	47512.92	79	Andrea PERRINO	(ITA)	(20)	15144.90
30	Federico COLOMBO	(ITA)	(21)	46626.50	80	Steve LEWTON	(ENG)	(14)	15142.50
31	Jan-Are LARSEN	(NOR)	(20)	45677.45	81	Philip GOLDING	(ENG)	(13)	14766.63
32	Victor RIU	(FRA)	(22)	45501.78	82	Matthew BALDWIN	(ENG)	(13)	14509.51
33	Christopher Ryan BAKER	(USA)	(11)	43184.92	83	François CALMELS	(FRA)	(17)	14275.49
34	David VANEGAS	(COL)	(16)	38974.82	84	Michael LORENZO-VERA	(FRA)	(11)	13774.80
35	Andrew MARSHALL	(ENG)	(14)	38177.50	85	Mads VIBE-HASTRUP	(DEN)	(18)	13772.95
36	Ben EVANS	(ENG)	(23)	37976.03	86	Jake ROOS	(RSA)	(10)	13745.83
37	Jamie MCLEARY	(SCO)	(20)	37811.82	87	Jorge CAMPILLO	(ESP)	(13)	13594.90
38	Stuart DAVIS	(ENG)	(21)	37605.00	88	Olivier DAVID	(FRA)	(13)	13385.00
39	Daniel DENISON	(ENG)	(17)	35746.31	89	Ricardo SANTOS	(POR)	(13)	13368.75
40	Jesus Maria ARRUTI	(ESP)	(14)	33804.33	90	Alex HAINDL	(RSA)	(9)	13214.33
41	Julien CLÉMENT	(SUI)	(19)	33136.25	91	Lasse JENSEN	(DEN)	(17)	13065.50
42	Edouard DUBOIS	(FRA)	(19)	32288.38	92	Jean-Nicolas BILLOT	(FRA)	(16)	12699.00
43	Colm MORIARTY	(IRL)	(17)	31788.08	93	Anders SJÖSTRAND	(SWE)	(12)	12579.00
44	Mikko KORHONEN	(FIN)	(18)	31362.99	94	Roland STEINER	(AUT)	(18)	12577.37
45	Adam GEE	(ENG)	(20)	30047.01	95	Oliver WHITELEY	(ENG)	(16)	12552.46
46	Pablo DEL GROSSO	(ARG)	(17)	28023.89	96	Jamie MOUL	(ENG)	(16)	12394.28
47	Thomas FEYRSINGER	(AUT)	(19)	26978.73	97	Mark LASKEY	(WAL)	(13)	12285.00
48	Tommy FLEETWOOD	(ENG)	(6)	26206.31	98	Antti AHOKAS	(FIN)	(19)	12244.77
49	Adrien BERNADET	(FRA)	(21)	26166.31	99	Florian PRAEGANT	(AUT)	(19)	12005.00
50	Andreas HARTØ	(DEN)	(4)	25466.38	100	Vince COVELLO	(USA)	(4)	11759.98

Charl Schwartzel - January

Ian Poulter - February and November

Ernie Els - March

Rory McIlroy - April

Luke Donald - May

THE 2010 RACE TO DUBAI EUROPEAN TOUR GOLFER OF THE MONTH AWARDS

The Race to Dubai European Tour Golfer of the Month Awards are presented throughout the year followed by an Annual Award. The winners receive an engraved alms dish and a jeroboam of Moët & Chandon champagne

GOLFER OF THE YEAR WINNERS

2010	Martin Kaymer and Graeme McDowell	1997	Colin Montgomerie
2009	Lee Westwood	1996	Colin Montgomerie
2008	Padraig Harrington	1995	Colin Montgomerie
2007	Padraig Harrington	1994	Ernie Els
2006	Paul Casey	1993	Bernhard Langer
2005	Michael Campbell	1992	Sir Nick Faldo
2004	Vijay Singh	1991	Severiano Ballesteros
2003	Ernie Els	1990	Sir Nick Faldo
2002	Ernie Els	1989	Sir Nick Faldo
2001	Retief Goosen	1988	Severiano Ballesteros
2000	Lee Westwood	1987	Ian Woosnam
1999	Colin Montgomerie	1986	Severiano Ballesteros
1998	Lee Westwood	1985	Bernhard Langer

George O'Grady and Matteo Manassero - October

Graeme McDowell - June

Louis Oosthuizen - July

Martin Kaymer - August

John Parry - September

Richard Hills and Ian Poulter - February

Noh Seung-yul - March

Lee Westwood - April

THE 2010 EUROPEAN TOUR SHOT OF THE MONTH AWARDS

The European Tour Shot of the Month Awards are presented throughout the year followed by an Annual Award

SHOT OF THE YEAR WINNERS

2009	Rafa Echenique	
2008	Padraig Harrington	
2007	Angel Cabrera	
2006	Paul Casey	
2005	Paul McGinley	
2004	David Howell	
2003	Fredrik Jacobson	

Martin Kaymer - January and August

Luke Donald - May

Graeme McDowell - June and October

Miguel Angel Jiménez - July

Edoardo Molinari - September

Blueprint for the Future

London Golf Club – host of The European Open 2008 & 2009

The enterprising establishment in 2009 of a joint venture partnership between The European Tour and London Golf Club has galvanised the development of a highly selective network of world-class venues to be branded European Tour Destinations and European Tour Courses.

Recognised as the perfect strategic fit for The European Tour, with two Championship courses and a proven record in hosting major tournament golf, London Golf Club provided the essential foundation to advance and cultivate a diverse but fully integrated company incorporating a portfolio of golf and real estate projects.

European Tour Properties demonstrated the way forward when, in June 2010, Belek Golf Club, which will be the first integrated golf and residential community on Turkey's Mediterranean coast, followed London Golf Club in becoming a European Tour Destination. This will ensure top-flight professional golf being staged in Turkey on a new José Maria Olazábal designed golf course. The opening date is planned for 2012 by which time 630 homes should also be complete.

Even so, the evolution of European Tour Properties – and the growth of a meaningful network - essentially began on May 31, 2009, with the announcement that a joint venture partnership with London Golf Club, which is owned by the Bendinat Group, would spearhead the new Property and Venue strategy of The European Tour. London Golf Club is better known as the outstanding host venue of The European Open in both 2008 and 2009 and for having successfully hosted several European Senior Tour events.

Charles Fairweather, Chairman of London Golf Club, explained: "We are proud of the superb feedback we received from the players on both The European Tour and the European Senior Tour, especially on the condition of the course, and, significantly, of the record crowds which visited us for The European Opens. The Joint Venture Partnership with The European Tour is enabling us to combine our mutual resources and professionalism to further develop London Golf Club and maximise its full potential on the global stage."

George O'Grady, Chief Executive of The European Tour, said: "London Golf Club is the perfect joint venture partner for The European Tour and we look forward to working with Charles Fairweather and his team at London Golf Club to further develop this venue to the high standards that both parties demand."

European Tour Properties regard the mutually beneficial development of London Golf Club, with the Jack Nicklaus-designed Heritage Course and the equally celebrated International Course, as a dynamic component of the progression of their network.

David MacLaren, Director of Property and Venue Development for The European Tour, said: "The existence and development of European Tour Properties is founded on the strong partnership forged with London Golf Club which demonstrated the commitment of both parties to work together in originating a blueprint for the future."

Alongside Destination venues London Golf Club and Belek Golf Club, the blueprint has benefited from and been enhanced by the expansion of the network through those branded as European Tour Courses. Each and every one of these is regarded as being among the highest quality venues in their respective countries. Such eminence will be a requisite of any European Tour Course united to the European Tour Properties network.

The impressive plans for Belek Golf Club

London Golf Club, eighth hole on The International

LONDON
GOLF CLUB

London Golf Club
The Pursuit of Perfection

London Golf Club is proud to be the first club to become a Joint Venture partner with The European Tour as well as the first European Tour Destination property within the European Tour Properties portfolio.

Every day we are inspired by those around us to innovate, improve and perfect what we do. At London Golf Club we continually strive for perfection on behalf of our members and guests.

The perfect balance between technical excellence and effortless comfort means you can experience the rolling fairways of the Jack Nicklaus designed courses, relax, and enjoy stylish surroundings in a world attended to by our courteous and professional team.

Welcome to London Golf Club, a European Tour Destination.

To find out more call 01474 879899, or email us at info@londongolf.co.uk

www.londongolf.co.uk

London Golf Club, Stansted Lane, Ash, Nr Brands Hatch, Kent TN15 7

MacLaren points out: "European Tour Properties is pursuing, through a strategic alignment with the appropriate development partners , a portfolio of golf and real estate projects which, through their diversity, optimise the commercial opportunities provided by the value of The European Tour brand."

This is emphasised by the current portfolio of European Tour Courses which comprises Vanajanlinna Golf and Country Club in Finland, Estonian Golf and Country Club, Fleesensee Golf and Country Club in Germany, PGA Catalunya Resort in Spain, Quinta do Lago in Portugal, and Kungsängen in Sweden.

Vanajanlinna Golf and Country Club, ranked by Golf World in the 2010 Top 100 European Courses, played host to the European Amateur Championship in 2010, one year after successfully staging the SK Golf Challenge on the European Challenge Tour.

Estonian Golf and Country Club, also ranked by Golf World in the top 100 European Courses, is to be found only 20 minutes from Tallinn, one of the most beautiful and lively of European cities. The Club hosted the Omega Mission Hills World Cup European Qualifier in 2009.

Fleesensee Golf and Country Club is an exceptional golf venue resort comprising five courses including the Schloss championship course. Designed by European Golf Design and rated as one of the top three in Germany by Golf Magazine, the course is characterised by large undulating greens and rolling fairways. Fleesensee is a regular host for European Qualifying for The European Tour Qualifying School.

The first hole on the Schloss Course at Fleesensee Golf and Country Club

The stunning view from the Sea Course, Estonian Golf and Country Club

15th hole, Vanajanlinna Golf and Country Club

PGA Catalunya Resort is situated in the north east of Spain between Barcelona and Girona and features two courses – the Stadium and Tour – both designed by two of the most renowned figures in European golf, England's Neil Coles and Spain's Angel Gallardo, in conjunction with European Golf Design. PGA Catalunya Resort, voted 88th best course (Stadium) in the world by Golf Digest (US) in 2010, hosted the 1999 Gene Sarazen World Open, the 2000 and 2009 Open de España, the 2001 European Senior Tour Championship and in 2010 The European Tour Qualifying School Finals for a third successive year.

Quinta do Lago in the Algarve of Portugal was the host venue of The European Tour Qualifying School in 1979, 1980 and 1981 and the Open de Portugal on no fewer than eight occasions – including in 1989 when Colin Montgomerie won the first of his 31 European Tour titles.

Kungsängen, located only 25 minutes from Stockholm, has two impressive courses – the Kings and the Queens – and first hosted the Scandinavian Masters in 1998 when Jesper Parnevik won and subsequently in 2000 (Lee Westwood), 2002 (Graeme McDowell) and 2005 (Mark Hensby).

The attraction of all the venues in the European Tour Properties network is the challenge of the courses blended with their locations, and in announcing Belek Golf Club as the second European Tour Destination the company underlined its aspirations to target

growth areas of the future. Turkey's government is seeking to emulate the Iberian peninsula by using golf to expand its national tourist industry with the purpose of encouraging top end travellers and international second home buyers.

The Belek region of Turkey has become the biggest hotspot for travelling golfers in Europe with 17 high quality courses and more than 40 resort hotels all located in a highly concentrated area. Belek Golf Club will be the first world class venue in the region to have a real estate component – offering the opportunity to own a home within an exquisite residential and resort community benefiting from year round warmth and sunshine.

José Maria Olazábal, who is designing the Castle Course on which a tournament will be played on The European Tour International Schedule within seven years, said: "This is my first design work in Turkey and I am honoured to be part of a development of such high international standard. I am relishing the challenge of creating a course that will not only be a spectacular venue for The European Tour but, as importantly, an enjoyable and memorable experience for future residents and guests."

Hasan Besneli, Chairman of the Board, Belek Golf Club, said: "Our partnership with The European Tour through European Tour Properties is significant as it guarantees our residents, hotel guests and golfing visitors outstanding facilities and levels of service. This partnership will position Belek Golf Club among the finest clubs in the world. José Maria Olazábal, who has taken a close personal interest in the project, is designing a remarkable golf course that will be both fitting and challenging for a European Tour event."

As the first European Tour Destination, London Golf Club occupies a privileged position within this new portfolio of venues. This role will be given further prominence when, in July 2011, the Kent venue will stand as a geographical gateway to Royal St George's, host of the Open Championship. The European Tour is justly proud of this new and exciting partnership.

Honorary Life Vice Presidents

The European Tour welcomed six new Honorary Life Vice Presidents in 2010, with Gaston Barras, Claude-Roger Cartier, Masato and Akito Mizuno, Don Jaime Ortiz-Patiño and Johann Rupert accepting awards for their colossal contribution to the Tour over the past quarter of a century.

Gaston Barras, the irrepressible driving force behind the Omega European Masters, has been a member of the golf club committee at Crans-sur-Sierre since 1954, and has been President of the club since 1981. He has also been President of the Organising Committee of the European Masters since 1964 and a committee member of the Swiss Golf Association from 1969 to 1997, serving as President for the last six years of his tenure.

Claude Roger Cartier, Honorary President of the Federation Française de Golf, has played a key role in the development of golf across Europe. When John Jacobs was appointed the first Tournament Director-General of the Professional Golfers' Association, tasked with uniting Great Britain and Ireland with the continent of Europe, Cartier's support was vital and unstinting in immediately seeing and believing in the vision of 'One Europe' for the professional circuit, which would later become The European Tour.

Masato Mizuno, Chairman of the Mizuno Corporation, and Akito Mizuno, President of the Mizuno Corporation, accepted their awards during The Open Championship at St Andrews in recognition of The European Tour's longest running agreement with the world renowned golf club manufacturer. The Mizuno workshop has become a familiar sight on the driving ranges of The European Tour for the past 27 years and featured at 25 tournaments in 11 countries on The 2010 Race to Dubai. The Mizuno team of expert technicians continue to provide a service of club repair and adjustment to all players, irrespective of which brand of club they play.

Don Jaime Ortiz-Patiño is the Bolivian-born owner of one of The European Tour's most iconic venues – the magnificent Valderrama on Spain's southern coast. It was Patiño's vision that saw The Ryder Cup being played on European soil for the first time in 1997, when Seve Ballesteros's European Team sealed a dramatic 14½ - 13½ over the USA to retain Samuel Ryder's famous trophy. That historic week was the culmination of a journey that began in 1956 and saw Patiño build one of the best courses in the world that would stage one of The European Tour's most prestigious events, the season-ending Volvo Masters from 1988-1996, and from 2002-2008, and the Andalucia Valderrama Masters on The 2010 European Tour International Schedule.

Johann Rupert, Chairman of the Swiss-based luxury goods company Richemont, is one of the Tour's most valued sponsors with an association spanning 25 years having brought the Alfred Dunhill Cup to St Andrews in 1985. His tournament has evolved into the Alfred Dunhill Links Championship, a unique event that brings together the world's best golfers, notable sportsmen and women as well as celebrities from film and television in a festival of golf over the Old Course at St Andrews, Carnoustie and Kingsbarns. Rupert also serves as the Chairman of the South African PGA Tour, The European Tour's oldest co-sanctioning partner, and the South African Golf Development Board. He developed the Gary Player-designed Leopard Creek Golf Club in Malelane, which is consistently rated as one of South Africa's best golf courses and host venue since 2005 of the Alfred Dunhill Championship.

George O'Grady and Gaston Barras

Claude Roger Cartier

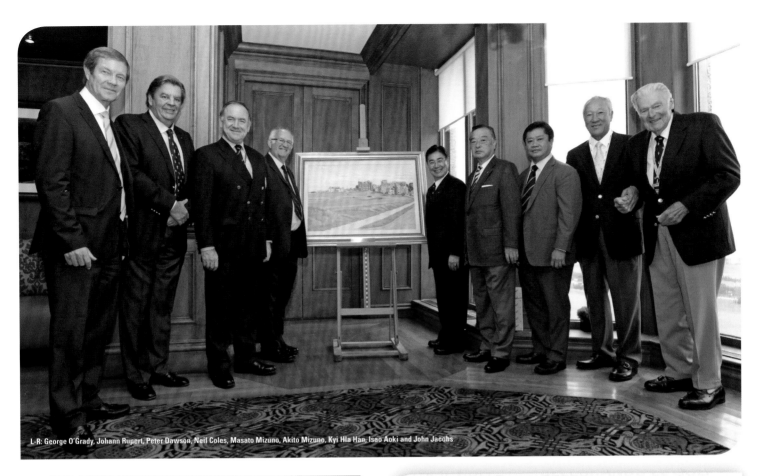

L-R: George O'Grady, Johann Rupert, Peter Dawson, Neil Coles, Masato Mizuno, Akito Mizuno, Kyi Hla Han, Isao Aoki and John Jacobs

L-R: Jose Maria Olazabal, Don Jaime Ortiz-Patiño, George O'Grady and Angel Gallardo

L-R: George O'Grady, Johann Rupert and Ernie Els

EUROPEAN TOUR HONORARY LIFE VICE PRESIDENTS

Mr Gaston Barras	Mr Akito Mizuno
Sir Michael Bonallack OBE	Mr Masato Mizuno
Mr Claude Roger Cartier	Mr Padraig O'hUiginn
Mr Bernard Gallacher OBE	Mr Len Owen
Mr W Graham	Mr Jaime Ortiz-Patiño
Mr Ulf Lauren	Mr Johann Rupert
Lord Macfarlane	Ms Emma Villacieros

THE EUROPEAN TOUR

DIRECTORS

Neil Coles MBE, Chairman
Angel Gallardo, Vice Chairman
Maurice Bembridge
Paul Eales
Chris Hanell
David Jones
Robert Lee
John O'Leary
Mark Roe
David J Russell
Ove Sellberg
Jamie Spence
Sir Michael Bonallack OBE
(Non Executive Tour Group Director)
Peter Davidson
(Non Executive Tour Group Director, Finance)
Björn Nordberg
(Non Executive Tour Group Director)
Nigel Northridge
(Non Executive Tour Group Director)
Keith Owen
(Non Executive Tour Group Director, Broadcasting)

TOURNAMENT COMMITTEE

Thomas Björn, Chairman (DEN)
Paul Casey (ENG)
Darren Clarke (NIR)
Gonzalo Fernandez-Castaño (ESP)
Richard Finch (ENG)
Joakim Haeggman (SWE)
David Howell (ENG)
Raphaël Jacquelin (FRA)
Miguel Angel Jiménez (ESP)
Robert Karlsson (SWE)
Barry Lane (ENG)
Paul Lawrie MBE (SCO)
Paul McGinley (IRL)
Colin Montgomerie OBE (SCO)
Henrik Stenson (SWE)

EUROPEAN TOUR EXECUTIVES

CHIEF EXECUTIVE

	GEORGE O'GRADY CBE
Chief Operating Officer and Director of International Policy	Keith Waters
Ryder Cup Director	Richard Hills
Group Marketing Director	Scott Kelly
Financial Director & Company Secretary	Jonathan Orr

EUROPEAN TOUR MANAGEMENT

Director of Tour Operations	David Garland
Managing Director, European Senior Tour	Andy Stubbs
Director of Challenge Tour	Alain de Soultrait
Director of Broadcasting & New Media	Mark Lichtenhein
Director of Corporate Affairs & Public Relations	Mitchell Platts
Director of Property & Venue Development	David MacLaren
Director of International Championships	Peter Adams
Director of Championship Management	Jamie Birkmyre
Chief Referee	John Paramor
Ryder Cup Match Director	Edward Kitson
Assistant Director of Tour Operations & Senior Tournament Director	David Probyn
Senior Tournament Director & Qualifying School Director	Mike Stewart
Director of Communications	Gordon Simpson
Sales Director	Tim Shaw
Brand Director	Tim Hunt
Senior Referee	Andy McFee
HR Director	Rose'y Buchanan
Deputy Director of International Policy	Ben Cowen

PHOTOGRAPHERS

getty images®

Krafft Angerer
David Cannon
Stanley Chou
Tom Dulat
Julian Finney
Stuart Franklin
Victor Fraile
Sam Greenwood
Scott Halleran
Richard Heathcote
Harry How
Phil Inglis
Ross Kinnaird
Chris Lee
Warren Little
Andy Lyons
Ian MacNicol
Andrew Redington
Jamie Squire
Ian Walton

ADDITIONAL CONTRIBUTORS

Asian Tour
Claudio Scaccini
David Williams - Photolibrary Wales
Gallo Images
Luke Walker - Sunshine Tour
Matthew Harris - Golf Picture Library
Media Wales
Montana Pritchard - PGA of America
OneAsia
Parallel Media Group plc
PGA of Australia
PGA TOUR
Sport Progress
Sports Illustrated
Steve Pope Sportingwales

Martin Kaymer and Graeme McDowell

EUROPEAN TOUR
RACE TO
DUBAI
2010

1 ARGENTINA
Number of wins: 30
Number of winners: 11
Leading performers:
Eduardo Romero (8); Angel Cabrera (5);
Vicente Fernandez, Ricardo Gonzalez (4)

2 AUSTRALIA
Number of wins: 106
Number of winners: 36
Leading performers: Greg Norman
(14); Graham Marsh (10); Rodger Davis,
Adam Scott (7)

3 AUSTRIA
Number of wins: 3
Number of winners: 2
Leading performer: Markus Brier (2);
Martin Wiegele (1)

4 BELGIUM
Number of wins: 1
Number of winners: 1
Leading performer:
Phillipe Toussaint (1)

5 BRAZIL
Number of wins: 1
Number of winners: 1
Leading performer: Jamie Gonzalez (1)

6 CANADA
Number of wins: 3
Number of winners: 2
Leading performers: Mike Weir (2);
Jerry Anderson (1)

7 CHILE
Number of wins: 1
Number of winners: 1
Leading performer: Felipe Aguilar (1)

8 CHINA
Number of wins: 2
Number of winners: 2
Leading performers: Zhang Lian-wei,
Liang Wen-chong (1)

9 DENMARK
Number of wins: 22
Number of winners: 7
Leading performers: Thomas Björn (10);
Anders Hansen, Søren Kjeldsen (3);
Søren Hansen, Steen Tinning (2)

10 ENGLAND
Number of wins: 257
Number of winners: 81
Leading performers:
Sir Nick Faldo (30); Lee Westwood (20);
Mark James (18); Howard Clark (11);
Paul Casey, Ian Poulter (10)

11 FIJI
Number of wins: 13
Number of winners: 1
Leading performer: Vijay Singh (13)

12 FINLAND
Number of wins: 2
Number of winners: 1
Leading performer: Mikko Ilonen (2)

13 FRANCE
Number of wins: 23
Number of winners: 10
Leading performers: Thomas Levet (5);
Grégory Bourdy, Grégory Havret,
Jean-Francois Remesy (3);
Christian Cévaër, Raphaël Jacquelin,
Jean Van de Velde (2)

14 GERMANY
Number of wins: 60
Number of winners: 6
Leading performers: Bernhard Langer
(42); Martin Kaymer (8); Alex Cejka (4);
Sven Strüver (3)

15 INDIA
Number of wins: 7
Number of winners: 3
Leading performers: Arjun Atwal, Jeev
Milkha Singh (3); SSP Chowrasia (1)

16 IRELAND
Number of wins: 46
Number of winners: 14
Leading performers: Padraig
Harrington (14); Des Smyth (8);
Eamonn Darcy, Paul McGinley,
Christy O'Connor Jnr (4)

17 ITALY
Number of wins: 15
Number of winners: 8
Leading performers: Costantino
Rocca (5); Baldovino Dassu , Edoardo
Molinari, Francesco Molinari
(2); Emanuele Canonica, Matteo
Manassero, Massimo Mannelli,
Massimo Scarpa (1)

The European Tour International
Schedule embraces the world. In total
no fewer than 37 countries have hosted
competition on The European Tour and
players from no fewer than 35 countries

MOST VICTORIES BY PLAYER
THE TOP TEN

1. Seve Ballesteros — 50
2. Bernhard Langer — 42
3. Tiger Woods — 38
4. Colin Montgomerie — 31
5. Sir Nick Faldo — 30
6. Ian Woosnam — 29
7. Ernie Els — 25
8. José Maria Olazábal — 23
9. Sam Torrance — 21
10. Lee Westwood — 20